MW01714968

Computers Made *Ridiculously* Easy

Computers Made *Ridiculously* Easy

Srully Blotnick

McGraw-Hill Book Company
New York St. Louis San Francisco Auckland Bogotá
Hamburg London Madrid Mexico
Montreal New Delhi Panama Paris São Paulo
Singapore Sydney Tokyo Toronto

Library of Congress Cataloging in Publication Data

Blotnick, Srully.
Computers made ridiculously easy.

Includes index.
1. Computers—Popular works. 2. Microprocessors—Popular works. I. Title.
TK7885.4.B56 1984 621.3819'5 83-23858
ISBN 0-07-006123-8

4567890 DOC/DOC 898

The editors for this book were Stephen G. Guty and Lynne Lackenbach, the designer was Naomi Auerbach, and the production supervisor was Teresa F. Leaden. It was set in Baskerville by *Byrd* Data Imaging Group.

Printed and bound by R. R. Donnelley & Sons Company.

Part of Chapter 1 appeared, in revised form, in *Forbes*.

Contents

Preface

Learning about computers can be made easier and more fun by making use of everyday analogies. What starts out seeming strange and remote can be rendered in this way understandable and even familiar. Some analogies make a point crystal clear; others may prove less helpful. In order to find the most effective ones, we've tested the contents of this book on diverse groups of readers for nearly three years: small business owners and managers, airline pilots, high school students, lawyers, doctors, marketing and sales pros, and architects.

What all these people had in common was little or no background in computers and/or electronics. There are many excellent science and engineering texts geared to the highly trained reader who has no trouble absorbing complex technical material. This isn't a book for them. They're likely to think we're making computers look ridiculous (we aren't), rather than trying to laugh and learn at the same time (we certainly are).

To prevent anyone from becoming lost along the way, we have made it a point to restate, usually in a more serious manner, the major concepts already covered that will be needed for an understanding of a new one about to be introduced. The book also makes extensive use of a pedagogical tool that resulted from the field testing. Whenever readers found a topic difficult to understand or not described in sufficient detail, they were invited to rephrase the text briefly in a way that helped illuminate the point, once they'd grasped it. When a majority of readers came up with pretty much the same phrasing, it was included. At more than 100 places in the book the words "that is," followed by an explanation, therefore appear. If you don't need the additional or alternative explanation, skip it and go on to the next sentence. However, most readers should find the added comments useful.

The most important piece of advice we can give readers who come upon a point they don't understand is to keep reading. By all means, reread the material once or twice before going on, but instead of feeling defeated if you don't understand it, and stopping, go ahead anyway. The text deliberately repeats every important point on a number of subsequent occasions, each time in a slightly different manner that may prove much easier to grasp. Our field testing shows that the vast majority of readers who did this later absorbed all the points that had stumped them earlier.

Srully Blotnick

chapter 1 entering the gates

Tables for Two

If you've ever been in an expensive French restaurant or a budget-priced Chinese one, you can understand how a modern digital computer works. Digital computers don't speak English, or French or Chinese, for that matter. Their language is binary—that is, all they understand is zeros and ones (actually, high and low voltage).

To see what eating out has to do with learning about computers, suppose that there are two restaurants, one French, the other Chinese, right next to one another on the same block. Both decide to get rid of the maitre d' at the door. Each owner wants to save money, eliminate favoritism due to tipping, and is convinced that a machine can do the job better and more fairly. The big question is: How should the machine decide whether or not to admit someone to the restaurant? The answer depends on the kind of place it is. Different rules apply at the French as opposed to the Chinese restaurant.

To enable the machine to "see" what is happening at the door, suppose that sensors are installed in the floor. The sensor signals a "1" when somone stands on it and a "0" otherwise. To make life easier for the machine, the entranceway to each place has been designed to hold just two people at a time. It's the same story inside the restaurant: All the tables in both restaurants have only two chairs.

When there are two people in the entranceway, the sensors will therefore signal a pair of 1s. A 1 and a 0 mean that there is only person there. Finally, two 0s mean that no one is waiting to be seated.

For the sake of simplicity, the same signals, 0 and 1, are to be used instead of red and green to tell people whether or not they can enter. When no one is standing in the entrance foyer, the owners want the machine to produce a 0—a "Stop, you can't go in"—and keep on producing it until it's ready to seat people who are standing there waiting. Then, it can signal a 1—a "Please, come in." Since all the tables in both restaurants are tables for two, any time there is a *couple* waiting in the entranceway and an empty table is available, the owners want the machine to signal a 1 without delay. In short, two 0s as inputs should produce a 0 as output. And two 1s as inputs to the machine should produce a 1 as the machine's output.

The third possibility, namely, that a person arrives alone at the entranceway, is the tricky situation. What makes this a complicated case? Because, as we've said, different rules apply at the two restaurants.

The owner of the French place has decided that someone seeking to dine alone should not be admitted. His reason is that having one person at a table takes the rest of it out of commission. Even though only one customer is sitting there, the entire table is essentially occupied. So a 1 and a 0 at the entranceway of the French restaurant produces a 0 from the machine—that is, a "Stop, you can't go in." At the Chinese restaurant, on the other hand, a different attitude prevails: A 1 and a 0 as inputs to the machine (because only one person is standing in the entranceway) produces a 1 from the machine—that is, the message the hungry table seeker gets is: "Come on in. As long as there is an empty seat somewhere in this joint, you'll be served."

The situation at the French restaurant is therefore summarized by the following truth table for AND:

A	B	C
0	0	0
0	1	0
1	0	0
1	1	1

It's easy to read; just read it one row at a time. A and B are the sensors in the floor of the entrance foyer, and when someone stands on them, they light up with a 1. The third column, C, is the yes or no the machine generates. A 0 means that no table is available. A 1 means yes, you may have a table (or in the Chinese restaurant, at least a seat, perhaps at a table with other people).

The situation at the Chinese restaurant can therefore be summarized by the following truth table for OR:

A	B	C
0	0	0
0	1	1
1	0	1
1	1	1

Note that the only difference between this chart and the one above it occurs in rows 2 and 3. The difference is no minor matter, though, since it tells you whether you will get into the restaurant if you arrive there alone.

A chart such as this is called a *truth table*. However, at this stage you can learn more about the operation of digital logic circuits by thinking of the chart as "the truth *about* the table."

The first table, the one summarizing the situation at the French restaurant, is called an AND gate. Why? Because the machine, which is acting as a gate, determining who gets in and who doesn't, wants you *and* someone else there before it will admit you. The second chart, the one summarizing the situation at the Chinese restaurant, represents an OR gate, because if either you *or* someone else (or both) is present, you can go on in.

These gates are so important to the operations of computers, and appear so often in the diagrams representing what goes on inside these machines, that they have their own symbols (see Figure 1-1). The difference between the two symbols is that the AND gate is shaped like the last letter of the word "AND." That is an easy way to remember its shape. The OR gate, on the other hand, is shaped like the bow of a boat. If you think of the oar of a rowboat, you'll remember that OR has a more pointed shape than AND. As microelectronic devices and circuitry become more widespread, you'll see symbols like these increasingly. They are worth remembering. Drawing them a few times helps.

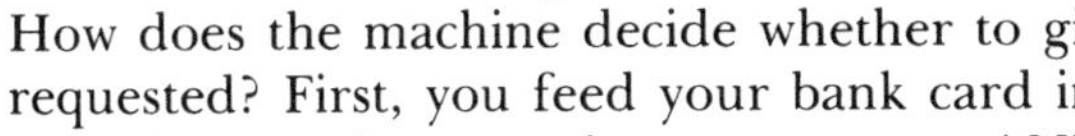

Figure 1-1 An AND gate and an OR gate.

The computers we come into contact with in our everyday lives make extensive use of these gates. Take automated bank tellers, for example. How does the machine decide whether to give you the cash you have requested? First, you feed your bank card into the machine. Then, if there is enough money in your account AND the number of the card matches your account number, out come the nice crisp bills you wanted.

Here, the card is being used as a key. When you stick a key into a lock, *every* notch in the key must match one of the tumbler pins. And when you use a plastic card as a key, everything must match as well. You wouldn't want someone who gets only part of the information right to gain access to either your house or your bank account. In short, the device acts primarily as an AND gate, much like the maitre d' at a French restaurant.

In other major applications—for instance, a computer that is monitoring an industrial manufacturing process for errors—OR gates are more important. When the production process begins to go awry, even a single error in the sequence should be brought to someone's attention. If there are two steps in the manufacturing process, A and B, the computer should inform the operator if either one OR the other of them starts to screw up. Both steps shouldn't have to fail before a signal is sent. When all is said and done, in this instance the computer acts in a manner that is analogous to the host of a Chinese restaurant.

Note that the situation is the reverse of the one at the bank. There, we want the transaction to go through only if *everything* is in order. Here, we want a signal to be issued if *anything* is out of order—and we want to know what and where it is. (We don't want the customer to be given this information at the bank, though, since a thief would then know what to fix, by trial and error, in order to make a fraudulent transaction go through.)

The logic systems in computers are combinations of AND and OR gates etched into tiny silicon chips. One hears a great deal about integrated circuits—in particular, LSIs and VLSIs—and will be hearing even more about them in the near future. However, once you understand even a little about gates, there is no longer any reason to be intimidated by the concept of an integrated circuit, no matter how complex it may be. There are four categories to keep in mind. A small-scale integrated (SSI) circuit is a silicon chip that has a dozen or fewer gates, whereas a medium-scale integrated (MSI) circuit has anywhere from 13 to 99 of them. A large-scale integrated (LSI) circuit is a chip that contains anywhere from 100 to 999 gates. Very-large-scale integrated (VLSI) circuits are those that contain 1000 or more such gates. Each gate is simple, but working together on a chip, they can be made to handle quite sophisticated tasks, as we'll soon see.

Tables for Three or More

There is no reason for a restaurant to have tables only for two, and similarly, there's no need for the logic gates in a computer to be limited to only two inputs. If a party of four arrives at either a French or Chinese restaurant, the owner will want to be certain that any machine that is acting as a host admits them as soon as a table is ready. The same goes for the gates in a computer. Sometimes gates with three or more inputs are absolutely essential if the machine is to do what it's supposed to.

For instance, we described a plastic card that you use at an automated teller machine as being in some sense like a key. Instead of notches in a piece of metal, the bank card uses numbers. But a key with only two

notches or a credit card with only two numbers woul
number of possible combinations to accommodate t'
who use them. So if there are 10 numbers on your
gate would be used in the machine.

The same goes for OR gates that are being useu, -
industrial manufacturing process. For example, sneakers u-
well, just sneakers. One model in one color was used for almost ..
sport, while another that was higher on the sides was used for basketball. Now, sneakers have become a fashion item and a multibillion-dollar-a-year industry, with a wide variety of models to choose from for every conceivable sport. Runners alone have more than 200 styles from which to choose. If the manufacture of a sneaker takes three machine-monitored steps (such as putting in the insole and glueing on the bottom), a three-input OR gate could be used to let the operator know if *any* of the three steps is malfunctioning.

What do a four-input AND gate, say, and a three-input OR gate look like? Exactly what you'd expect (see Figure 1-2). Notice that although the AND gate in this picture has four inputs and the OR gate has three, both gates have only one output. That is important, because the whole idea behind these devices is to feed in information from a variety of sources at one end and get an unequivocal yes or no, true or false, stop or go, at the other. Since the only language the machine understands is binary—that is, 0s and 1s—that's what is fed into the device at each of its inputs, and that is what it will give us as an output: a 0 or 1 that summarizes the information it received at its inputs.

Figure 1-2 (a) A four-input AND gate. (b) A three-input OR gate.

If there are more than two inputs to a gate, you may be uncertain just looking at the thing what the output will be for any given arrangement of 1s and 0s on its inputs. There is always an easy way to find out what the output will be: Make a truth table. Later we'll see how it's done, even when the gate is more complicated than the ones we've been discussing.

"No, I Won't Go, and You Can't Make Me"

Besides AND and OR gates, there is a third kind of logic gate: the NOT gate. Anyone who has ever watched an irritable three-year-old or a defiant teenager taking a stand against a parent knows exactly how the e works. Whatever you feed into it, it gives you back the reverse. Say We're going to Grandma's," and the immediate reaction is "No." Say "We're not going to Grandma's," and the instant reply is "I don't care if *you* don't want to go, I do. Grandma gives me cookies." There is so much of this in the world, and not just from youngsters, that a computer would reflect reality only poorly unless it too were capable of acting the same way (on request, of course).

The NOT gate is the simplest gate, because it merely takes 1s and converts them to 0s, and vice versa. There are only two possible values at each of its inputs, a 1 or a 0, and whichever is there, the device produces the opposite at its output. The symbol for a NOT gate looks like a triangular arrowhead with a small bubble at the tip—without the bubble it is symbol for an amplifier (see Figure 1-3). Since the output, D, is merely the reverse of the input, C, the NOT gate is often referred to as an *inverter*.

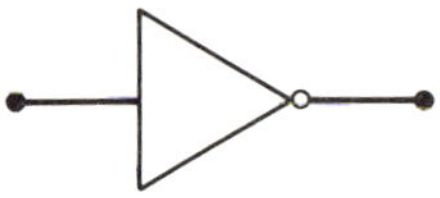

Figure 1-3 A NOT gate.

Four Bouncers on a Chip

The NOT gate can be combined with either the AND or the OR gate to produce some very useful devices. Far from being just an empty exercise, the resulting combinations are extremely important. In fact, they provide a more realistic embodiment of what occurs in many commonly encountered situations.

For example, Henry is the 6′3″, 230-lb, muscle-bound bouncer at a popular New York-area singles bar. He takes his job seriously, and therefore does everything precisely by the rules. The first rule is that if you are with a member of the opposite sex, you aren't admitted to the place. Smiling pleasantly, he says to each couple that arrives at the door seeking entrance: "Hey, you can't go in, this is a singles bar."

Henry may be a simpleton, but he is quite a logical fellow, so logical in fact that we should have no trouble modeling his behavior as a bouncer in terms of the three logic gates at our disposal, AND, OR, and NOT. To begin with, then, let's see if he can be replaced by an AND gate. Remember, the truth table for AND goes as follows:

A	B	C
0	0	0
0	1	0
1	0	0
1	1	1

Here, A is a male, B is a female. Column C is the yes or no; 0 means no, you can't enter; 1 means yes, go on in. Hence row 2 of the table states that a lone female who arrives at the entranceway is not admitted. Neither is a lone male, as row 3 tells us. Row 4 means that a man and woman who arrive together *are* admitted. This is obviously not what is supposed to occur at the door to a singles bar.

It is apparent that we must modify the AND gate in some way in order to make it match what Henry does. But how? Simple. By combining it with a NOT gate. The truth table for a NOT gate could hardly be more straightforward:

C	D
0	1
1	0

The truth table can be understood immediately if you think of a table with only one chair, or a bar stool. If someone is already sitting there (row 2), you can't. If no one is, you can (row 1).

The correct combination of gates needed to capture what Henry does is therefore an AND followed by a NOT gate, and is called a NAND gate. The resulting truth table reveals that this combination provides the appropriate inputs and outputs at the entrance to a singles bar. The truth table for a NAND gate is therefore:

A	B	D
0	0	1
0	1	1
1	0	1
1	1	0

That is, everyone gets the green light—except couples (row 4). Notice that column D in this table differs from column C in the AND gate truth table in a very simple manner: 1s have become 0s, and 0s have become 1s. This table, then, really does represent AND followed by NOT, and should thus be called an AND-NOT gate. But euphony prevails here instead of literal description, so it is always referred to as a NAND gate. Keep in mind, though, that NAND means AND followed by NOT. There is another reason to keep this gate in mind: It is the single most important logic gate in a computer.

We've already seen that an AND gate looks like a capital D with the inputs along the flat side. Since a NAND gate is merely an AND gate followed by a NOT gate, it looks like Figure 1-4. Notice that the symbol

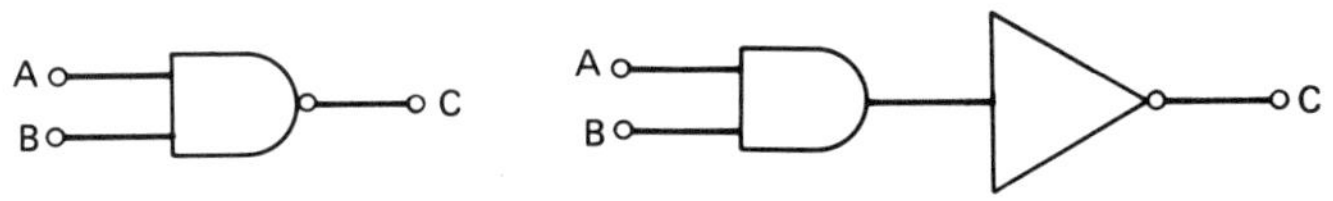

Figure 1-4 NAND = AND + NOT.

for a NAND gate differs from the one for an AND gate only slightly—namely, the NAND gate has a small bubble added at its output. The bubble means that the output is inverted (0s become 1s, and vice versa).

Column C in the truth table for AND and column D in the truth table for NAND are the reverse of one another, so it is clear that the truth tables and the symbols of the two gates really do reflect the fact that they produce opposite results.

Why are NAND gates so important to computers as well as singles bars? For two primary reasons. First, they are very easy to fabricate, especially in integrated circuit (IC) form. For instance, pictured in Figure 1-5 is a schematic of an actual IC available from a variety of domestic and foreign semiconductor manufacturers. It contains not one but four NAND gates. Hooked up correctly to four singles bars, it could replace Henry (who acts as a NAND gate, as the truth table clearly demonstrates) and three more guys like him. However, as the bar owner put it: "The customers would miss that stupid grin of his."

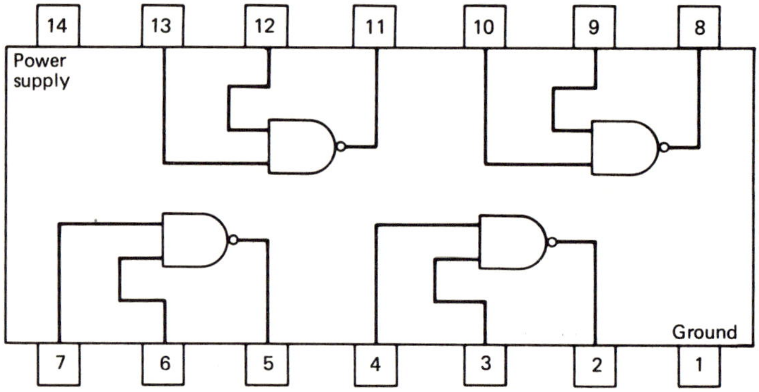

Figure 1-5 A quad two-input NAND gate.

The lingo used to describe this IC, which costs less than 50¢, is worth knowing. Since one row of connecting pins sticks out of each of the two long sides, this layout is called a dual in-line package (DIP). Also, since there are four NAND gates in the IC pictured in Figure 1-5, and each NAND gate has two inputs (there is also a pin for the power supply and another for grounding the device, to avoid a shock), the IC is fully described as "a DIP 14-pin quad two-input NAND gate." But if you like, you can refer to it as "four Henrys on a chip."

Lonely Saturday Nights

We've just seen that if you take an AND gate and follow it with a NOT gate, you get a NAND gate. You might be wondering: "What happens if I take an OR gate and follow it with a NOT gate?" You should, of course, get something called an OR-NOT gate. However, the same considerations (of euphony) that applied before apply here as well, so it's called a NOR gate instead. Let's see what its truth table and electronic symbol look like.

We already know that the truth table for OR goes as follows:

A	B	C
0	0	0
0	1	1
1	0	1
1	1	1

We also know that the NOT gate has a very simple effect on the output of an OR gate, or any gate for that matter: It merely inverts the output. So the truth table for NOR must go as follows:

A	B	D
0	0	1
0	1	0
1	0	0
1	1	0

Notice that column D here is simply the reverse of column C above.

Its symbol for use in circuit diagrams is subject to the same rules of formation as we encountered in the case of NAND (see Figure 1-6). The bubble at the tip of the NOR gate means that it yields the inverse of whatever the gate would otherwise have produced as an output.

What is a NOR gate used for? Lots of things, and a second look at the truth table for NOR may give you a hint as to some of them. A good example of an everyday situation that is accurately described by a NOR gate is the following: Harold is 38, recently divorced and doesn't intend to spend any more Friday or Saturday nights at home alone if he can possibly help it. He hasn't found anyone he's crazy about just yet, but that's less important to him than he thinks. Above all, as he puts it: "I want to be sure I've always got *someone* I can call up—even at the last minute—and say, 'Let's go out.' " Since Harold sells insurance, he knows about limiting his risk and has done just that: He has two women whose numbers he can call. Since one or the other of them is usually free, he sees both regularly, though neither has met or knows anything about the other.

What in the world does this have to do with NOR gates? Plenty. As long as Harold is able to arrange a date with at least one of the women

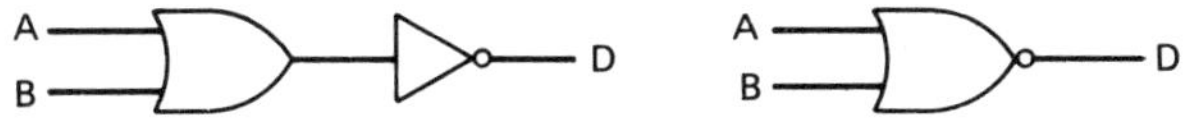

Figure 1-6 OR + NOT = NOR.

each weekend, he's happy. If he sees both, one on Friday and the other on Saturday, all the better as far as he's concerned. However, on those weekends when neither woman is available, Harold is miserable. "I don't know anyone else off the top of my head that I can call," he grumbles, "and I don't want to hit the singles bars. I always feel so uncomfortable there."

Harold's emotional state each weekend can therefore be summed up nicely by the truth table for a NOR gate. It is only when a weekend arrives and he scores a 0 with both A and B that he becomes upset and registers a 1 as a result.

"One for You, One for Me"

NAND and NOR gates do a good job of characterizing how certain bouncers and bachelors, respectively, behave on evenings and weekends, but the gates also perform a feat of crucial importance in a computer: allow it to remember.

Anyone who discusses computers even casually with friends, much less buys one for personal or business use, will quickly find the subject of the computer's memory moving to the fore. That's only natural, since memory is what makes a computer so much more than a mere calculating machine. The key to grasping how a computer remembers is the concept of a *flip-flop*, which we'll describe in a moment. By contrast with the glories of the human mind, a flip-flop may strike you as an underwhelming, even trival, device. Nevertheless, it is the single most important—and most common—circuit in a computer.

At the beginning of this chapter we talked about two restaurants, side by side, one French, the other Chinese. However, the best way to understand how NAND gates allow a computer to remember is for us to look at two singles bars, side by side. Earlier we saw that a bouncer at such a place who took his job literally could be replaced by a NAND gate, whose symbol and truth table are shown in Figure 1-7.

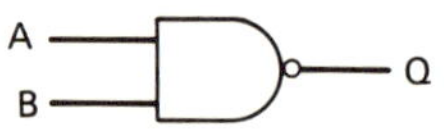

(a)

		Q	
A	B	AND	NAND
0	0	0	1
0	1	0	1
1	0	0	1
1	1	1	0

(b)

Figure 1-7 (a) A NAND gate. (b) Truth table for AND and NAND.

Notice that the only difference between this NAND gate truth table and symbol and the one we gave previously is that now the output is labeled Q instead of D. The lettering really doesn't matter, since the output of any given gate depends solely on the inputs to it, and is therefore the same regardless of the letter used to describe it. Where flip-flops are concerned, though, Q is the label traditionally used for its output.

We are assuming, then, that there are two singles bars right next to one another on the same street, each with a NAND gate at its front door. Let's also assume that the owners of these businesses grow tired of battling one another continually for customers and therefore decide to divide the available business between them. Each partner to the collusion remains uneasy, though, afraid that the other will get a bigger piece of the pie. What should they do? How can they watch one another to guarantee that everything stays balanced? The answer is to install a digital electronic device that makes certain that the rule, "one for you, one for me," is followed.

Most people have the impression that such devices are fiendishly complicated inside, even if they display simple, legible numbers on the outside. Yet in this case, the device can be implemented in a very straightforward manner by running a wire from one singles bar to the other. To be more specific, the wire should run from the *output* of the NAND gate at the first bar to the *input* of the NAND gate at the second. The top NAND gate is labeled H, after its bouncer, Henry; the lower one is labeled L, after its bouncer, Larry (see Figure 1-8).

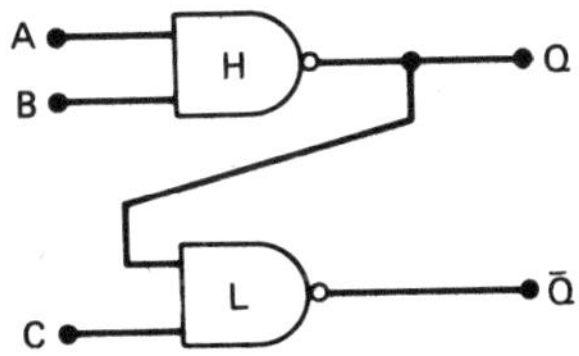

Figure 1-8 A flip.

The diagram may seem complicated at first glance, but it really isn't, as will be clear if we discuss it step by step. To begin with, we know that if a couple shows up at Henry's, he will turn them away. This is, A = 1 and B = 1 as inputs at NAND gate H produces Q = 0 as the output (see row 4 of the truth table in Figure 1-7). However, if only one person shows up, whether it be a man or a woman, A = 1 and B = 0 in the first case, and A = 0 and B = 1 in the second, the output, Q, is 1. That is, the person is given the go-ahead to enter (see rows 2 and 3 of the truth table).

That output signal is not only carried to Q, but Figure 1-8 tells us that it is *also* carried to the other singles bar by the connecting wire. Therefore NAND gate L knows immediately and exactly what the output of NAND gate H is. That is, it knows instantly if Henry is admitting people to his bar at that moment. A 1 means that he is, a 0 means that he's not.

Notice what happens if Henry is lucky enough to have only one person at a time come to the entrance to his bar. In that case, one of A or B will always be equal to 0, and therefore Q will always be equal to 1, as rows 2 and 3 of the truth table indicate. Key question: What effect does that have on NAND gate L? A major one: No one can enter Larry's bar! For even if only one person is present, that is, C = 1 in the diagram, NAND gate L is fooled into thinking that *two* people are.

Thanks to that connecting wire, NAND gate L is getting signals from two sources. It is receiving a 1 from Henry's bar, and simultaneously, at its other input, C, it is being told that a single has shown up. However, that looks like a couple to Larry's NAND gate—since both inputs are 1s. So, in accordance with the truth table for NAND, it produces a 0, that is: "Stop, you can't come in."

It's worth noting that the output of NAND gate L has a line over the top of it. The line means "opposite" or "complement." Thus, $\overline{Q}$ is read as "opposite of Q," and as we've just seen, it really is. If Q = 1, then $\overline{Q}$ = 0. On the other hand, if Q = 0 (because a couple tries to get past Henry), then and only then could $\overline{Q}$ = 1, which would allow a single who shows up at Larry's to go on in.

Henry may be very pleased with the arrangement, since it allows what happens at his bar to determine what happens at Larry's. But Larry would be right to consider the arrangement woefully lopsided.

The solution: *Each* bar gets to connect a wire to the other, so that neither place has the upper hand. The electronic device pictured in Figure 1-8 (a flip) therefore turns out to be only half of what is needed (a flip-flop), which is depicted in Figure 1-9.

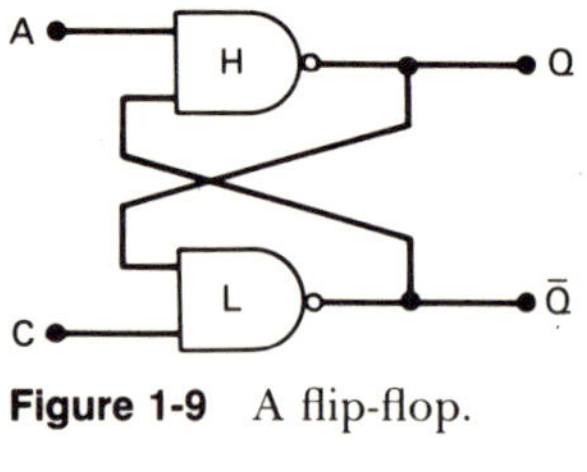

Figure 1-9 A flip-flop.

Once again, the diagram may seem complicated at first glance but really isn't. Keep in mind that this is just two NAND gates keeping a watchful eye on one another's output, through cross-coupling. Drawing the figure a few times will not only help you understand how it works, it will also allow you to remember it more easily when it is referred to in the future. (For readers who've had absolutely no previous exposure to circuit diagrams, it may be worth noting that at the point where the two wires cross—the middle of the X—the wires make no electrical contact with one another. One wire just sits on top of the other, in the same way that the wires from the lamp and clock radio next to your bed may rest on top of one another on the floor near the outlet into which they are both plugged.)

To a computer engineer, flip-flops are of enormous value, because a flip-flop is either in one state or the other. That is, either $Q = 1$ and $\overline{Q} = 0$, or else $Q = 0$ and $\overline{Q} = 1$. Since Q and $\overline{Q}$ are always opposite to one another, we need to know only one of them to know the state of the other one as well. Output Q is therefore normally taken to be *the* state of the flip-flop.

When all is said and done, a flip-flop allows computer designers to have a way of capturing and holding one binary digit. That is, a 0 or a 1 can be parked as Q's output, and it will stay that way until something is done to input A or C to change it.

The Impulsive and the Inert

We have arrived at a crucial question: Why does a flip-flop deserve to be called a memory cell? What does it do to justify so glorious a name? The answer given by computer engineers is clear and precise: A flip-flop demonstrates memory capability because it *retains* its previous output state even when the inputs that produced that state in the first place both go back to zero—that is, return to $A = 0$ and $C = 0$.

"So what?" you may reply. "So does a light switch. It too will stay where I put it—in either the on or off position—when I take my hand away." That is true, and therefore by the simple criterion that we've just cited for determining whether or not a particular device does or doesn't have a memory, a light switch does indeed have one.

Nevertheless, engineers, in the field have something much more important in mind than the (admittedly) simple nature of the building blocks they utilize in this instance. After all, a pile of plain old red bricks can be used to erect a wide variety of complex houses and office buildings. It's what you do with the pile of basic units, not the units themselves, that really counts in the end.

More to the point, in saying that flip-flops *have* memory, engineers are indicating something essential about AND, OR, and NOT gates—namely, that these units *lack* one. For instance, if both inputs to a two-input AND gate are 1s, the AND gate's output will also be a 1 (see row 4 of the AND-gate truth table on page 2). If one of the inputs is subsequently changed to a 0, then the two inputs become a 1 and a 0. The output therefore is a 0 (see row 2 or 3 of the same table). Key question: Does the AND gate remember that it was previously in the state when both its inputs were 1s? It does not. All these gates do is *combine* whatever inputs happen to be present at that particular moment, and produce the output required by the appropriate truth table.

As we've mentioned, flip-flops, on the other hand, *do* remember what the previous state was. For instance, suppose the inputs to the pair of cross-coupled NAND gates that constitute the flip-flop in Figure 1-9 are A = 1 and C = 0, and the output is Q = 1 (and therefore, of necessity, $\overline{Q}$ = 0). If A is then changed from 1 to 0, so that the inputs are now a pair of 0s, will Q change? The answer is no. It retains its previous state, and in this sense does indeed remember—or at the very least, reflect—what happened before. The sequence of input states (how one follows another) matters. For that reason, a circuit that uses logic gates such as AND, OR, and NOT is called a *combinational* circuit, whereas those circuits that employ devices such as flip-flops are said to be *sequential* circuits.

In case all this strikes you as much ado about nothing, a mere splitting of hairs, consider how deep the distinction is between combinational gates and flip-flops when human behavior is viewed in this light. There are people whose everyday actions show little evidence of a memory faculty. They react, that's all. Put them in a situation, surround them with co-workers, friends, or events, and they go off, like a firecracker. Psychologists frequently label such people impulsive, yet it is revealing to think of them as "combinatorial," in the sense that they combine the large number of inputs present *right then* and produce an output that is probably logical in terms of some truth table, if only one could figure out what it is.

At the other end of the spectrum are people who are clearly present, at least bodily, yet who seem almost impervious to the impact of present events. They do not react. Events of prior periods are clearly holding sway, and unless one can find the right magical mixture of new inputs, the past will continue to dominate behavior in the present. This group remembers too well. Steadfast, even stubborn, these flip-flops often seem determined not to live up to their name.

To a modest extent we all do this, and in fact, it is one of the greatest gifts granted to us by memory: independence. We don't need the continuing presence of a stimulus or an event in order to derive benefits (or anguish) from it later. Years after the fact, we can still react to it. Our rich, inner store of memories may keep us fully occupied even in a dark and quiet room, a troublesome by-product if we happen to be attempting to fall asleep at the time. When all is said and done, memory does much to liberate us from our surroundings. Trivial though each may seem when viewed individually, flip-flops help guarantee our freedom.

Strings of Flip-Flops

Flip-flops are used in a wide variety of common but quite important devices, such as fire and burglar alarms. Why? Because once smoke or an intruder triggers the device, causing it to change state from 0 to 1 and thereby setting off the alarm, it is desirable to have the alarm keep on ringing. If a burglar alarm rang only as long as a burglar was standing in the path of the beam of light, say, that had to be interrupted in order to sound the alarm, the device would be almost worthless. For in that case, someone who sprinted at top speed through the beam of light, interrupting it for one-tenth of a second, would set off an alarm that rang for only one one-tenth of a second. That would never do, since the signal might be missed. Flip-flops are therefore extremely useful in such an instance because once the beam is broken, even if for only a fraction of a second, the flip-flop will change state and keep on sounding the alarm.

Until? Until someone who knows how to reset the flip-flop, information that may be known solely to the owner or that requires a key, deliberately returns it to its original state. If the person or key isn't around, and the alarm is set off accidentally, the device can become annoying instead of informative. That has been happening with increasing frequency in cities. If the burglar alarm happens to be serving as an antitheft device in a car, and a youngster eating an ice cream cone momentarily sits on the hood or another car trying to park in back of it bumps it, the alarm sounds. And sounds. And sounds. At that moment, anyway, flip-flops may seem a little less than wonderful to residents of the neighborhood.

Once people, particularly those with something to protect, find out that there are flip-flops in many of the electronic devices with which they come in contact each day, they often ask: "How come *every* device doesn't have at least one?" The answer is instructive: Sometimes you don't want an electronic device to have a memory. For example, warning lights on a car's dashboard; when they *don't* go off after the condition has been remedied, they represent a common area of owner complaints. Another place where memory isn't needed is in the exit to a supermarket. Mats near the door, when stepped on, cause the door to open, but only as long as someone is standing on the sensor. (The door is adjusted to shut slowly, however, since otherwise it might end up heaving customers and their groceries head first into the frozen food section.)

To repeat: As far as computer engineers are concerned, each flip-flop serves as a temporary storage slot for one binary digit—that is, a 0 or a

1—which we'll call a *bit* from now on (a contraction that results from keep the "b" in the word "binary" and the "it" at the end of the word "digit"). Each flip-flop is a "one-bit register," where "register" means recording device.

One-bit registers aren't enough, though. The numbers we make use of in our everyday personal and business lives are often two, three, seven, or more digits long. All around us are meters and counters: on gas pumps at the filling station; in the basement for fuel oil; on the side of the house for electricity—and, as we'll later see, in the "accumulator" of a computer, which is its central register, the one with which the user has the most contact. These are all just strings of flip-flops.

Why do these registers, these strings of flip-flops, play such a pivotal role in the operations of computers? An illuminating answer is as follows: "A very large part of the operations in a computer consists of nothing more than the transfer of words from one register to another. That isn't surprising if we note the manipulations we perform when doing a calculation using pencil and paper. First we transfer numbers to the paper. We may then need to transfer several numbers to a single column so that we can add them, and then we may want to transfer the sum to some other location. It is not gross exaggeration to say that the manipulations performed in a digital computer consist of a great deal of register-to-register transfers mixed with a few arithmetic and logic operations."*

It is by becoming fully comfortable with the mechanics of register-to-register transfers that both the hardware and software aspects of a computer emerge as truly meaningful. Before we go on to describe, first, how flip-flops are strung together to form registers, and later, how information is moved from one register to another, we should note that the flip-flops we've been discussing thus far have been composed of a pair of cross-coupled NAND gates. It turns out that a pair of cross-coupled NOR gates can be—and often is—used for the same purpose (although the truth or excitation table, as it is frequently called, which describes the next state in the sequence, would have its output column inverted). Also, it turns out that a variety of different kinds of flip-flops can be constructed, many depending for their change of state on the pulse of a clock. The details are fascinating, and we hope you'll pursue them when you've finished reading this work, with the aid of the annotated bibliography at the end of the book. However, the details aren't needed in order to understand the rest of the material we'll cover. Above all, register-to-register transfers will form our main focus.

---

* H. Taub, *Digital Circuits and Microprocessors,* McGraw-Hill Book Company, New York, 1982, p. 160.

chapter 2 counters and counting

To learn more about registers and, simultaneously, about binary arithmetic, in this chapter we'll look at *counters*. These are the registers with which most people already feel somewhat comfortable. The units are indeed everywhere, keeping track of the number of cars that go through a toll gate and the number of people born each day.

"I'm a Little Flip-Flop, Short and Stout, Here Are My Inputs, Here Are My Out—"

Near the end of Chapter 1 we learned that flip-flops can be constructed out of either cross-coupled NAND or NOR gates. Which ones are used makes little difference, so from now on we'll represent a flip-flop by a square box and not worry about what's in it, just so long as it does the job.

To review briefly: A NOT gate has *one* input and *one* output, as we saw in Figure 1-3. AND and OR gates have *two or more* inputs and *one* output, as we saw in Figure 1-1. Finally, flip-flops usually have *two* inputs and *two* outputs, in which one of the outputs is always the reverse of the other, as we saw in Figure 1-9. Therefore the box we will draw from now on to describe a flip-flop looks like the one in Figure 2-1. Since all we can see are the inputs, A and B, and the outputs, Q and its opposite $\overline{Q}$, and not the electronic devices inside the box, this picture is usually referred to as a "black-box" version of a flip-flop.

Something is missing from this picture, though, if we intend to use the device to keep track of the most important everyday situation we want to monitor. Which situation is that? What *is* the most widespread use by far to which counters are put in our everyday lives? Keeping track of time. On our wrists and walls are the counters we refer to most often each day.

What is interesting is that when clocks had two hands (three, if a second hand was included), people eventually came to realize that the insides consisted largely of gears. As the gears whirred, the hands moved. Now that clocks are increasingly becoming digital, and have only numbers and not hands on their faces, it is essential to realize that something electronic has taken the place of the mechanical gears. What is it? Flip-flops, arranged in strings, to form registers. When the flip-flops change state, the numbers on the face of the clock also change.

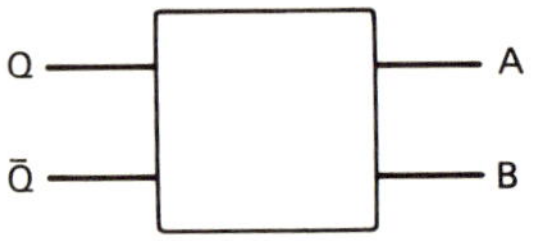

Figure 2-1 A "black-box" version of a flip-flop.

The element that is missing from our simple, black-box picture of a flip-flop, then, is a clock input. If the unit is to keep track of time for us, it needs to be hooked up to a clock. The unit that we need therefore has three inputs: the two it had before and a new one, from the clock, as shown in Figure 2-2.

The diagrams in this chapter have usually been turned around (inputs on the right side of the device, outputs on the left) because numbers increase in size from right to left; for instance, 111 versus 11.

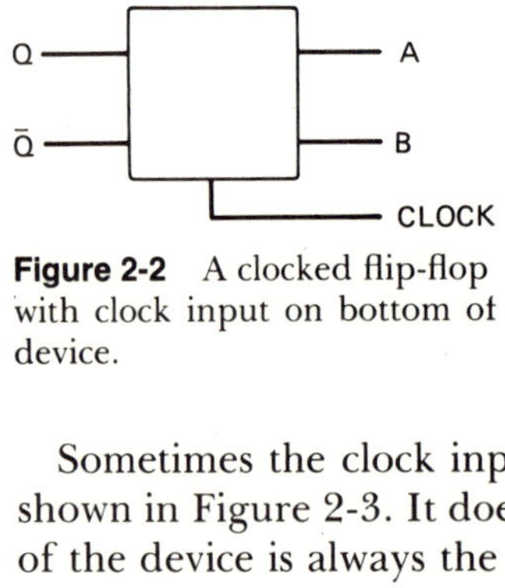

Figure 2-2 A clocked flip-flop with clock input on bottom of device.

Sometimes the clock input is drawn between the A and B inputs, as shown in Figure 2-3. It doesn't matter what the layout is: The operation of the device is always the same.

The key point here is that the inputs to the flip-flop are effective only when they occur synchronously (meaning at the same time) with an input signal from the clock. That is, input signals A, B, and C must arrive at the flip-flop simultaneously if they are to cause the output state to change. For that reason, a clocked flip-flop is called a *synchronous flip-*

flop. By contrast, the first flip-flop we encountered, in Figure 1-9, is called an *asynchronous flip-flop,* and its output depends solely on the signals it receives at its two inputs, here labeled A and B.

You may be wondering where the clock pulse comes from. In both a watch and a computer it is usually generated by a quartz crystal. Why? The crystal can be made to vibrate millions of times per second by applying a voltage across it. (The phenomenon is called the *piezoelectric effect*—pronounced "pee-ay-zo"—and we mention it only so that you can pursue the subject further through the references at the back of the book, if it's of interest to you.) A piezoelectric quartz crystal provides a highly stable frequency source, one that is little affected, for instance, by normal temperature changes.

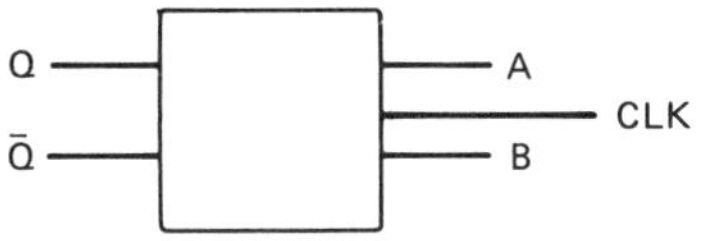

Figure 2-3 A clocked flip-flop, with clock input on side of device.

People who are having their first encounter with the material we're discussing often ask an interesting question at this point: "How does the additional input—input #3 from the clock—become smoothly integrated into the operation of the flip-flop? That is, isn't it hard to make a synchronous flip-flop from one that was originally asynchronous?"

Not at all. Odd as it may sound at first, what is required is an AND gate. This seemingly innocuous little device can be made to work wonders where timing is concerned. Getting two impulses to combine so that they produce their effect simultaneously (or not at all) merely requires that each signal be made one of the inputs to a two-input AND gate.

An example drawn from everyday life serves to illustrate how simple this seemingly complicated process really is. When a group of equally skilled runners, say, three of them, Tom, Dick, and Harry, are all lined up in their starting blocks at a track meet, each is set to run. The adrenaline is pumping, the desire to win is present in abundance. What's missing is the sound of the shot from the starter's pistol. Looking at each runner as an AND gate helps us understand the many electronic devices that have a structure similar to this one (see Figure 2-4). The large dot drawn where two lines intersect is intended to convey the fact that the two lines are connected at that point; otherwise they just overlap, making no electrical connection.

Since an AND gate needs two 1s as inputs in order to produce a 1 as an output, if either the starter's gun doesn't go off, or it does but the desire

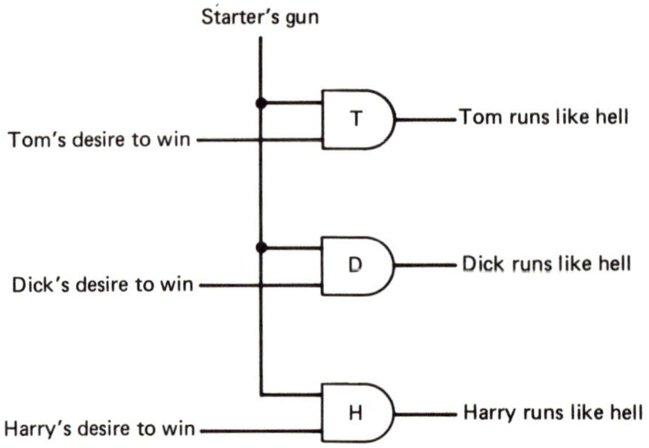

Figure 2-4 Three runners awaiting the starter's signal.

to win isn't present, the runner will produce a 0. In a similar manner, when we want a number of electronic events to occur simultaneously, all we have to do is use AND gates in the appropriate places.

Fidex: Automating Your Dog

If we're to succeed in making a counter from the limited tools at our disposal, we're obviously going to have to hook them up in the right way. One thing is clear: A single flip-flop just isn't enough. All it can do is go back and forth between one state and the other (remember, it has only two of them, a 0 and a 1). That might be useful at a railroad crossing where we need a flashing light—at 0 the light would be off and at 1 the light would be on, with the clock pulses determing when the switching takes place—but we require a more complicated device for the purpose of counting.

What is called for is *a string of flip-flops in which the output of one serves as the input to the next.* In that case, information will pass from flip-flop #1 to flip-flop #2, and so on, down the line. Let's see how the process works with just two flip-flops. Specifically, what we want to do is transfer the contents of flip-flop #1 to flip-flop #2 in the device pictured in Figure 2-5. The two input lines to each flip-flop are labeled J and K, instead of A and B, because the kind of flip-flop that is normally used in this situation is called a JK flip-flop. (Recall that at the end of the last chapter we mentioned that computer engineers have a variety of different types of flip-flops from which to choose, depending on the task at hand. The most important feature of a JK flip-flop is that when both its inputs are 1s, its output state, Q, changes with the arrival of each and every clock pulse. Since it acts like a toggle switch that repeatedly opens and closes—think of a light switch wiggling back and forth—this flip-flop is said to toggle each time it changes state. For that reason, it is sometimes referred to as a type T flip-flop.) Don't let the lettering in this or the other diagrams confuse you. It doesn't matter what letters are used to label the inputs; the operation of the device is the same. How it's manufactured and hooked up is how it operates.

What *does* matter, and should indeed be noted, is that there is a clock input connected to flip-flop #2. The signal from the clock serves the same purpose that the starter's gun serves at a track meet. Namely, no information will move from flip-flop #1 to flip-flop #2 until a signal from the clock arrives and *enables* it to do so.

The word "enable" will be encountered many times in the remainder of this or any other book about computer hardware, and for good reason: Having data move around in a computer in an uncoordinated manner would produce the same chaotic effect as having all the runners at a track meet leave their starting blocks whenever they felt like it, even though other events were in progress on the track. Whether a clock pulse or some other signal coordinates the information transfers in a computer isn't the point. Something *has* to do the coordinating. At least when two runners collide, they both still exist after the collision. In a computer, a similar collision will usually result in the loss of one or both of the pieces of information involved. The enable signal allows the transfer to occur in an orderly manner, assuming that it was ready to take place to begin with. (That is, the sound of the starter's gun at a track meet is wasted if the runners aren't in their starting blocks waiting for it).

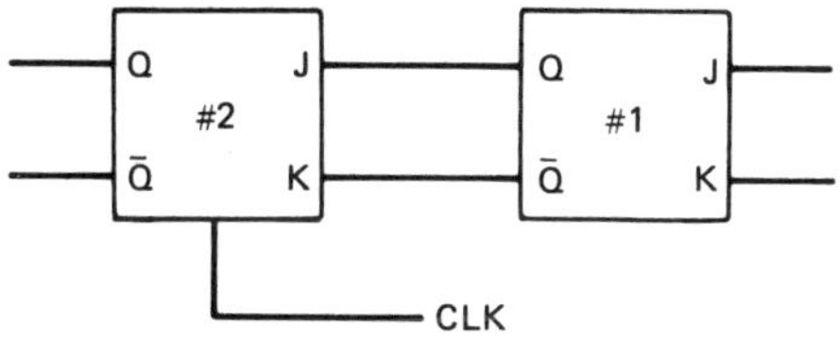

Figure 2-5 Information transfer between flip-flops.

After the enable signal is received, thanks to the arrival of the clock pulse, the contents of flip-flop #1 are transferred to flip-flop #2. Question: Is there a difference at this point between the bit of data stored in #1 and the bit stored in #2? The answer is no. The bit stored in #1 has been transferred to #2—more precisely, admitted into flip-flop #2—thanks to the enable signal from the clock. However, nothing has happened to #1 to make it change state. That is, no new signals have arrived at its J and K inputs to cause it to change. The upshot is that both flip-flops now hold the same bit; both are 0s or both are 1s.

If we want flip-flop #1 as well as #2 to change (and simultaneously, at that), then the clock pulse that enables the change in #2 must also reach #1. Moreover, it obviously must do so in much the same way it is enabling a change in #2. The resulting arrangement is shown in Figure 2-6. What is this arrangement of flip-flops called? The most natural name: a *shift register.* If there were four flip-flops linked together in the manner pictured in Figure 2-6, like pearls on a string, data would enter at one end (one bit at a time) and exit at the other of the string (also one bit at a time).

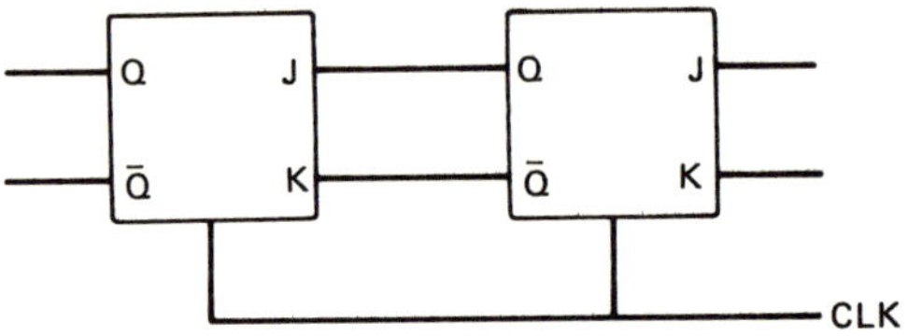

Figure 2-6 A shift register.

As is done with a string of pearls, the two ends of the string of flip-flops can be connected. Then data will move round and round the circle that has been created, instead of going in one end and out the other. If we call the four flip-flops on the string A, B, C, and D, and assume that in the beginning of the period in question A = 1, while B, C, and D = 0, the motion would go as follows:

	Flip-flops			
Time	A	B	C	D
$t = 0$	1	0	0	0
$t = 1$	0	1	0	0
$t = 2$	0	0	1	0
$t = 3$	0	0	0	1
$t = 4$	1	0	0	0

By reading each row of the chart, then moving down to the line below it, we can see that with each clock pulse, the 1 moves to the next flip-flop in the sequence. It's almost like a runner doing laps around a track. Instead of a 4-minute mile, here the completion time for each trip around the loop takes 4 units of time (seconds, millionths of a second, or whatever the time units we're using happen to be). This device is called a *ring counter,* that is, a counter that is effectively arranged in a ring (even if the physical device isn't in the shape of a circle).

When they learn about ring counters for the first time, many people are underwhelmed. The device strikes them as too simple to be of much use. Be that as it may, ring counters are used in a substantial portion of the industrial world's manufacturing operations. A four-step manufacturing process, such as the making of a long-playing record or eyeglass frames, may well be controlled by a ring counter that has four flip-flops. Thanks to the counter, one step in the process follows another in the correct order, each for a specified period of time.

The device can even be used to automate your dog. If the cost of Alpo is getting you down, or you don't feel like trailing behind Fido any longer with a pooper-scooper in hand and a gallant smile on your face for passers-by, there is an alternative—or there soon will be. People worry that automation will eventually cost them their jobs, but pets will probably be automated before people are. When and if that happens, ring counters will play a role.

Why? One of the first things people learn to say to a dog is "fetch." They want the dog to chase after any sticks they throw and bring in the morning newspaper. Real dogs don't always cooperate, but an automated one wouldn't balk, or bite. When you yelled FETCH (the word is now in capital letters because instructions to a computer are normally written that way), it would do as you requested.

Let's assume that you decided to spring for only the economy-model automated hound, named Fidex, and as a result, it has to get you the Sunday paper one section at a time. If Fidex contains a ring counter consisting of four flip-flops, then the first two operations it controls could be called the *fetch cycle*. Fetch 1 and fetch 2 (it should sound like "hup one, hup two" in football) will net you, say, the sports and business sections. The third and fourth flip-flops are responsible for setting into motion—that is, executing—actions that depend on what you've read in the first and second steps of the cycle. Let's call these latter two steps, then, the *execution cycle*

What does all this have to do with computers? Everything. It is worthwhile for us to take a glimpse now at material we will be examining in detail later. If some of it seems puzzling, don't worry: When we return to the subject in subsequent chapters and look at the process step by step, it won't be any harder to understand than the idea of telling an automated dog to fetch your paper and then call your stockbroker for you, thanks to what you learned in the fetch part of the dog's behavior.

A computer is hardware, and needs software—a program—to run it. The program consists of a numbered sequence of instructions. What is being fetched, then, in a computer is the next instruction. Executing the contents of the instruction is the second half of the fetch-and-execution process. The process, called a *machine cycle*, consists of two parts. First there is a fetch cycle, with one or more trips to the computer's memory (where the program is stored). Then there is an execution cycle, usually with another trip to the computer's memory (where the raw data to be manipulated are also stored). Who is commanding all the fetching and executing? With Fidex, it is you. In a computer, it is the microprocessor, the brain of the machine, a unit we'll look at more closely in Chapter 4. Makes a point of noting even at this early stage that the words microprocessor and microcomputer refer to different things. A microprocessor is only *part* of a microcomputer. A useful analogy can be drawn between a microprocessor and the human brain, on the one hand, and a microcomputer and the entire human body, on the other. We'll make this much more precise later.

For the moment, the main reason we're interested in seeing how to construct a general-purpose counter is twofold: It turns out that most people come to understand binary arithmetic better once they learn a little about the device that actually helps perform the arithmetic, and how it does it. Second, there is an important counter—the program instruction counter (the PC)—in the microprocessor that keeps track of the sequence of instructions.

A Universal Gate

Shift registers of all sorts, including ring counters, will be our focus again later when we examine the connection between hardware and software. For the time being, we're looking for an economical counter (that is, one that uses the smallest number of flip-flops). It doesn't seem that we've found one yet. One modification that we should clearly make concerns the number of inputs to each of the flip-flops we use. Until now, there have been three, each independent of the other two.

Is that necessary? We certainly need the clock input, otherwise various parts of the computer's operations might get out of sync with one another and cause serious problems. However, the other two inputs, J and K, can be combined. In fact, the process of counting shouldn't require that each flip-flop in the sequence have its J and K inputs independent of one another. After all, unlike the situations at restaurants and singles bars that we examined in the first chapter, in which there were men, women, and couples to consider, here we're dealing with a simpler case. All the individuals—whether they be people, cars, or seconds—are to be viewed as the same for the purpose of tallying them up.

There is a time-honored tradition in microelectronics that calls for the use of complex devices to handle even simple tasks. That way, if a difficult task also needs to be handled, the hardware is already available or in place to tackle it. There are major advantages on the manufacturing end as well, since one unit can be produced to serve a wide variety of purposes. It may be necessary to modify the hardware so as effectively to reduce its complexity and bring it down to the level of the problem to be solved, but this is usually easy. In this case, it requires us to tie the two input leads, J and K, together. This could also be done with the logic gates we looked at in Chapter 1. What, for example, does a two-input AND gate look like once its two inputs are tied together? Just what you'd expect (see Figure 2-7). In other words, instead of two inputs, there is now effectively only one. For if A = 1 in the AND gate with its inputs tired together, then both inputs are 1s simultaneously, so the output, C, is also a 1. Conversely, if A = 0, then both inputs are 0s, so the output is also 0. That's all there is; there are no other cases to consider in this instance.

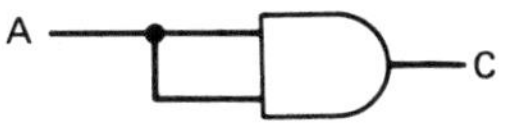

Figure 2-7 A two-input AND gate with its inputs tied together.

As long as we're hog-tying logic gates, let's do the same thing to a NAND gate and see what we get (Figure 2-8). When A = 1 in a NAND gate with its inputs bound together, both input signals to the gate are 1s and therefore the NAND gate's output state, C, is equal to 0. (See the truth table for NAND in Figure 1-7.) In fact, this is the only time that C = 0. Conversely, when A = 0, both inputs seem to the gate to be 0, so the output, C, is equal to 1. If we summarize these results in a truth table, something fascinating surfaces:

A	C
1	0
0	1

The table, when read one row at a time, tells us that whatever we put into the device, we can expect the reverse back. In that case, we have created an inverter, a NOT gate. If two seemingly different logic gates have the same truth table, for all intents and purposes they're the same. So, if we start out with a collection of NAND gates and happen to need a NOT gate along the way, we can easily make one.

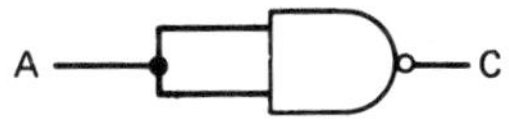

Figure 2-8 A two-input NAND gate with its inputs tied together.

The same goes for an AND gate, if we need one; it too can readily be constructed from NANDs. If you recall the definition of NAND, you'll quickly see why: A NAND gate is nothing more than an AND-NOT gate (see Figure 1-4). And a NOT gate followed by another NOT gate brings us back to where we started. The two NOTs in succession cancel one another. The string of gates in Figure 2-9 is therefore, in effect, an AND gate. It is just an AND-NOT gate followed by a NOT gate. But AND-NOT-NOT = AND, which is just what we were looking for.

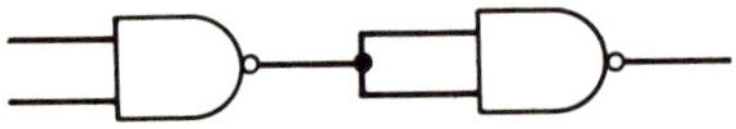

Figure 2-9 An AND gate constructed from two NAND gates.

Finally, NAND gates can also be used to construct an OR gate. It is for this reason that NAND gates are said to be *universal*; using them alone we can construct AND, OR, and NOT. The same universality also happens to apply to NOR gates; using them alone we can make the three basic gates, AND, OR, and NOT. In short, computer engineers usually don't have to use a wide variety of logic gates to achieve the various goals they have in mind. NAND gates (out of which the others are made) suffice, particularly since NANDs are so easy to manufacture in intergrated-circuit (IC) form.

What we did with logic gates we can also do with flip-flops. Tying the J and K inputs to a flip-flop together—and then keeping the common JK input at 1—means that the flip-flop will toggle with every clock pulse. That is, the flip-flop will go from 1 to 0 and back again every time a clock pulse goes by.

We need to pause for a moment and be absolutely certain that we understand what happens during any given clock pulse. Nothing connected with the timing mechanisms in a computer is a minor matter. The most important issue here is for us to know precisely when the flip-flop changes state. Ideally, it does so instantaneously, going from 0 to 1 (or vice versa) in a flash, so that we're never confused about which of its two states it is in at any moment. If it takes its time making the transition and loiters at ½ for a while, there is a good chance that a mess will be created. For the machine understands only 0s and 1s, and this is neither. It is hardly surprising, then, that we want any changes of state that do occur during a clock pulse to do so with the greatest possible speed.

When, precisely when, should a flip-flop make the transition from one state to another? The answer is: right between the tick and the tock that, taken together, define each clock pulse. (Although it's not essential, from here on we'll assume that the tick and tock both take the same amount of time.) The appropriate picture of the pulse is shown in Figure 2-10. The 0-to-1 transition is always called, by definition, *the rising edge*; the 1-to-0 transition is defined as *the falling edge*. Some people ask at this point: "Isn't it possible to become confused about which tick to pair with any given tock, the one before it or the one after it? After all, if you jump in in the middle of an endless series of tick-tock-tick-tocks, maybe the place to begin counting is a tock, not a tick."

Actually, it doesn't matter whether you use the rising edge or the falling edge to trigger the nearly instantaneous switch in the flip-flop's state. Either edge will do, but not both. It is essential to be consistent: Either all the flip-flops must change state (if they were going to at all) when the rising edge of the clock pulse arrives, or they must do so when the falling edge arrives.

Figure 2-10 Clock pulses. The diagram should be read from left to right, the direction of increasing time.

Clocks and Counting

Now, at last, we're in a position to construct a general-purpose counter, one that uses the smallest number of flip-flops, *and* learn a good deal about binary arithmetic as well. Let's gather the few simple facts we'll need in order to assemble the device correctly.

First, the flip-flops we'll be using change state with every clock pulse. (If the technical details interest you, the units are JK flip-flops with both inputs tied together and maintained at 1. Therefore J = 1 and K = 1, which forces the output, Q, to go back and forth between 0 and 1 with the falling edge of each pulse from the clock.)

Second, only the first flip-flop is connected directly to the clock.

What does such a device look like? Using two flip-flops, it would look like Figure 2-11.

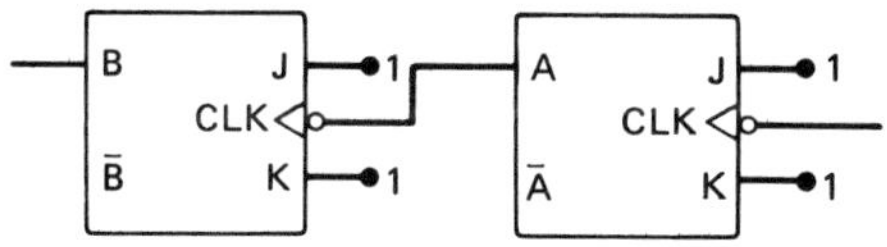

Figure 2-11 A counter.

There are four things worth noting about Figure 2-11.

1. We haven't drawn the J or K input lines to either of the flip-flops because there's no need to; all J and K inputs are assumed to be held at 1 while the device is operating.
2. The triangle drawn at the clock's input point into the flip-flop means that this flip-flop is edge-triggered. That is, it doesn't care whether the voltage on the line is high or low; the flip-flop will change state when either the rising or falling *edge* (we don't know which yet) of a clock pulse arrives. Read the triangle, then, as "edge-triggered."
3. The little circle at the clock input—you may remember it from the NOT gate in Figure 1-3—tells us that it is the *falling* edge that triggers the change. That is, when the signal from the clock goes from 1 to 0, the flip-flops output state (A in the case of the first flip-flop, B in the case of the second) changes to the reverse of whatever it had been until that moment.
4. Last but by no means least, note that flip-flop A's output goes into B's clock input. That is, A serves to "clock," or more accurately, trigger, changes in B's output state. That being the case, we haven't drawn $\overline{A}$, since it is merely the reverse of A (until now, we've been using Q and $\overline{Q}$ as labels for the two complementary output states of each flip-flop).

After all these preliminaries, let's see if we've accomplished anything. Specifically, we want to know: Can this device actually count?

It is clear that flip-flop A simply goes from 0 to 1 and back again with each clock pulse's falling edge. That is, A merely toggles. When does B change? As the little circle at its clock input tells us, it does so only when A goes from 1 to 0, for that is when flip-flop B thinks the falling edge of a clock pulse has just arrived. Putting these results in chart form helps clarify the situation:

B	A
0	0
0	1
1	0
1	1
0	0
0	1
1	0
1	1

Although we've been asking you to read the tables presented up to now row by row, this table and the next should be read column by column first, starting at the right. Column A, as you can see, merely has 0 and 1 alternating regularly. Why, then, doesn't column B do the same? Because—and this a key point—B changes state only when 1 goes to 0 in column A. Therefore B changes state with *every other* pulse of the clock. The result is that two 0s are followed by two 1s in succession, and so on, down the column.

If there were a third flip-flop, C, in Figure 2-11 and hence a third column in the truth table, you can probably guess what the sequence of 0s and 1s would be. Like the other two columns, C would start out at 0. How long would it stay at 0? Until the flip-flop before it, represented by column B, made the transition from 1 to 0. As you can see, that happens during the fourth clock pulse—and every four clock pulses after that. The resulting table thus looks as follows:

	C	B	A
Before the first clock pulse arrives	0	0	0
After the first clock pulse	0	0	1
After the second clock pulse	0	1	0
After the third clock pulse	0	1	1
After the fourth clock pulse	1	0	0
After the fifth clock pulse	1	0	1
After the sixth clock pulse	1	1	0
After the seventh clock pulse	1	1	1

Read row by row, this table provides a list of the first seven binary numbers!

It is very important that you understand what's going on here—so important, in fact, that we'd like to ask you to forget everything you've already read in this book. Let's pretend for a while that the first line of the next section is the first line of the first chapter (it almost was). We're going to start over again, from scratch, and discuss binary numbers without reference to any electronic device that is used to count them. Then we'll compare the results of the arithmetic versus electronic approach and see how each illuminates the other.

"Lend Me a Hand, Will You?"

We have 10 distinct, single-digit numerals—0 through 9—in our everyday number system because we have 10 fingers and a similar number of toes. (Who knows what would have happened if we'd have had 8 fingers and 10 toes?) When we get to the number 11, we therefore have to begin again, having used up all 10 fingers. One solution is to use someone else's fingers in addition to our own.

Notice how economically we can do that. We only have to ask someone to lend us a hand after 10 objects have been counted, and even then, we need only one extra finger at a time. Therefore if we finish counting a pile of objects and we have seven fingers raised and our friend has six, we've obviously counted 67 objects.

Now consider what would happen if all human beings had only one finger on one hand and none on the other. Just one digit per individual. Doing finger math would now require a lot more friends. (It would be hard on the glove industry and nail polish companies, but it might do wonders for people's social lives.) How many friends would it take to count three objects? Well, let's see, the first one you could count yourself by raising your finger. The second object, though, would require you to put your finger down and your friend to raise his. Finally, counting the third object would require you to raise your finger as well. End result: The number 3 would be represented by two people standing side by side, each with a finger raised. If you call yourself Column A and your friend column B, the number 3 would be represented by 11.

How about the number 5? How many friends do you need in order to count this high? We already know that getting as high as the number 3 requires two people, each standing there with a finger raised. That is clearly the highest number these two can represent. To get to 4, then, they'll have to call on a third person to help. Let's do this formally, as our first example of binary arithmetic. We'll ask Tom, Dick, and Harry (you may remember them from the track meet) each to lend us a hand—or more precisely, a finger.

At the start, then, we have the number 3;

Tom	*Dick*	*Harry*
0	1	1

Here 0 means that the person has his hand clenched, in the shape of a fist, with no finger raised; a 1 means that he's standing there with his finger upright. We want to take the next step—that is, add 1—and get to 4. Harry already has his finger raised, so all he can do when an additional unit is to be added to the total is put his finger down and say "Over to you, Dick." That's his way of communicating the most important rule in binary arithmetic: $1 + 1 = 0$ and carry the 1. In other words, $1 + 1 = 10$. (By 10, here, we mean that Dick has his finger raised and Harry doesn't.)

If Dick already has his finger raised, the same rule applies: "$1 + 1 = 0$ and over to you, Tom." The end result: $4 = 100$ in binary. To add one more to this total, and hence finally get to 5, is easy: Harry merely has to raise his finger. (Remember, it was down at this point, so by raising it he can represent the fact that one more unit has been added to the total.) Therefore 5 = 101 in binary. And so it goes; the other numbers are constructed in the very same way. What, then, have we learned? The first thing is that anyone who tells you that binary arithmetic is hard has either too many fingers or too few friends.

The second thing is that using 10s to count things seems natural to us only because of our abundance of fingers and toes. Be that as it may, having gotten used to the system, it is hard for most people to get used to another. The best way to bridge the gap between the decimal system we all use every day and the binary number system that computers use is this: start thinking about numbers—in both systems—in terms of columns.

In the garden-variety base-10 system, the first column is units (that is, 0 through 9). The second column (counting from right to left) is tens, the third column is hundreds, and so on. Therefore, 7356 really means $7 \times 1000 + 3 \times 100 + 5 \times 10 + 6 \times 1$. The key point here is that to get from one column to the next (that is, the one to the *left* of it) requires us to multiply by 10 each time. Thus, $10 = 10 \times 1$, $100 = 10 \times 10$ and $1000 = 10 \times 100$. To repeat: Multiplying by 10 shifts our position one column to the left.

It's the same in binary arithmetic, only this time multiplying by 2 is what takes us from any given column to the one to the left of it. Once again, the first column is units, although in binary there are only two of them, a 0 and a 1. The second column is 2×1, so a 1 here really stands for $2 \times 1 = 2$. Finally, to get to the third column, we again multiply by 2, so a 1 here stands for $2 \times 2 \times 1 = 4$. Therefore, 111 in binary means $1 \times 4 + 1 \times 2 + 1$, which equals 7. As another example, 10101 in binary = $1 \times 16 + 0 \times 8 + 1 \times 4 + 0 \times 2 + 1 \times 1 = 21$.

There isn't much memorization that has to be done to understand computers. The subject isn't like botany or human anatomy. However, there is one piece of memorization that is worthwhile and is very easy besides, because you can *figure out* the rest of the numbers after the first few, which you already know. Specifically, what you should be thoroughly familiar with is what happens when you keep multiplying the number 2 by itself. The first 11 members of the sequence are 1, 2, 4, 8, 16, 32, 64, 128, 256, 512, and 1024. Notice that getting from one number to the next in the sequence is simple, and merely requires you to multiply the given number by 2. The importance of this sequence of numbers is that they play the same role in binary arithmetic as 10, 100, 1000, and so on, do in ordinary arithmetic: They are the *headings* on each successively greater column.

Powers of Two

Scientists and engineers are used to dealing with large numbers and have therefore devised a shorthand for them that is quite useful. Since a hundred is 10 times 10, and a thousand is 10 times 10 times 10:

$100 = 10 \times 10 = 10^2$ (This is read as "10 to the second power," or "10 squared.")

$1000 = 10 \times 10 \times 10 = 10^3$ (This is read as "10 to the third power," or "10 cubed.")

That is, 10^3 simply means "three 10s multiplied together." That not only makes large numbers easier to write, it makes them less awesome as well. A million can be written either as 1,000,000 or 10^6, six 10s multiplied together. One of the nice features of working with a number system based on 10 instead of 2 is that you can easily check to see if you've written the number correctly in this more compact manner. How? The 6 in 10^6 means that there should be 6 zeros in the result.

Multiplying the number 2 by itself repeatedly does not give us such instantly recognizable results, but the compact scientific notation is still very useful. In some ways, it is even more so, because 16 takes up only two spaces in the ordinary decimal system but takes up five spaces in the binary system: 16 in binary is 10000. That is, $16 = 1 \times 16 + 0 \times 8 + 0 \times 4 + 0 \times 2 + 0 \times 1$.

Most people have seen this kind of shorthand notation for base 10 (that is, they've seen numbers such as 10^3 before), but those who've had little contact with computers may not have seen numbers such as 2^5, two to the fifth power. Yet understanding what 2^5 means is just as easy; all it takes to become comfortable with it is a little practice. Read it as "five twos multiplied together."

This is the point where the memorization comes in handy. Unless you remember that $2^5 = 32$ (or are willing to figure it out each time by multiplying 2 times itself four times—that is, $2 \times 2 \times 2 \times 2 \times 2$), the shorthand will give you a nice, neat expression that means little or nothing to you.

So spend a few minutes memorizing the following eight expressions. The minor effort involved will pay surprisingly large dividends later.

2^0 is *defined* as being 1*	$2^6 = 64$
$2^3 = 8$	$2^7 = 128$
$2^4 = 16$	$2^8 = 256$
$2^5 = 32$	$2^{10} = 1024$

*If you remember high school algebra, you can prove this easily instead of having to accept it on faith. Since $x^{a+b} = x^a \cdot x^b$, we have $2^0 = 2^{n+(-n)} = 2^n \cdot 2^{-n}$. But $2^{-n} = 1/2^n$. So $2^0 = 2^n/2^n = 1$, since any number divided by itself, except 0, is equal to 1.

To repeat: even if you forget them—and you will—you can always figure them out again quickly. However, the goal here is to become sufficiently at home with the shorthand form of binary numbers that when you encounter them again—and you will—they will be thoroughly familiar to you, like a bunch of old friends.

Once that happens, you'll have no trouble figuring out what, say, 1101 1011 means in binary. (A space is often inserted after every four numbers in a long binary number; it's the equivalent of commas in the base-10 system, where they're used to group numbers in clusters of three. Besides making a binary number more readable, the space has no meaning.) By referring to the headings at the top of the columns, you'll know how many of that particular power of 2 there are:

2^7	2^6	2^5	2^4	2^3	2^2	2^1	2^0
128	64	32	16	8	4	2	1
1	1	0	1	1	0	1	1

That is, we have $1 \times 128 + 1 \times 64 + 0 \times 32 + 1 \times 16 + 1 \times 8 + 0 \times 4 + 1 \times 2 + 1 \times 1$, which is equal to 219. Or, $2^7 + 2^6 + 2^4 + 2^3 + 2^1 + 2^0 + =$ 219. When all is said and done, it is clear that a binary number is nothing more than a recipe for adding together certain powers of 2.

Multiplication Is a Moving Experience

Now let's see if what we've learned about binary numbers casts light on the electronic devices (particularly flip-flops) used to count them, and conversely, whether our knowledge of flip-flops helps deepen our understanding of binary arithmetic.

Figure 2-12 shows an arrangement of flip-flops similar to the one in Figure 2-11, except that now there are four of them instead of two. By way of review, this is an asynchronous counter, asynchronous because the clock input is directly connected only to the first flip-flop, not the other three. It is usually called a *ripple* counter, since the signal to the first flip-flop takes time to propagate to and through the other flip-flops in the sequence, until, like a row of falling dominos, the last one is affected.

Suppose we know that this string of flip-flops—which we will depict

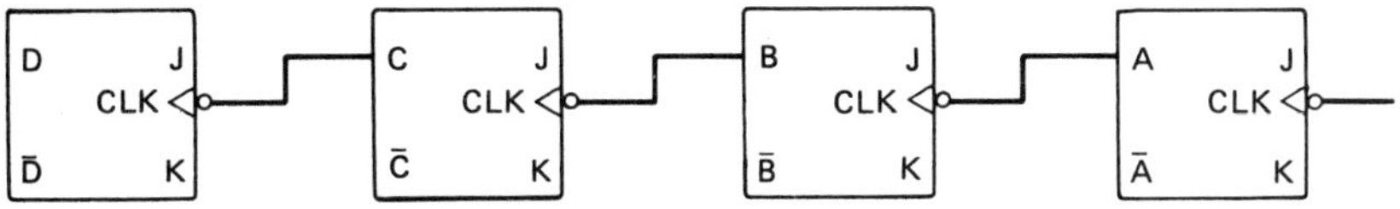

Figure 2-12 A 4-bit asynchronous ripple counter.

from now on in the form of boxes, side by side, with the space between them removed—is in the state

1	1	0	1

First question: What number does this represent? Answer:

$$1 \times 2^3 + 1 \times 2^2 + 0 \times 2^1 + 1 \times 2^0 = 8 + 4 + 0 + 1 = 13$$

The second question is: What happens when any given binary number is multiplied by 2? The answer can help substantially to deepen your understanding of binary arithmetic. Let's look at one example and then state the general rule. Suppose the binary number we're given is 5; that is, the four flip-flops in Figure 2-12 are in the state

0	1	0	1

since

$$0 \times 2^3 + 1 \times 2^2 + 0 \times 2^1 + 1 \times 2^0 = 0 + 4 + 0 + 1 = 5$$

We know that $5 \times 2 = 10$, so what we now must do is convert 10 into binary form and see how it compares to the number 5 in binary, 0101, with which we began. Well, what is 10 in binary? It is 1010, as you can readily determine, since

$$1 \times 2^3 + 0 \times 2^2 + 1 \times 2^1 + 0 \times 2^0 = 8 + 0 + 2 + 0 = 10$$

How do 0101 and 1010 compare with one another? Simple. To make 10 in binary from 5 in binary, all you have to do is push all the numbers to the *left* one space, and fill the empty space with a 0. This is exactly what one does in ordinary base-10 arithmetic anyway, but the result is that the number is multiplied by 10, not 2. Thus 35 shoved to the left one space to become 350 is indeed 35 multiplied by 10. If we repeat the process, shifting still another space to the left, we have 3500, which of course is 350×10. Let's try the procedure with one more binary number and see if it works. Take 0111, which is

$$0 \times 8 + 1 \times 4 + 1 \times 2 + 1 \times 1 = 4 + 2 + 1 = 7$$

If we push it to the left one space, it becomes 1110.

But

$$1110 = 1 \times 2^3 + 1 \times 2^2 + 1 \times 2 + 0 \times 1 = 8 + 4 + 2 + 0 = 14$$

So the procedure works in this case too, since 7 doubled is 14. Actually it works in every case, assuming that we have enough flip-flops to hold the number that represents the product. For example, if we try to double 1110 by pushing all the binary digits—the bits—over one space, we wind up with 1100. That is 12, not the 28 (= 2 × 14) we expected to find. The problem is that there aren't enough flip-flops available here (we'd need five of them) to hold the correct answer, 11100, which is 28 in binary.

Most computers, no matter how small, have a way of indicating that you've used up all your flip-flops. To be more specific, the result of any calculations you make on a computer are stored temporarily in a string of flip-flops called the *accumulator*. This is the microprocessor's most important register, the one with which the user has the most contact. Suppose the microprocessor is an 8-bit device, meaning that eight flip-flops have been strung together to make up its accumulator. If the result of any addition or multiplication you do is 9 bits long, a ninth flip-flop, separate and apart from the accumulator, registers that fact. This extra flip-flop, called the *overflow*, changes state and let's you know that something is wrong.

One flip-flop can't send much of a message, but then again, in this instance no complicated message is called for. The situation is the same as the one that occurs on the dashboard of a car. There, there is a whole string of flip-flops, each of which, independent of the others, can switch from 0 ("your oil level is OK") to 1 ("something is wrong with your oil level"). Since it's just a flip-flop, it can't tell you the details of what's amiss the way a finely calibrated oil gauge—or better still, a pair of them, one for quantity of oil, the other for oil pressure—could. All it can do is warn you that there's trouble.

Let's look at one more example of overflow and we'll see something simple but important. The largest binary number a 4-bit counter—that is, four flip-flops strung together—can hold is 1111, which is 15 (since 8 + 4 + 2 + 1 = 15). If we add 1 to 1111, the result is 10000, because the rule "1 + 1 = 0 and carry the 1" would be applied here four times in succession. We had only four flip-flops in our counter to begin with, so the counter will now read

0	0	0	0

The 1 that overflowed is actually a carry. That's not usually the case; carry and overflow normally differ. Each flip-flop may not be able to tell us much, but for that very reason, two of them would be better here than one. Most microprocessors therefore have one flip-flop to indicate what the carry is and another to let us know that the result of the computation has overflowed (it may be an enormous overflow). In everyday use, the overflow flip-flop, usually labeled V, is the one more often referred to.

Overflows are common and, as long as you're aware that they've occurred, easily handled. Once they happen, though, the content of the carry flip-flop at that moment is usually of secondary importance.

Other flip-flops are used to monitor a variety of conditions in a microprocessor. Although these flip-flops operate independently of one another, they are usually clustered together, just as they are on the dashboard of a car. That doesn't mean a great deal; they're together only for convenience. In both cars and computers, the fact that one flip-flop communicates that there is trouble should have nothing to do with what the other flip-flops are saying. Each is to be read independently of the others, even if it turns out there is something sufficiently out of whack to cause more than one flip-flop to change state. You'd certainly not want the gas gauge in your car to suddenly register "empty" just because your oil pressure is low.

Summing up, microprocessors contain a string of flip-flops called a *status register*. It is also called a *flag register*, since each flip-flop can act as a red flag. This register is different from the accumulator inasmuch as each flip-flop in it independently monitors a different condition: The C flip-flop monitors carries and the V watches for overflows. There is also an N flip-flop to let you know that the result in the accumulator is negative. Finally, there is a Z flip-flop (or flag) to let you know that the result in the accumulator is zero.

You may be asking: "Why would anyone care whether the result in the accumulator is zero? Having a V flag available to let me know that there is an overflow makes sense, but why would a zero result in the accumulator be sufficiently important to warrant a flip-flop, Z, all its own?"

The answer goes right to the heart of how computers are used in many everyday applications: namely, to perform repetitive tasks. If you personally do something 10 times in a row, you're likely to start at zero and count to 10 to keep track while doing it. A computer would just as soon start at 10 and count to zero, since arriving at zero will always let it know, definitively, that it has finished with one task and is therefore free to handle another. (Space launchings always use this kind of countdown.)

Let's end this chapter with one quick quiz question: If shifting a binary number one space to the left *multiplies* it by 2, how do you *divide* a binary number by 2?

Answer: Move it one space to the right.

chapter

3

how a computer reads and writes

Everyone knows what a TV serial is. One episode follows the last, usually at the same time each week. Cars going through a tunnel that has only one lane may be said to be traveling in serial form too, since each has to follow the one in front of it. Similarly, data go into the counters we looked at in Chapter 2 one binary digit at a time. The string of flip-flops that make up the counter might as well be a tunnel, given that binary numbers enter it from only one end. If we overdo it, and the register overflows, data exit from the other end. The picture looks as shown in Figure 3-1.

However, neither cars nor data bits always have to travel one behind the other. If a highway has two lanes going in the same direction, two cars can travel on it side by side. In that case, we say that they are traveling in parallel. Similarly, there are many occasions when we want data bits, 0s and 1s, to travel side by side. Why? Because it's faster, even though we have to provide additional lanes to allow it to happen. But in some cases the additional speed of transfer is worth the extra cost. Moving data quickly from one location to another allows us to monitor certain complex processes or solve difficult problems whose solution would otherwise elude us. Data bits are therefore made to move from one register to another simultaneously. The picture looks as shown in Figure 3-2.

There's nothing complicated about any of this, and if you think of the many situations that occur each day which are basically parallel in nature, the concept will become well fixed in your mind. For instance, to say that the work world is largely "9 to 5" means that millions of people have tacitly agreed to accept these hours as the time frame during which they will all simultaneously be at work. It certainly makes coordination of their activities easier. Similarly, if a group of friends or a family sits down to eat, one person doesn't have to wait for another to finish, though they may all wait for one another before beginning.

In a computer, however, timing considerations play a paramount role. It doesn't really matter that one person finishes dinner first and another does so a few seconds later. But to the typical modern-day microprocessor, a few seconds is an eternity. Making certain that data bits being transferred in parallel are received simultaneously—that is, with split-second accuracy—is essential.

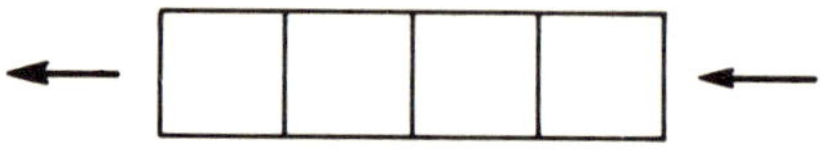

Figure 3-1 Serial data entry.

What is the easiest way to guarantee that that will happen? By using our old friend ENABLE. We first encountered ENABLE at the track meet, where the sound of the starter's gun as well as the will to win had to be present before the runners could head down the track successfully. However, we need a slightly different version of that analogy here in order to describe what typically happens during a register-to-register transfer in which data are being moved in parallel.

Suppose that you are the manager of a large sporting goods store, and the store's owners have decided to hold a "once-in-a-lifetime" sale to clear out some of the excess inventory. To excite public interest in the event, the owners have also decided to sell three 25-inch color TV sets for $1 each, first come, first served, one to a customer.

The event we're describing did indeed happen, and although the store's normal opening hour was 9:00, by 7:30 there were more than 2000 people milling around outside, eagerly waiting to get in. At exactly 9:00, you, as the manager, signal the 10 salespeople positioned at the 10 entrances to the store to throw the doors open.

How is this like an important aspect of computer operation? It turns

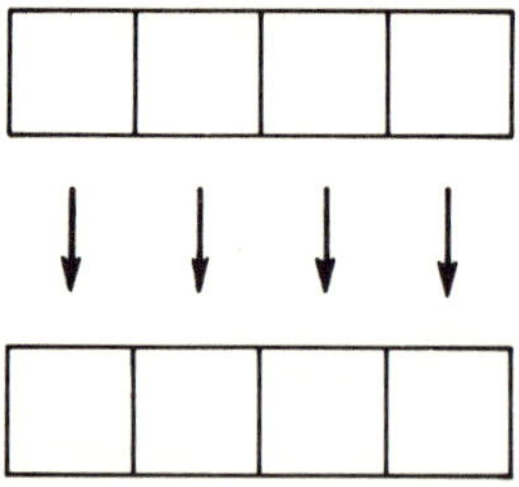

Figure 3-2 Parallel data entry.

out to be quite difficult to keep electronic signals that represent 0s and 1s traveling on parallel paths moving at exactly the same speed. Unfortunately, even if the signals are all sent at the same time on their respective parallel lines, they don't all arrive at precisely the same moment. What to do? Play store manager, and make them wait. When you are absolutely certain that each and every signal in the group has arrived at the end point of its respective line, then and only then do you give the ENABLE signal and admit them to the awaiting register. The resulting arrangement is shown in Figure 3-3.

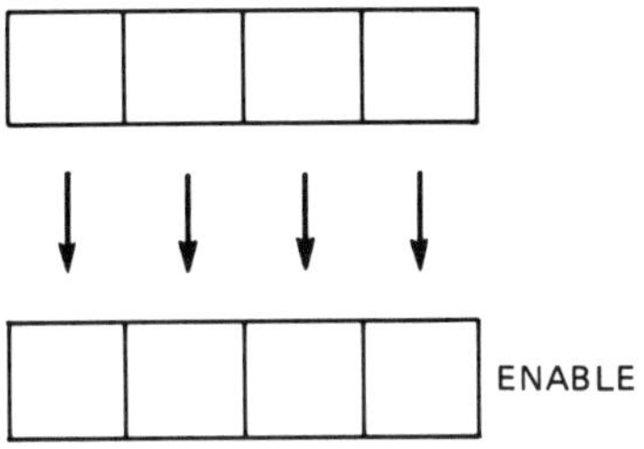

Figure 3-3 Parallel data entry, with an input-control ENABLE.

Although we have drawn the ENABLE input in a way that makes it appear to be connected only to the first flip-flop, it is in fact connected to all four and therefore makes them simultaneously receptive to the message from the flip-flops directly above them. Now it doesn't matter that one signal travels slightly faster than another on the line next to it; only when the ENABLE signal is given is the register on the receiving end ready to receive. ENABLE is the input-control signal that allows truly parallel register-to-register transfers. It is also frequently called the LOAD signal, since it allows the flip-flops in the destination register to "load up on" the new signal.

Summing up, previously we used ENABLE to send messages (or runners at the track meet) on their way simultaneously. Here we're using LOAD or ENABLE to allow messages (or customers at the store) to be received simultaneously.

Filling a Computer's Memory

It's all well and good to talk about register-to-register transfers and the crucial role they play in computer performance, but at this point you may be wondering: "Which registers are involved, and why? Also, where are the registers located?"

The registers we've become most familiar with up to now have been counters, that is, strings of flip-flops that get to the binary number 7 (which is 0111) by starting at 0000 and incrementing the counter by 1 each time a clock pulse arrives. However, suppose that we want to *start* with the number 0111 in our 4-bit register. It would be a nuisance to have only counters as registers, particularly because we might want to start our count with a number representing the current population of the United States in one of our registers. (That would obviously require a register that was wider than 4 bits; but 8 or 16 bits can be made to handle such numbers, and frequently are.) What we want, then, is a register that permits us to put into it any combination of 0s and 1s any time we want. With counters we have to wait; with general-purpose registers we don't. They are the electronic equivalent of writing paper.

Think about it for a moment: What *is* the surface you write on when you're interacting with a computer? Most people reply: "You don't write, you type, and the surface you do it on is a television screen."

That may be how it looks, but the electronic surface you are actually writing on is a register, or more accurately, thousands of them. All the letters, numbers, and other symbols you type in by using the keyboard are translated by the computer into strings of 0s and 1s that uniquely represent each character. A keyboard that has both letters and numbers on it is said to be *alphanumeric* ("alpha-" for alphabet, and "-numeric" for numbers), and may include some special characters, such as $, @, and =.

How, specifically, are alphanumeric characters represented in binary form so that the computer can understand them—that is, so its registers can record them? You already know that $2^7 = 128$. So if we use binary numbers that are 7 bits long, we can represent at most 128 different letters, numbers, and symbols. Is that enough to cover everything that's on an ordinary typewriter keyboard? Let's check: There are 26 lowercase letters in the English alphabet (a, b, c, . . .) and 26 more that are uppercase (A, B, C, . . .). Also, there are 10 single-digit decimal numbers (0 through 9). With these 26 + 26 letters and 10 numbers we can construct any word ("Shazam") or number (the earth's population) that interests us. There are a few other symbols that are present as well, such as $, @, =, +, *, and last but by no means least, a blank so that we can insert a space between words. As it turns out, $2^7 = 128$ possible combinations is more than enough different 7-bit sequences of 0s and 1s to represent the entire keyboard.

The most frequently used standardized binary code for representing alphanumeric characters is the ASCII (pronounced "as-key"), which stands for American National Standard Code for Information Interchange. A portion of the code is shown in Table 3-1.

Notice that the ASCII representation of the numbers 0 through 9 is

TABLE 3-1 *American National Standard Code for Information Interchange (ASCII)*

Character	*Binary Code*	*Character*	*Binary Code*
A	100 0001	0	011 0000
B	100 0010	1	011 0001
C	100 0011	2	011 0010
D	100 0100	3	011 0011
E	100 0101	4	011 0100
F	100 0110	5	011 0101
G	100 0111	6	011 0110
H	100 1000	7	011 0111
I	100 1001	8	011 1000
J	100 1010	9	011 1001
K	100 1011		
L	100 1100		
M	100 1101	blank	010 0000
N	100 1110	.	010 1110
O	100 1111	(	010 1000
P	101 0000	+	010 1011
Q	101 0001	$	010 0100
R	101 0010	*	010 1010
S	101 0011	)	010 1001
T	101 0100	—	010 1101
U	101 0101	/	010 1111
V	101 0110	,	010 1100
W	101 0111	=	011 1101
X	101 1000		
Y	101 1001		
Z	101 1010		

simply 011 followed by the number in binary (for instance, 7 is 011 0111). To repeat: Every letter, number, or symbol on a typewriter keyboard is represented by a 7-bit sequence of 0s and 1s because 0s and 1s are all that a computer's registers can hold. Let's assume that the microcomputer we're talking about is an 8-bit machine; that is, all its registers are 8 bits wide. When you type CAT (we've written it all in capital letters because many less expensive micros have only caps, not lowercase), the machine therefore uses three of its registers to record the following information at three successive locations in memory:

0	1	0	0	0	0	1	1	Meaning: C

0	1	0	0	0	0	0	1	Meaning: A

0	1	0	1	0	1	0	0	Meaning: T

It is essential for you to realize that nothing has changed merely because the letters C-A-T have been translated into three distinct, 7-bit strings of binary numbers. The same thing happens all the time at the

United Nations. A representative from one country speaks, and those who aren't familiar with his or her native tongue listen to a simultaneous translation of the words via a headset provided for the purpose. Although important connotations of many words are lost in the process, the translator does a good job of conveying at least the literal meaning of what's being said. In a computer, it isn't words that are translated but letters. All the connotations of the word CAT are therefore omitted right from the start. Since computers use an extremely literal translation process, everything has to be spelled out—that is, described in minute detail—for them.

Having letters and numbers both represented by 7-bit strings of 0s and 1s is confusing to many people who are encountering this aspect of computer operation for the first time. After all, in no other language-translation process (say, English to Russian) does this occur. Letters are letters, numbers are numbers, and that's all there is to that. The distinction between them even survives the language-translation rules.

Not in a computer. Here everything is translated into numbers—binary numbers. Every letter, number, and symbol on the keyboard of a typewriter becomes a 7-bit sequence of 0s and 1s. That may strike you as an extreme trivializing process—"everything reduced to 0s and 1s"—yet it is the only way for computer's registers to house the information we want it to work with.

The idea that everything that goes into a computer, even formatting instructions, will be represented by a string of 0s and 1s is a little strange at first, but it is something to which people soon become accustomed. After all, each of us has a social security number, and that is how the government keeps tabs on our income, regardless of the host of individual characteristics we each possess that make us unique. Moreover, this is one translation process that can be reversed: Associated with each name is a social security number, and conversely, to each social security number that has been assigned to someone is the name of that particular person. When the Internal Revenue Service has the number, it can look up the name.

It is enormously important to realize that the same thing does not apply in a computer. Every letter, number, and symbol is translated into a 7-bit string of 0s and 1s and recorded in a register, but looking at a string of 0s and 1s in a register doesn't in and of itself tell you what you're seeing. For example, in ASCII the symbol "$" is represented as 010 0100 (see Table 3-1). Key question: How would you know, just looking at that string of 0s and 1s in a register, that it doesn't represent the number 36 in binary—that is, $0 \times 64 + 1 \times 32 + 0 \times 16 + 0 \times 8 + 1 \times 4 + 0 \times 2 + 0 \times 1 = 32 + 4 = 36$?

The registers in a computer not only have to hold the raw materials—

letters and the numbers 0 through 9 in binary form—they also have to hold the *results* of working with those letters to form words and the numbers to form larger numbers. If we multiply 6 times 6, get 36, and store the result in a 7-bit register, it will look like 010 0100 or $ in ASCII. Which is it? If you don't know what occurred before or where you are in the computer's memory, looking at the 0s and 1s won't help you. In short, in a computer you cannot reverse the translation process merely on the basis of what's in a given register. Everything translates into 0s and 1s easily enough and in a standardized manner, but going in the reverse direction is difficult and in many instances impossible.

How Do You Handle a Murderer? Very Carefully.

What is the solution? How do we find our way out of this dilemma? The following situation highlights the basic issue involved here and points to its resolution.

You are the sheriff of a small town. The countryside is pretty, the place is peaceful, and the citizens are law-abiding. The cells in your jail are usually empty, with the exception of an occasional visit from the town drunk or an overnight stay by someone picked up on disorderly conduct charges at 3 a.m.

On a cold winter night when the town drunk is once again using your jail as a hotel, you get an emergency call. A homicide is in progress; the neighbors hear the screaming and want you to come quickly. You do, but it's too late. Apprehending the murderer, who hasn't yet had time to escape, is all you can do. When you take him back to your office and are about to put him in a cell, you discover something very disconcerting: The murderer and the town drunk look like identical twins.

What to do? Switch your focus. Instead of concentrating on the particular characteristics of the person in each cell, concentrate on the *address*—the number of the cell—in which each prisoner is housed. So you write on the blackboard next to your desk: "The drunk is in #3, the murderer in #4." To make certain that there are no slip-ups, you write the same words again on a piece of paper and put it in your pocket.

The two men may look the same, but one is guilty (you caught him in the act) and the other is innocent (he was in your jail cell at the time of the murder). To confuse the two would be unforgivable. When deputies from the county seat come to collect the murderer for his arraignment there, you make it a point to look at the blackboard and check the note in your pocket as well. Then you give them the man in #4. The guy in #3 can't help you, or himself; he doesn't even remember where he was the night before.

To make the situation more akin to what happens in a computer, let's imagine that you get a promotion. You handled your job as local sheriff so well that you've been appointed warden of the state penitentiary. This time, you don't have just two prisoners, you have 2 to the tenth power prisoners—that is, $2^{10} = 1024$ of them. The guards and prison officials there have been eagerly awaiting your arrival. They have a problem, a big one, and you are the only person who can solve it. What's the problem? All 1024 prisoners look exactly alike.

At first that upsets you too. Then you remember the lessons you learned as a small-town sheriff and decide to implement the same procedure here, on a large scale, that worked so well before. "It doesn't matter what any of these men look like," you tell the guards. "From now on, we're going to worry about their address—the number on each cell—and only their address."

"Couldn't that lead to trouble?" one of the guards inquires. "I mean, suppose we arrive one morning and find that there's a baboon in one of the cells."

"Doesn't matter," you reply. "Orders are orders. The procedure is to be followed strictly. If it's cell number 357's turn to do KP, and there's a baboon in there, teach him how to wash dishes."

Until now, the most important concept we've been focusing on has been that of a register—that is, a string of flip-flops—since registers serve as the writing paper on which data and word processing take place. From now on, the most important concept will be that of the address of a register. You already understand why. Translating words, symbols, and decimal data into strings of 0s and 1s is easy; making sense of a given string of 0s and 1s may be difficult or impossible. It can represent too many things.

Problems similar to this arise continually in everyday life, for instance, in the maternity ward of a hospital. Newborns do indeed all look alike to many observers, and mix-ups have caused great distress and sizable lawsuits. A plastic bracelet, bound securely to the child's wrist, solves the problem. Later we'll see that data being transferred from one computer to another at a distant location are similarly "tagged" to facilitate identification. However, within any given computer installation, the solution is to keep careful track of the addresses of the registers that hold your data and the instructions (that is, the program) that will be used to manipulate it. The computer can't tell the two apart merely on the basis of their appearance; data and instructions are both just strings of 0s and 1s and therefore look alike. You as the programmer or user need to know which is where, so you don't accidentally end up multiplying two instructions together.

Keeping track of *where* data, on the one hand, and computer programs, on the other, are stored in the computer's memory is obviously a task to be approached with care. This is one place in which the attention paid to good bookeeping is well worth the bother. What we need to do now is take a closer look at what a computer's memory is. We've used the term on a number of occasions without seeing exactly what it means. Specifically, we need to examine how a computer's memory is structured. That sounds like a formidable task—"examining the structure of a computer's memory"—but as you'll soon see, it isn't.

Memories That Need Refreshing

Even people who are aware that computers have memories often state that an air of mystery surrounds the subject in their minds. Why? "This is *really* a high-tech field," is a typical reply. And so it is. However, once we become familiar with an object, we know what to do with it. Take the Sunday paper, for example. Our reactions to its many sections fall into two categories: Either we are interested in a particular section or we're not. The two inclinations, then, are READ or DISCARD.

The next time you hear or read the term "computer memory" it would be worthwhile to have a similar pair of reactions, only this time let it be READ or WRITE. That is, from now on, think of a computer memory as something either to be read or written into.

We've already seen that each flip-flop is a 1-bit register that can store a binary digit, a 0 or a 1. One bit doesn't tell us much, so flip-flops are strung together to form registers that are usually 8, 16, or 32 bits wide. That allows us to form 8-, 16-, or 32-bit data words. What needs to be kept in mind, then, is that a typical computer memory is nothing more than an ordered (that is, numbered) collection of such registers. In the previous pages of this book, the development of the subject matter has proceeded from NAND gates to flip-flops to registers and, now, to main memory.

Here comes the important part: Your reaction to the unit. Once you become as comfortable with computer memories as you are with the Sunday paper, it will be natural for you to think "READ" or "WRITE." After all, registers in particular, and memories in general, are the (electronic) writing paper in a computer. Some groups of registers in a microprocessor, placed there to hold information temporarily, are even called the "scratch pad." The question in your mind should therefore be: "Do I want to read what is stored in this memory, or write something new into it?"

The question is answered for you in certain instances because the unit won't let you write into it. What is this kind of memory called? A read-only memory, of course; ROM, for short. Bear in mind that there were only two possibilities to begin with, READ or WRITE. So with WRITE excluded, READ is all that's left. Note well, then, that ROMs don't need or use flip-flops. A different type of device is used instead, one that houses a pattern of 0s and 1s that have been *permanently* etched into its registers.

That's not so different from each newspaper page you read. The ink that makes up each word has been placed on the paper in what is intended to be a permanent manner. For that reason, it is often called "hard copy." By contrast, the image on a television screen is intended to be only temporary. For that reason, it is often referred to as "soft copy." In fact, if the same image stays on the screen too long—a TV station's test pattern, say—it may harm the coating of phosphors on the inside of the screen, causing the image to persist even when it's no longer supposed to be there.

In certain situations it is a major advantage to have a computer memory be much like a page of print. For instance, if you turn off the power to a ROM and then turn it back on, it still contains exactly the same information. Its pattern of 0s and 1s is permanent. Pulling the plug doesn't destroy the data bits it was storing. That is *not* so when flip-flops are used. As long as the power remains on, flip-flops have the delightful ability to remain in the last state they attained: $Q = 0$ and $\overline{Q} = 1$, or $Q = 1$ and $\overline{Q} = 0$. For that reason, they are called *static* memories (as opposed to *dynamic* memories, which we'll discuss in a moment). However, if power is lost even briefly, the flip-flops in each register will be in a different, unpredictable state once power is restored. As computer engineers are fond of saying: "Pulling the plug turns the contents [on such a memory] into garbage."

There are many computer installations in which a continuous source of power is therefore a critical consideration. Should power from the local electric company fail, an in-house backup power supply attached to the computer is ready to take over instantly. In fact, this generator will click into action if power hasn't been shut off completely, but has merely dropped below a certain fixed level, say, as a result of a brown-out. In smaller machines, especially the growing number of portables, a battery serves the same purpose, allowing the machine to maintain its memory while the unit is temporarily in transit.

There is an important class of memories whose binary contents quickly degrade through leakage of electrons, even though power to the unit remains on continuously. This highly leaky memory has to be *refreshed* approximately 250 times per second. That sounds like a real nuisance, doesn't it? Nevertheless, miniaturization has been the name of the game in electronics in recent decades, and dynamic memory cells (using capacitors) require only about one-fourth the space on a semiconductor chip that static memory cells (using flip-flops) do. That's a big enough difference to compensate for the bother of having to refresh them so many times per second if you need more than approximately 65,000 bits of memory.

Microprocessors in an automobile or home appliance—for instance, in a carburetor or microwave oven—don't require the owner to program them. An accompanying ROM that has already been programmed (permanently) at the factory is incorporated in the device. However, if you buy a microcomputer for business or personal use, the ability to WRITE into as well as READ the machine's memory becomes essential.

In that case, the appropriate memory is a RAM, a random-access memory. It is called random access because each memory cell within it takes the same to access—that is, get to and use. That is not so, of course, with information stored on a reel of magnetic tape. The data stored in the middle of the tape obviously takes longer to access than that at the beginning of the reel. The slower access time is a disadvantage that is offset by an important advantage of magnetic tape, disks, and drums: They don't lose their memories when power is shut off. As you know from taking a cassette with music on it and putting it in your cassette player, even years later the information (in this case, musical notes) is still available to be heard.

"Wait a minute," you may be saying at this point. "I thought you said that the words READ or WRITE were all I had to keep in mind where computer memories are concerned. So why are we talking about RAMs and then SAMs (sequential-access memories), such as disk and tape?" It is worthwhile because you'll encounter terms such as ROM and RAM (static and dynamic) again both in this and other books about computers. The terms are also popping up with increasing frequency in casual and office conversation, not to mention newspaper and magazine advertisements for the machines themselves.

Nevertheless, we meant what we said: The most important thing to keep in mind about a RAM is that you can WRITE into it. Having done so, you'll want to READ what you've written, both to check on its accuracy *and* to retrieve the information should you want it at a later date. In short, and this is what needs to be remembered: ROMs are read-only memories, whereas RAMs are READ-and-WRITE memories.

There are a few other types of memory whose names are worth knowing, even though you are unlikely to make much use of them. One is PROM, which stands for *programmable* ROM; that is, you can program the device yourself instead of having the factory do it. The problem is that any mistakes you make are permanent, and even if you make no mistakes, whatever pattern you etch (or "burn") into its memory cells cannot later be changed.

The other type, clearly more versatile, is *erasable* PROM; that is, *erasable programmable read-only memory.* With this device, any mistakes you make can indeed be corrected, though the process is a bit laborious. Advances in technology will no doubt reduce the labor involved. Both PROM and EPROM are relatively expensive and used primarily for systems development work, where their extra cost is readily justified.

Learning to Address a Register

Let's return again to the prison and see how the setting helps us understand how computer memories are generally structured.

It may seem like a trivial thing to you to put numbers on jail cells, each of which holds a prisoner who looks exactly like the others. Yet this seemingly simple act instantly creates order out of chaos. It is the same in a computer. We've already seen that the sequences of 0s and 1s which are in the registers that make up a computer's memory cannot be read like so many words of a foreign language. Some elementary arithmetic casts an interesting light on the underlying issue.

If the registers we're using are 8 bits wide, how many *different* binary words can we make? The answer is $2^8 = 256$. What are they? The binary equivalent of the numbers 0 through 255:

| 0000 | 0000 |, | 0000 | 0001 |, | 0000 | 0010 |, . . . , | 1111 | 1111 |

(The line inserted after every 4 bits is solely to make them easier to read; other than that it has no meaning.)

It is standard when discussing binary words to say that one which is 8 bits wide is a *byte.* The definition is especially useful for us because the analogy we're using is between a prison with 1024 cells, each containing one prisoner, and a computer with 1024 memory cells, each containing 1 byte. A memory this size is usually referred to as 1K, where K stands for "kilo." Elsewhere kilo would mean a thousand, but in the world of computers, where everything is binary, the word means 2^{10}, which is 1024, not 1000 (Quick quiz question: If K = 1024, what is 64K? Answer: Just multiply the two numbers, 64 × 1024, and you'll see that the product is 65,536.) To repeat: Each prisoner corresponds to an 8-bit register which is part of a larger memory bank. In fact, you can imagine each inmate being photographed with that particular string of 0s and 1s on a plaque held in front of his chest.

Unfortunately, after the first 256 prisoners have been given 8-bit numbers, we'll have used up all the available distinct byte-sized combinations of 0s and 1s. That means we've numbered only one-fourth of the prisoners that are present, since 256 × 4 = 1024. Summing up, not only do all our prisoners look alike, every binary number we assign to one of them will end up being shared by three others. We simply don't have enough 8-bit binary numbers to give each prisoner a unique one, so in using the same sequence (0 through 255) over and over again, three other prisoners eventually wind up with that number as well.

It is something of a minor miracle that this problem can be handled with such ease simply by numbering each *cell*, not each prisoner. Since there are $2^{10} = 1024$ cells, assigning them the numbers 0 through 1023 gives each one a unique numerical hang tag. (As you've probably already noticed, it is common in the world of computers—as well as on roulette wheels and football jerseys—to start the numbering at 0 instead of 1.)

The picture of what's going on here looks as follows:

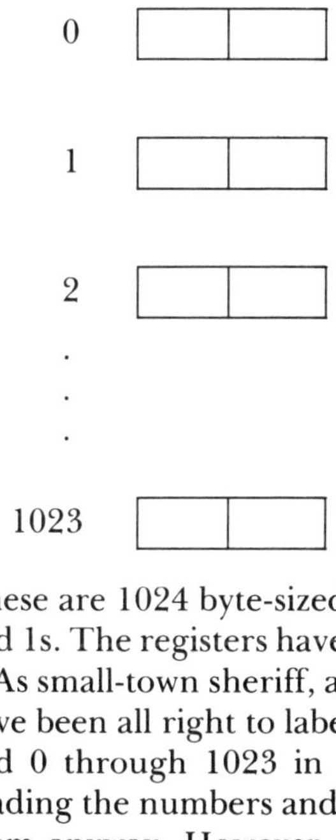

These are 1024 byte-sized registers, each full of some combination of 0s and 1s. The registers have been numbered consecutively from 0 to 1023.

As small-town sheriff, and later, as warden of the state prison, it might have been all right to label cells using decimal numbers, 0 to 9 in the jail and 0 through 1023 in the prison. Human beings were going to be reading the numbers and that's the form in which they're used to seeing them anyway. However, in a computer, even the address of the cells must be written in binary. When the microprocessor wants something from memory, it asks for it by giving the address of the cell, in binary. Since in the machine we're discussing there are $1024 = 2^{10}$ such cells, we need a 10-digit binary number for each, if they're all to have a unique address. Keep in mind that whether we're dealing with prisoners who look identical or byte-sized registers in a computer that look alike, it is crucial for them each to have a distinct number that allows us to identify them unmistakably.

Students encountering this material for the first time often say that they find it a little confusing that putting a 10-bit address into a computer ends up producing an 8-bit string of data. For some reason, they intuitively expect the length of the address and the length of the data word that is being addressed to be the same.

As a topic in abstract arithmetic the point may seem vague and confusing yet the event happens every day in a more concrete form. For instance, you could dial one digit on the phone—0, for Operator—and have three fire trucks show up at your house. Or you could dial three digits, 911, and end up with four police cars outside your door. Finally, you could dial the local grocery store using seven digits and have two bags of groceries show up later. In short, there needn't be (and usually isn't) any correlation between the width of the number (that is, the number of places it takes up) that goes into a system and the width of the number that comes out. All that matters is that you use the right input number—the address—in order to get what you want out of the computer's memory, namely, instructions and data. Dialing 911 or 0 won't get you two bags of groceries, though it might net you a free trip to the nearest mental hospital. If there is a fire truck in front of the A&P, either the barbecued chickens in the deli section have just set off a blaze, or a few firefighters are picking up food to take back to the station house.

The second topic students often find confusing at this point has to do with how the computer handles 10-bit addresses. The specific question usually asked is: "If all the registers in an 8-bit microcomputer are 8 bits wide, how can the machine handle a 10-bit address?"

The answer is: by taking two 8-bit registers and linking them together to form a register 16 bits wide. It's not hard. After all, the eight flip-flops that make up each register had to be linked together in the first place. Linking the last flip-flop in one 8-bit register with the first flip-flop in another 8-bit register doesn't present any real problems. The result, called a *memory address register* (MAR), is shown in Figure 3-4.

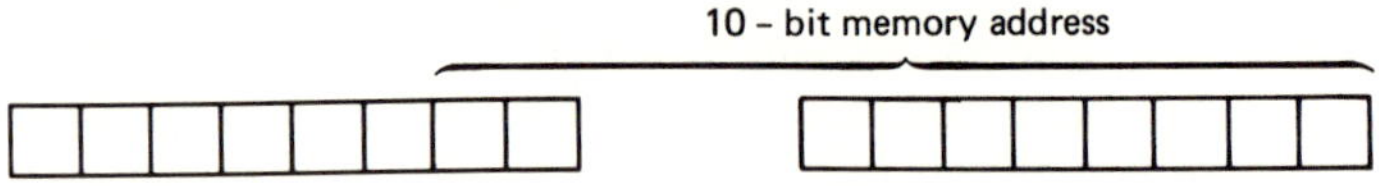

Figure 3-4 A 16-bit memory address register (MAR).

Since 8 + 8 = 16, and we've used only 10 of the 16 available bits for addressing all 1024 of the cells, you may be wondering what happens to the other 6 bits. Are they used at all? The answer will be immediately clear if you imagine that you did your job as warden of the state penitentiary so well that you were promoted once again. This time, you don't have just one prison to oversee, but 64 of them. And what do you know, the prisoners in the other 63 prisons all look exactly like the prisoners in the state pen from which you were just promoted; that is, all the prisoners in all the prisons look identical.

That being the case, it becomes extremely important to make certain that every prison as well as every prisoner is carefully numbered. A friend of yours who works at the phone company laughs a little when she hears of your plight. "We've had the same problem for years," she says, "since we know few if any of our customers personally. We solved it by giving every telephone number a prefix, called its *area code*. That helps us distinguish between the number of John Doe in New York and the number of another John Doe in Los Angeles, both of whom even have the same regular seven-digit number."

Since the telephone company uses ordinary decimal telephone numbers, a three-digit area code is sufficient for the entire nation. As manager of dozens of prisons that have to be given *binary* numbers in order to identify them uniquely, you need six digits in your prefix, not three. The 64 prisons are therefore numbered 0 through 63; that is, 0000 00, 0000 01, 0000 10, . . . , 1111 11.

How does that compare to what actually happens in a computer? Remarkably well. Few microcomputers have 64 memory chips, each 1K in size (that is, each containing 1024 cells). But all have both ROM and RAM semiconductor memory chips in them, and it is important to see why.

Programming your own computer is great fun to some people, and gives them much the same pleasure they might otherwise derive from successfully completing a jigsaw or crossword puzzle. Most people, though, find the activity an unwelcome nuisance. To begin with, they don't know any programming languages, such as BASIC, COBOL, FORTRAN, or Pascal. So if the computer is going to run a program for them, they'd just as soon buy it ready-made, perfected for them by someone else. Knowing the language would be worthwhile anyway, if for no other reason than the fact that one could then proceed to modify the program, should that be necessary to make it better suit one's personal requirements. In fact, most of the best and most widely used programs are constantly being revised and improved.

Assuming that the program is satisfactory for your purposes, you might not want to tamper with it any further. In that case, it would be worthwhile for you to have the program on a ROM chip. Why? That way, should something happen to the power supply to your computer—for instance, someone trips over the cord that plugs into the wall and pulls it out—the program won't be lost. If the program was being stored on a RAM chip, a power outage could be disastrous.

It's clear, then, why someone would want ROM chips in a computer, and when we later look at a concept called "operating systems," we'll see other reasons why every microcomputer now contains at least one ROM chip. RAM chips, on the other hand, have an important place as well, since the data one is working with may change from one day to the next, even though the program that will manipulate that data stays the same, day after day.

Reading and Writing

Let's summarize what we've learned in the previous few sections. When a microprocessor wants something from memory, whether it be an instruction from one of its ROM chips or some data housed in one of its RAM chips, it sends out the appropriate address. The address is long, in our example, 16 bits, but the length is needed in order to be precise about the location of the instruction or data bit that is being sought. Keep in mind that as manager of 64 prisons filled with 64 × 1024 = 65,536 identical people, you too would have to specify the correct six-digit prefix, followed by a 10-digit cell address, if you wanted to FETCH any particular prisoner and have him brought to your office.

What should be emphasized here is that although you put a 16-digit number in the memory address register (which serves as the new, modern version of the blackboard you used to have in your office when you were a small-town sheriff), you get back only eight-digits: the 8-bit number of the prisoner in that cell. Similarly, in an 8-bit microcomputer with a 64K memory, the memory address register holds a 16-bit address that fetches an 8-bit data word and houses it temporarily in an 8-bit register, called the *memory data register*, before using it.

(There is a piece of terminology that is frequently used in this situation, and you should know about it. We've already mentioned that perfecting a computer program is a long and difficult process, one that may take hundreds or even thousands of hours. Moreover, some of the nation's best computer programmers would insist—correctly, we feel—that a good program never attains a final state of perfection, but is always being refined to improve both its performance and readability. Preserving what one has achieved thus far on any given program therefore makes sense, and that's where ROM chips come in.

(Data, however, constantly change, since the world does. Rarely are we afforded the luxury of analyzing a problem that is just sitting there, static and complete; instead, there is usually a fresh batch of data arriving before we've barely finished digesting what we already had. Parking data somewhere *temporarily* is therefore essential. The registers in which it is parked are called *buffer* registers, and since registers are what a memory is made of, it is hardly surprising that one frequently runs into the term *buffer memory*. All it means is a place to park data short-term. A memory data register is just such a short-term parking space, but this one happens to be in the microprocessor. The next few pages will make clear precisely how it is used.)

What happens when you want to put the prisoner back in his cell or place a new one there? Simple: You reverse the process. Once again you send out the same carefully specified address consisting of 16 bits. That's the first step, and it identifies the cell to which the prisoner will be sent for the first time, or sent again, if that's where he was before. Notice something extremely important here; addresses go only one way, and that is *out*. You're the one who sends them, whether a prisoner is being brought *to* you or is being sent *by* you to his cell.

The same thing happens in a computer. A microprocessor sends an address to memory whether it wants to get a data word *from* memory or it wants to send one *to* the memory chip. Either way, the address travels in only one direction: from microprocessor to memory. Data, on the other hand, move in both directions, from memory to microprocessor and microprocessor to memory, although always from and to the address specified in the memory address register.

There is no standard word to describe the process of putting a prisoner in this cell ("incarcerate?") or dragging him out of his cell and bringing him to your office ("interrogate?"). However, there are indeed standard terms used to describe the comparable process in a computer, and fortunately, you already know them. A little while ago we said that the two most important terms to keep in mind whenever you hear the word "memory" are READ and WRITE. Lo and behold, they turn out to be what we've been describing all along.

How? When the microprocessor sends out a 16-bit address and an 8-bit data word as well, the data word ends up being written into memory. This is a WRITE operation, one we'll look at in more detail later. Conversely, when the microprocessor sends out a 16-bit address and as a result receives the 8-bit data word housed at that particular address, that is a READ operation.

chapter

4

inside a microprocessor

When you're the manager of 64 prisons, it's easy to decide how to move prisoners about—easy, that is, once you are certain that each cell has been uniquely numbered. However, suppose you decide that you need a brief break from work and want to replace yourself temporarily with a machine, one that is as comfortable handling the necessary addressing procedures as you are after the experience you've gained at the local, regional, and now federal level. You might even find yourself saying: "Since I'm going to have a machine answering my phone while I'm away, another might as well be doing my work for me in my absence."

Fine, but what should such a machine look like? That is, what kind of structure would it need in order to do what you do? One thing it could make good use of is some buffer registers. When you were the sheriff of a small town, with 10 prisoners at most to deal with at any one time, you could talk to them right from your desk. Now, you've got 64K—that is, $64 \times 1024 = 65{,}536$—of them. They may all look alike, but they're all in the clink for different reasons; each has a story of his own to tell. Since there are so many of them, it's hardly surprising that you often have to deal with more than one problem prisoner at a time. That's where the buffer registers come in.

Instead of having to send for a particular troublemaker each time he causes trouble, you might decide to move him into one of the buffer cells—that is, temporary storage places right nearby. That way, whenever he acts up, he doesn't have to travel so far to be brought to your office once again. (Since he misbehaves regardless of which cell he's in, it clearly has little to do with the presence of other prisoners and is apparently connected with the phases of the moon and the chow in the mess hall. On nights when the moon is full and something that smells like old overalls and is called lamb stew is served, the guy is totally off-the-wall.)

What does any of this have to do with designing a microprocessor? Quite a bit, actually. Regardless of the use to which the machine will be put, there are certain pieces of data that are nice to have right at hand. Having to FETCH them from memory each time is not only a nuisance, it's also time-consuming. In short, a few general-purpose—that is, buffer—registers included in your microprocessor is not only convenient, it helps speed things along.

[What the optimal number of such registers should be is a subject about which reasonable people at Texas Instruments and Intel, say, two distinguished manufacturers of microprocessors, might disagree. Some computer engineers (at Intel) think a half-dozen or even a dozen makes sense, while others (at Texas Instruments) think there shouldn't be any. Those who hold the latter view would prefer to use a portion of the memory chip (rather than the valuable real estate on the tiny microprocessor itself) as general-purpose registers. When people speak about differences in microprocessor *architectures,* this is one of the things they're referring to. The vast majority of microprocessor manufacturers include some registers, and for that reason, the unit is said to be "register-oriented." Since microprocessors are often referred to as *central processing units* (CPUs), you'll also encounter the phrase "a register-oriented CPU."]

It's all well and good to have established procedures for addressing and then moving prisoners—or data—from one place to another, but the activity is supposed to serve a worthwhile purpose: making license plates or cracking rocks in a prison and processing data in the case of a computer. Having the needed devices included in your microprocessor to accomplish that end is the next step.

The material covered in the first few chapters showed us that there are two ways in which we might want to combine data: arithmetically and logically. The words may seem the same to you and therefore redundant; to most people, nothing is more logical than arithmetic. But to computer engineers, the word "logic" means gates—specifically, AND, OR, and NOT gates, or their universal equivalent, NAND or NOR gates. "Arithmetic," on the other hand, means the same thing to a computer engineer that it means to you, except in binary form, of course.

An example will highlight the different results that are obtained if 2 bytes are combined (1) logically and (2) arithmetically. Combining the 8-bit words 1011 0101 and 1101 0011 logically, using AND, for instance, produces the following byte:

```
1011  0101
1101  0011
──────────
1001  0001
```

That is, we'll find a 1 in the result only if there are 1s in both of the lines directly above each bit. Remember, a 1 and a 0 fed into an AND gate produce a 0 as an output.

Combining the same two numbers arithmetically yields an altogether different result. It is a simple exercise in binary arithmetic to add these two bytes, starting at the right of course, and using the rule "1 + 1 = 0 and carry the 1." The result of adding the two binary numbers is

```
 1011 0101
 1101 0011
 ---------
1000 1000
```

Not only are these two results different merely as 8-bit strings of 0s and 1s, the latter result is actually 9 bits long. Why? Because there was a carry in the last column, the one all the way to the left. The carry flip-flop, C, in our flag register would therefore switch from 0 to 1 to record that fact.

What do you mean, we don't have a flag register? We'd better, and now is as good a time as any to make certain that one is included in the design—the architecture—of our microprocessor. This is one point on which everyone agrees: engineers at Intel, Texas Instruments, and all the other manufacturers as well. The status or flag register is a convenient little device to have around, as you can see.

What should we call the device in our microprocessor that handles data either logically or arithmetically? The unit, the arrangement of gates that performs logic and arithmetic combinations, has been given a strikingly original name that has become standard throughout the industry: It is called the *arithmetic and logic unit*, or the ALU, for short.

Putting Data in the Right Places

It would be ridiculous for us to have spent so much time carefully keeping track of prisoners and their cell numbers—or data and their register numbers—and not apply the same care at the next step: making computations with those numbers. Every microprocessor has at least one general-purpose register that is special. It is singled out as the one in which *results* are held. After all, combining data in the ALU isn't just another facet of a computer's operations; it is the main reason the computer exists in the first place. (For comparison, one could argue that the main purpose of the rest of the human body is to feed the brain and move it from one place to another.) This special register is called the *accumulator*, and it is present even in microprocessors that don't have any other general-purpose or scratchpad registers.

To see precisely how the accumulator is ordinarily used, let's go back to the example above, where two binary numbers were added. It is important to know that one of the numbers being added is always housed in the accumulator. In fact, if the accumulator is all 0s, a number must be placed into it as the first step in the addition operation. The other number is housed either in memory or brought, for convenience, to one of the scratchpad registers before proceeding with the actual addition.

If the number 1011 0101 is in the accumulator, and the other number, 1101 0011, is in the fifth scratchpad register, say, which we'll designate by R5, the two numbers are fed into the ALU and added together. Then, the result is placed—where?—in the accumulator.

Note that the accumulator has the same number of bits in it (here, 8) as are in each data word, not the address length (which is 10 here). The accumulator plays a central role in the microprocessor's operations. Students who want to show how much they know, while still appearing oh-so-casual and cool, sometimes say, "You know, in the new microprocessors, you can use *any* register as the accumulator." That's true, but it certainly doesn't diminish the status of that register—at least as long as it continues to act as the accumulator. The same goes for the Presidency of the United States. Theoretically, *any* American youngster can grow up to become President, but that doesn't diminish the power and importance of the particular person who ends up with the position—at least during the time that person is still in office.

Before, when we were discussing memories, we said that READ and WRITE are the two key words to keep in mind. READ means retrieving information that is housed in the memory chip's or scratchpad's registers, while WRITE means the act of placing information into the registers. However, if you look at a variety of computer programs, or one long piece of software used for performing a complicated task you'll see abbreviations for the words LOAD and STORE used repeatedly. LOAD what? That is, to what register does the word LOAD refer? The accumulator. This step in the program instructs the microprocessor to place a data word into the accumulator. Where was the data word until then? Either in one of the scratchpad registers or memory chips.

The term STORE accomplishes the reverse. When STORE is used, this step in the program instructs the microprocessor to take the contents of the accumulator and put it somewhere else. Where? Either in one of the scratchpad registers or memory chips. For that reason, LOAD and STORE are often referred to as "accumulator-specific transfers."

Other register-to-register transfers are needed in the normal course of events in a computer, but they are handled by a third kind of instruction: MOVE. Since, by definition, the accumulator is not involved in these transfers, the only possibilities are that (1) a data word is transferred from one scratchpad register to another, say from R5 to R3; (2) a word is transferred from a memory chip to a scratchpad register, or vice versa; finally, (3) a word is transferred from one location in memory to another.

The last two possibilities may seem somewhat similar to you, since the scratchpad registers are really part of the computer's memory but are located in the CPU for convenience and speed. Nevertheless, precisely because the machine can operate faster when the data it needs are housed in one of the CPU's registers, the two cases are sufficiently different to list them separately.

Summing up, we've learned three terms which go far to describe how a microprocessor uses the available hardware to achieve results: LOAD, STORE, and MOVE. LOAD means load the accumulator; STORE means store the contents of the accumulator in a scratchpad register or memory; and MOVE means transfer the contents of a scratchpad-or-memory location to another scratchpad-or-memory location.

If we take the two binary numbers we added before, and this time perform the addition operation one small computer step at a time, you'll see how everything fits together. The first thing we have to do is place a number in the accumulator. Let's assume that the number 1011 0101 is sitting in prison cell—I mean, memory location—X, where X stands for a 10-bit address. Our first instruction, then, would be: LOAD X → A. That is, load the contents of the register with address X into register A.

(Here, above all, we want you to reap the dividend of having spent some time thinking of computers as analogous in some way to prisons. Learning how to manage one jail or penitentiary, much less dozens of them, is of no interest whatever to the overwhelming majority of people trying to understand computers. Yet the experience gained from having been forced to come up with effective procedures for handling dangerous prisoners who look alike—as opposed to data words that look alike and can similarly cause real chaos if mishandled—is invaluable. The best solution turned out to be a switch in focus from the *contents* of a register to its *address*. Now, for the first time, that change in focus is embodied in an actual computer program for adding two binary numbers.)

Having loaded the contents of memory location X into the accumulator with the first instruction, we want to place the other number, 1101 0011, into register #5. Currently the number is in memory location Y. The second instruction step in our program should therefore be: MOVE Y → R5.

In the third step we add the two numbers by feeding both into the ALU. What are we going to do with the result? Knowing *that* is as important as knowing the result; remember, we have to keep careful track of data words whether they represent raw data or the final outcome of computations. The place we're going to park the result—in this case and almost every other as well—is the accumulator. Now and only now are we in a position to write the next step in our program: ADD R5, A → A. That is, add the contents of scratchpad register #5 to the number in the accumulator and leave the result in the accumulator.

Finally, we want to put the sum somewhere else temporarily, so that the accumulator is freed up for other purposes. The last instruction in the sequence, then, is: STORE A → Z. That is, store the contents of the accumulator in memory location Z.

Two aspects of what we've done deserve comment. First, it wasn't absolutely necessary to move the number in memory location Y into register #5 before adding it to the number already in the accumulator. In fact, that had better not be a mandatory first step in this microprocessor or any other. Why not? Because, as we've mentioned, some microprocessors don't have any scratchpad registers. They have only an accumulator and therefore must use some portion of the memory chip as a scratchpad to hold results temporarily. Even in CPUs that do have a scratchpad, however, moving a number from memory to one of the scratchpad registers cannot be mandatory before proceeding with a computation. Why? Because all the scratchpad registers may already be full. Results of prior computations, soon to be used again, may be sitting in every available register in the CPU.

The second noteworthy point is that it's especially valuable to be able to place a number in a scratchpad register if that number is going to be used repeatedly—not added only once to the number in the accumulator, but 50 times, say. Then, the instruction ADD R5, A → A can more easily be run 50 times in succession. Thanks to the fact that the number is nearby (in R5) and doesn't have to be retrieved from memory each time, the speed of the computation can be increased significantly.

You may be wondering how we could add the contents of R5 to A if we've already done so. Many students at this point ask; "Haven't we already used it up during the addition process?" The phrase "used it up" is very deceptive where electronic signals are concerned. For instance, if you're driving a car, come to a red light, and respond to it by stopping, in what sense have you "used it up" just because you responded to it? You may have reacted, but the signal is still being sent. Clearly, something other than your reaction—namely, another signal—will have to be sent in order to change the light from red to green. It's the same in a computer: Let's assume that the contents of R5 are added to the number already in the accumulator. Unless something else changes the contents of R5—for instance, another number being moved from memory into that register—it is still the same after the addition that it was before. In short, the number in the accumulator keeps changing as other numbers are added to it, and that's the reason it is called the accumulator. It keeps a running total of the computation. The other registers that are contributing to the arithmetic or logic operation being conducted in the ALU and housed in the accumulator, however, are not changed. They can therefore be used repeatedly, if desired.

Area Codes and Op Codes

Our microprocessor is coming along nicely, and ought to allow you to go on vacation soon. First, though, something has to be done about the word ADD. As an instruction to a small-town sheriff, warden, or prison-system manager, the word could hardly be more straightforward. But it's a word in the English language, and computers only speak binary. How, then, is the computer supposed to read and understand what the instruction ADD means? Ask yourself an even more basic question: How is the microprocessor supposed to know that the sequence of 0s and 1s that make up the letters A-D-D mean that the machine should obtain the sum of the two binary numbers that follow the word?

In short, while instructions such as LOAD, STORE, and MOVE must be translated into binary digits to be understood, all they involve is simple register-to-register transfers. Instructions such as ADD and SUBTRACT are more complicated, and we now turn to seeing how the microprocessor first reads and then carries out these instructions.

The first thing you should know is that certain aspects of computer design haven't changed at all in the last four decades. The rapid pace of technological innovation in the field has seen bulky tubes, primitive relays, and miles of copper wire replaced by devices fabricated of silicon semiconductors, while room-size machines have shrunk to the point where they now fit into an attaché case. However, one key feature is the same today as it was in the beginning: the concept of the *stored program.* That is, the program that tells the machine how to run is not fed into the machine one line at a time and executed, after which another line is fed in and executed, and so on. Quite the reverse; just as with a car, the gas one needs for a trip through an area with no filling stations is pumped in ("fill 'er up") before one sets out. Then one hopes to cover the entire distance with the fuel one already has on board.

It's much the same in a computer. The machine executes each instruction so quickly that the whole lot of them must be fed into it at the start. If that weren't done, the computer would spend the vast majority of time sitting idly, waiting for the next piece of the program to be entered. In some sense, then, computers are gas guzzlers, if instructions are thought of as fuel. The central point is that in order to make optimum use of that fuel, the gas tank must be full. That is what is meant by the concept of a stored program: The entire sequence of instructions is placed into one of the computer's RAM chips (by the programmer) or ROM chips (by the manufacturer).

Bear in mind that even if the entire *program* is already stored in the computer and doesn't require any further intervention from the programmer in order to run, *data* or *words* to be processed may be fed in one at a time later. Indeed, they are often fed in interactively—that is, a word or number is put into the machine and the user deliberately waits for a reaction before proceeding. More on this topic later.

In order to be housed in the computer's memory, every instruction must be translated into a string of 0s and 1s. Assuming that this has already been done, how does the CPU read correctly the many different instructions it receives? This seems like a quite complicated issue—until one remembers how useful the idea of a three-digit decimal prefix is for the telephone company ("area codes") and a six-digit binary prefix is for the 64 prisons you have to manage. This time, prefixes will be used for a different purpose: to identify various types of operations on data, such as ADD and MULTIPLY. For that reason, the binary prefixes are called *operation codes*—or "op codes," for short—instead of area codes. An example drawn from everyday life will make clear how simple and effective this approach can be, and will indicate how often we use op codes without realizing it.

We react differently to friends and relatives of various ages. Our response to a 5-year-old usually differs considerably from the way we react to a 15-, 35-, or 65-year-old. Although people don't walk around with a number in front of them, one might as well be there anyway, since we have an approximate idea of how old someone is and therefore how to behave toward the person. The invisible prefix tells us to some extent what to do with the person trailing along behind the number.

Something similar happens in a computer, but the guesswork has been removed. The prefix in every instruction word is there explicitly, and it tells the microprocessor precisely what to do with the addresses of the data words trailing along right behind it. Thus, if the entire instruction is ADD X, Y, the microprocessor knows when it sees the word ADD (in binary form, or course) that there is (1) more to come, and (2) what to do with the data that follow. When the area-code portion of this binary telephone number—that is, its op code—is 8 bits long, there is room for $2^8 = 256$ different possible op codes. They are 0000 0000, 0000 0001, . . . , 1111 1111. The instruction ADD might be represented, say, by the second number in the sequence: 0000 0001.

Some readers may be troubled by the fact that although the two-address instruction ADD X,Y (where X and Y are addresses of data, remember, not the data themselves) seems all right at first glance, it is actually missing something of great importance: namely, an exact specification of where to put the answer. When we were discussing LOAD, STORE, and MOVE, we saw that STORE is used to tell us where to park a result once it has been obtained. Better than a two-address instruction, then, would be one that is three addresses long:

ADD	X	Y	Z

That is, add the data word in location X to the data word in location Y and store the result in location Z.

On the basis of what you've been told thus far, do you know what the data words in locations X and Y are? Of course not. Just as happened in the prison, we're dealing here with the addresses of the data, not the data themselves. In fact, the addition operation can proceed perfectly smoothly without our ever knowing what the intermediate data words in locations X and Y are; all we really want is the final result anyway, the contents of location Z, and it can be printed out for us or displayed on the TV screen when we want it.

Although a three-address instruction would certainly be nice, as you can see, it is 38 bits wide here (that is, three 10-bit addresses and an 8-bit op code). Most microcomputers are 8- or 16-bit machines. The upshot is that the microcomputers you're likely to encounter often make extensive use of one-address instructions, which look as follows:

op code	address

Doing addition is still possible using this format, it just takes more steps—in fact, three times as many. Also, since all we're given is one address, the other address (the location where the contents of the given register are supposed to be parked) is implied. Thus, if the instruction is

LOAD	X

then what's implied here is that the contents of memory location X are to be put—where?—in the accumulator. The next could well be

MOVE	Y

It is clear that something is missing: namely, where the contents of memory location Y are to be moved. We know the *source,* which is Y, but we don't yet know the *destination.* What is it? How is it specified explicitly in the instruction? The destination is one of the scratchpad registers in the CPU, and the op-code portion of the instruction specifies precisely which.

You may be saying, as many students have at this point: "Gee, that's an awful lot of information to cram into one little space. I mean, the op-code portion of the instruction has only 8 bits to begin with. How can it hold both the instruction *and* information about the destination register within one byte?"

The answer can help deepen your understanding of why most microprocessors are designed the way they are. If there are eight scratchpad registers in the CPU, they can be numbered consecutively from 0 through 7, or more accurately (in binary) from 000 through 111. Note, then, that it takes *only 3 bits* to number all eight registers.

We had 8 bits in the op-code portion of the instruction to begin with, so even after we've used up 3 of them, we still have 5 left over. That allows us to have $2^5 = 32$ different kinds of operations, numbered 00000 to 11111. For instance, ADD could now be 00001, instead of the 0000 0001 we were using before. That was wasteful anyway, since we didn't have 256 different operations that needed numbering (very few machines do).

It is important to realize how easy it is to address the registers that are in the CPU. If there are eight scratchpad registers, we need only 3 bits to address them, since $2^3 = 8$. Even if there are 16 scratchpad registers in the CPU, we need only 4 bits to address them all, since $2^4 = 16$. By comparison, if there were no scratchpad registers in our microprocessor, we'd need 10 digits to address each location in a simple $1K = 1024 = 2^{10}$-byte memory. The difference between 3 and 10 bits is huge, thanks to the fact that we're dealing with cramped spaces to begin with.

In short, having some scratchpad registers in the CPU not only speeds up certain kinds of computations, it allows us to write some of the instruction steps in our program in a more compact form. Here we see the first example of the impact of hardware—the architecture of the CPU—on software—the way in which instructions are written.

Bringing the Program from Memory to Microprocessor

While we can get an op code and a scratchpad register address into the same 8-bit space, we usually need more bits than that. In fact, even a typical one-address instruction takes up more than 1 byte. From step to step in our computer program, the number of bytes needed to describe each instruction precisely varies considerably: Sometimes 1 byte is enough; other times, 3 bytes are necessary.

We've been assuming that the memory chip in our microcomputer has a word length of 8 bits. In that case, the memory chip can be thought of as a flat apartment building which is 8 bits wide and for convenience, say, 256 stories tall.

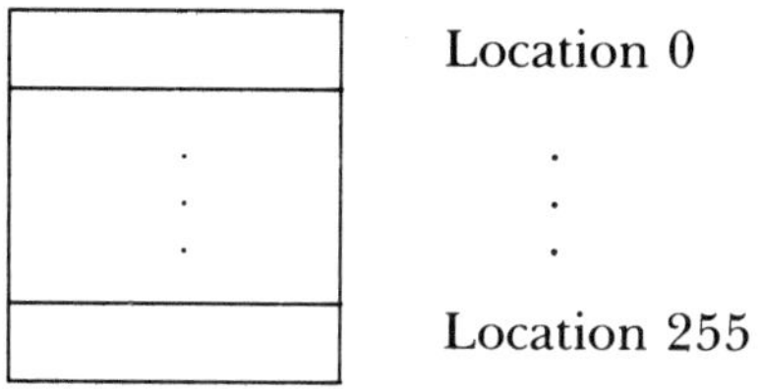

Whether this chip is a ROM or a RAM makes no difference; if it's only 8 bits wide, any multibyte instruction will have to be put in separate locations, one under the other. (Note that since there are only 256 registers on this chip, they can all be specified by 8-bit addresses. However, please don't confuse the address of a register with the contents of that register. Both may have only 8 bits, but the bits are almost certain to be different.)

It's easy for us to draw one-address instructions such as

LOAD	X

on one line of a piece of paper. Yet, since there is more than 1 byte in this one-address instruction, it will have to be placed on *two* separate floors in our memory-chip apartment building. A two-address, 3-byte instruction such as

ADD	X	Y

is also easily written on paper and is commonly encountered in computer programs, but it requires three separate registers on a byte-wide memory chip. It would look as follows:

ADD	Location 205, say, out of 256
X	Location 206
Y	Location 207

We've mentioned that from the time computers were first built more than four decades ago to this very day, the concept of the stored program has been one of their chief distinguishing features. The computer program is placed on the memory chip one line at a time, with each instruction taking as many locations (that is, addresses) as it needs. For instance, the instruction ADD X,Y above took three of them, locations 205, 206, and 207 of the 256 that were available to us on this chip. Any instruction needs at least one; some need three. Then the program runs. Since the steps in the program are numbered (and usually stored) in consecutive locations, it is easy to set a counter—in this case the *program counter*—to keep track of the program, one instruction step at a time.

Let's see how it actually works. Keep in mind that the computer is always doing one thing or another: either fetching an instruction or executing it. (You remember Fidex, the automated dog, don't you?) A more formal way of stating this is to say that each *machine cycle* consists of an *instruction* cycle (during which an instruction is fetched) and an *execution cycle.* The CPU thus begins the process by fetching from memory the first word in the first instruction in the program. How does it know where to go to get the first one? The program counter tells it. Since the program counter—the PC, for short—keeps track of instruction addresses, it usually has to be *2* bytes wide, thus allowing it to keep track of $2^{16} = 65{,}536$ possible addresses, each of which contains a word in our 8-bit microcomputer that is only *1* byte in width.

What happens to the word that is fetched? Let's assume that it is LOAD, and that it is part of the one-address, 2-byte instruction:

LOAD	X

The word is delivered to a register in the CPU that we haven't previously discussed, called, naturally enough, the *instruction register,* the IR.

The instruction register is needed in our CPU for a good reason—actually, two of them. First, it interprets (the technical term is "decodes") what the binary version of words such as LOAD and ADD mean. Second, and of great importance, it tells us whether there are more words to come, as part of the same instruction. In the case of LOAD X, there is indeed another word to come, namely, X.

Since the instruction tells us that the data word contained in location X is to be loaded into the accumulator, it too has to be fetched. Making that happen is simple: The address is placed in the memory address register, the MAR. Once it is there, the CPU knows the address of the register in its memory whose contents are to be fetched. That results in the arrival at the memory data register, the MDR, of the 1-byte data word that was being stored at location X. From the MDR, the word is placed in the accumulator. The instruction has been fetched and then executed. The program counter, which is incremented at the end of the instruction-fetch part of each machine cycle, therefore contains the address of the next instruction to be fetched. And so it goes, step by step, until the program is finished. The route is rarely simple and direct, however. As we'll later see, most programs use BRANCH, SKIP, and JUMP instructions to embody a very important degree of decision-making capability.

Notice that there has to be some feedback from the instruction register to the program counter. That is, after the instruction register reads the op-code portion of an instruction, it needs to communicate what it learns to the program counter, if the program counter really is to be able to point to the next instruction to be fetched.

To put it another way, we've just seen that the program counter is incremented after each instruction fetch, but the key question is *by how much* it should be incremented at the end of any given fetch. Only the instruction register can tell us. This information is contained in the opcode of each instruction, and it is the instruction register's job to decode that information—that is, to make sense of it. For instance, if the opcode is ADD, and the next two locations in memory contain the words X and the Y, this particular arithmetic operation involves three successive memory locations. It is a two-address, 3-byte instruction, so the *next* instruction should begin three addresses later. In terms of the diagram near the bottom of page 65, the next instruction should begin at location 208. That is the address we therefore want the program counter to contain as soon as it is finished decoding the word ADD.

The State of a Small Machine

Let's review a few simple facts about our microprocessor and see how they fit together. First, we know that the microprocessor contains some scratchpad registers, an accumulator, an ALU, and a status register, whose flip-flops let us know such things as whether the result in the accumulator is zero or negative and if there is a carry or overflow. We also know that the microprocessor contains a program counter and a memory address register which point to the location of the instruction and data words in memory that we need. The instruction words that are retrieved from memory are placed in the instruction register to be decoded. Finally, data words are usually sent to the ALU to be processed, unless they too happen to be addresses (as were X and Y in our examples), in which case they are sent to the MAR.

None of this happens by itself. Control and timing signals are being issued continually by the CPU to make certain that everything occurs when it should, and equally important, that whatever occurs was indeed supposed to. This aspect of microprocessor operation is established largely by the manufacturer. The user has little to do with the issuance by the control section of the CPU of the READ and WRITE signals that ENABLE data to flow out of or into the computer's memory chips or scratchpad registers. This is part of the normal fetch-and-execute process.

There is one more register it is very worthwhile for you to know about. We've left it for last for a number of reasons. Not only is it easier to understand than some of the other registers, it also operates in a more independent manner that they do. It can be studied in isolation, even though it functions as an integral part of every modern microprocessor. It is called the *stack pointer register,* the SP.

Most people associate the word "stack" with pancakes, but in this case it is more illuminating to associate it with plates. School cafeterias frequently have a spring-loaded tube into which dishes can be put. What the device does that makes it useful is have a plate at the level of the food selection. You just reach over and get one, not knowing how many others are underneath it. All you can see is that there is a plate available, and it's right where you want it.

There is need for a comparable device in a computer because information quite often has to be stored somewhere, and just as with the plates, one wants it to be right at hand when the time comes to make use of it again. You may be thinking: "I thought that's what the scratchpad registers were for. Isn't their purpose to store information temporarily?" It is, but if we look at a situation that happens to each of us almost daily—and occurs surprisingly often in computers too—we'll see why a slightly different storage arrangement is needed this time.

The key concept here is the idea of being interrupted. Think about it for a moment: If you're not doing anything, you can't be interrupted. It is when an activity of some kind is in progress that the word "interrupt" suddenly becomes meaningful. We've presented the activity of computers, the continual alternation of fetch-and-execute cycles, as being mostly linear: Starting at the beginning, the computer program runs straight through to the end, with no detours or other duties intervening along the way.

Life and computers are more complicated than that. Detours are common, and in a computer they're no accident. In fact, they may be very convenient, since there are a variety of standardized procedures incorporated in our program that are really independent subprograms. Taking a few seconds out to run one of them (perhaps repeatedly) may be a useful detour. The big difference between the interruptions that humans and computers experience is that, while a computer handles all acitivities in an equally unemotional manner, people tend to be more attached to the activity they're doing than the one they're abruptly asked to do. (Switching the two activities later may produce the same resentful reaction; once again, the emotional momentum has been snapped.) However, the technical requirements of people and computers in this situation are the same: Both need a place to store the details of the activity they were busy with when interrupted. Once the interruption has been attended to, the human is likely to ask: "Now, let's see, where was I?" The machine, on the other hand, must be able to obtain an answer to that question—and quickly—after handling the interruption.

Well, where *was* the machine? We don't mean its physical location so much as its mental state. What you've learned in this chapter should put you in a position to give a rather precise answer to this important question. Its state at any given moment can be described by the following pieces of binary data:

1. Where it was in the computer program it was running. Thus, we need to know the (instruction) address that was in its program counter.
2. The intermediate results it had obtained thus far. We'll therefore want to know what was in the accumulator at that moment.
3. The contents of the scratchpad registers, which may contain the addresses of data or the data themselves which the CPU was using, also help to define the state of the system at that time.
4. Finally, the status register contains information worth preserving about such things as carries, overflows, and negative results.

Summing up, to obtain a binary snapshot of the state of a working microprocessor at any given time, gather the data in its program counter, accumulator, scratchpad, and flag registers. In fact, the main reason we discussed the function of these registers first is that they are what must be saved if the microprocessor is to be interrupted, and after handling the interruption, return successfully to the task that occupied it in the first place. It should also be clear now why we cannot use the scratchpad registers to store this information temporarily. To repeat, it is often necessary to store the contents of the scratchpad registers themselves somewhere else, so that these registers can be free to handle effectively the task that serves as the interruption.

It's one thing to talk blithely about putting away data that will be needed later, but if you've ever been interrupted and been unable to remember what you were thinking or dreaming about, you know how easy it is to "lose your place" and not return to where you were. In order to be certain that computers don't become similarly confused when interrupted, a procedure has been established that guarantees an orderly return.

By now, you probably won't be surprised to hear that the procedure involves the address of the data, not the data bit itself. That is, without paying any attention whatsoever to the actual bits in the various registers—a register might even be full of all 0s or all 1s—they are stored in consecutively numbered locations in RAM. (It has to be RAM, not ROM, because one can't write into an ordinary ROM chip.)

The procedure is the same one you'd use if you were working in the school cafeteria and were asked to stack (there's that word again) plates in the self-leveling device near the steam table. However, the order in which you put in *these* plates—that is, the contents of the various registers—is important. The accumulator and flag register may both be 8 bits, say, but they're not likely to contain the same sequence of 0s and 1s. Also, as with plates in a self-leveling sunken tube, *the last one in has to be the first one out.* (They're not like a loaf of white bread; you can't reach around the stale slices at the top of the bag and get the moist, fresher ones underneath.) So LIFO—last in, first out—characterizes the stack. The order in which we put them in is the reverse of the order in which we'll be taking them out.

If pictures are usually worth a thousand words, where stacks are concerned they're worth two thousand. Suppose that we're going to save the contents of five registers, in the following order: the program counter, accumulator, registers 1 and 2 in the scratchpad, and the flag register. Then the results of our efforts, a five-layer stack in RAM, will look as follows:

flag
R2
R1
ACC
PC

However, *we* don't want to have to do any of this; this is something we'd like the CPU to take care of for us automatically whenever it's interrupted and has to turn its attention (that is, its registers) to handling a second task before it has finished the first.

How, then, does the CPU keep track of which registers were put (or "pushed," as the process is usually called) onto the stack and which ones have been removed (or "popped") from it? That is where the *stack pointer register*—the SP—comes in.

To be precise, suppose that we have set the stack pointer to all 0s when we first began using the machine. (You know what clearing your throat means; clearing a register means making certain that all its bits are 0s). Since the stack pointer will keep track of locations on a memory chip, the stack pointer has to have the right number of bits: If the microcomputer uses 16-bit addresses, the stack pointer register must also be 16-bits wide. Here, on our 256-byte memory chip, 8 bits are enough; previously, when we were using 10-bit addresses, the stack pointer would have to have been 10 bits wide.

When we push the contents of the first register, the PC, onto it, the stack pointer will be incremented by 1, so that it now reads 0000 0001. After we put the contents of the accumulator onto the stack as well, the stack pointer will have been incremented again and now reads 0000 0010. In this way, the stack pointer keeps track of how many registers have been pushed onto or popped from the stack. There is an insightful way of looking at this register that many computer engineers use as a shorthand: The stack pointer does the same thing for data that the program counter does for instructions. To get from one instruction to the next, all we have to do is increment the program counter the correct number of times. It then takes care of the job of locating the address of the next instruction for us, without our having to worry about its address. The stack pointer works similarly; by simply moving up or down a few numbers, it locates the data we just stored, without our having to worry about its address in memory.

When we were discussing scratchpad registers before, we often referred to them as general-purpose registers. By contrast, the stack pointer, and the instruction register as well, are clearly special-purpose (or *dedicated*) registers in the microprocessor. Speaking of dedicated, just as certain registers are set aside for special purposes, a preselected portion of RAM is set aside as the stack. Any group of registers in RAM could do the job, but it is very easy to forget *which* registers have been reserved for the purpose and are full of important instructions or data. Using them as ordinary registers, and writing right over the information housed there, can create a real mess.

By the way, don't let the words "push" and "pop" deceive you, even though they are widely used in discussions about stacks. Unlike what happens with dinner plates, no registers are physically added to or removed from the computer's memory bank. Instead, all that happens when something has been pushed onto or popped from the stack is that the stack pointer register points to a different register than the one it was pointing to before.

In our example, the stack pointer is *incremented* when the contents of yet another register is added to the stack, and is decremented when one of the registers is popped. That was the result of our thinking of the stack as a five-story building and the floors toward the top of the page as having higher numbers. However, in other diagrams we've drawn (for instance, the one on page 65), register 0 is toward the top of the page and registers with higher numbers are more toward the bottom. In that case, each time the contents of another register is added to the stack, the stack pointer will decrease. As long as we're consistent, it makes no difference whether we number from the top down or from the bottom up. Either way, the stack pointer allows us to keep track of the information we needed to store temporarily so that we can return it in an orderly manner to the registers in which it was initially housed.

chapter

5

take the bus

You wouldn't think that little Johnny and Fred, 7-year-olds who live next door to one another, are in the forefront of modern technology. Yet in talking to one another through two empty cans that have been strung together through a 25-foot string (see Figure 5-1), they are doing much the same thing that a digital computer does when it sends a message.

In the previous chapter we talked about dedicated registers, that is, registers such as the stack pointer and instruction register that serve a strictly limited purpose and are never used randomly to store data. What Johnny and Fred have is a dedicated communications link. When the phone is busy, Fred's father can't turn to him and say, "I need your corn can, I have to call the garage."

We know how important dedicated registers are in a computer, yet there is a much larger number of general-purpose registers. Similarly, while the dedicated communications links in a computer are important, there is an even greater number of general-purpose communications links. Each of them is called a *bus*.

When a technical term also has a commonplace meaning in everyday life, the word is usually the subject of a variety of puns, not all of them intentional. That is particularly likely to be the case when the everyday meaning of the term is what motivated scientists and engineers in part to adopt the word for technical purposes in the first place. However, you'll have a much greater understanding of what the word "bus" refers to in a modern microcomputer if you associate with it something other than a lumbering 8-wheel, 64-passenger vehicle.

Instead, think of the line that Johnny and Fred have hooked up as being an example of *point-to-point* communication. What is the reverse? *Broadcasting.* Assuming that they're nearby, the easiest way to send a message to a large number of people is to shout it. Although newcomers to the subject are always surprised to hear it, this is the most common form of communication in a computer. Who is doing the shouting? The microprocessor. How does it do it? By putting the message it wants to send on an electrical highway that goes to nearly every part of the computer. What is that highway called? The bus.

Figure 5-1

Note, then, that the most accurate analogy you can use involving the word "bus" in a computer isn't the vehicle itself but the road it travels on. People who are writing about or discussing high-tech subjects often make silly jokes about terminology (we've got a few of our own coming up), but in this case it's very important that the word convey the correct image: Bus should imply broadcast, since the CPU uses the bus to send messages throughout the system. That the words travel electronically through a solid instead of traveling acoustically through air makes no difference. The CPU is broadcasting its message, and just as happens when you shout to a friend of yours in a crowd, the CPU depends on the right listener—and only that listener—to recognize that it is being addressed.

As you've probably noticed by now, the CPU is a very gabby device. Since it is the center of so much activity, it does indeed have a lot to say. Fortunately, its messages fall into three quite distinct categories: addresses, data, and control signals (such as READ or WRITE). It won't come as news to you, then, that there isn't just one bus, there are three of them: an *address* bus, a *data* bus, and last but by no means least, since nothing can happen without it, a *control* bus.

Since these buses are really highways, it is reasonable to ask: "How many *lanes* are there in each of these buses?" Let's take them one at a time, because the answer differs in each case.

The address bus has to have enough lanes—or, since we're talking about electronic pathways, not concrete roadways, lines—to be able to send messages to every register in its memory bank. For example, if the machine's memory chip is a 256-byte RAM or ROM, then the address bus needs 8 lines. Why? Because that way, each register will have a unique address. What are they? The $2^8 = 256$ addresses are 0000 0000, 0000 0001, 0000 0010, . . . , 1111 1111.

Similarly, if the microcomputer has a $1K = 2^{10} = 1024$-register memory, the address bus should be 10 lines wide. A 1K memory is kind of small, though, so a $64K = 64 \times 1024 = 65{,}536 = 2^{16}$-register memory would be more useful. Larger memories, particularly 256K, are becoming more common by the day. Since 256K = 2^{18}, an address bus with 18 lines would be necessary here. Finally, memories with a 2^{20} (that is, approximately 1 million) bytes are also encountered frequently, and they require a 20-line address bus.

That is so many lines, it is only to be expected that engineers have found a variety of ways to cut down on the number required by making other lines (especially data buses) serve double duty. You'll see the same thing happening with increasing frequency in the major cities around the country. No one wants to build a 20-lane road into the downtown area for commuters, though it would ease congestion on the highways considerably. So some of the outgoing roads are made to serve incoming traffic in the morning, and vice versa in the evening. Be that as it may, we'd like to ask you for the moment to forget about the brilliant line-reducing schemes (such as tristate and multiplexing) that electronics engineers have developed in recent decades, although we will look at them in a later chapter. Once you have a good grasp of the underlying principles involved here, gaining an understanding of the line-saving tricks that have been developed is easy.

A prominent feature of the address bus is that it goes *from* the CPU *to* the memory registers. If buses are essentially highways, this one allows travel in only one direction. That is definitely not so in the case of the data bus. We've seen that the CPU may address a memory register either (1) for the purpose of retrieving the data housed in that register, or (2) in order to park some data there. The first operation might be a LOAD (the accumulator), the second might be a STORE (the contents of the accumulator in that register).

Finally, the control bus has signals, such as READ and WRITE, that originate in the CPU and go to every memory register. However, there are other signals, such as interrupts, that originate elsewhere in the microcomputer and have the CPU as their destination (more about this soon when we discuss input/output). The control bus, then, is clearly a two-way road, as is the data bus.

An areal survey of a cluster of highways and byways, with their intersections and cloverleafs, may not reveal a pattern to the traffic, but in a computer there is always a high degree of coordination. Signals must travel on both the address and control buses *simultaneously* if either message is to be effective. For instance, the CPU may shout the name of a memory register, by putting the address of that register on the address bus. And the register may realize that it is being addressed, thanks to its ability to recognize its own number (just as your friend in the crowd can recognize her own name).

Nevertheless, in a computer, unless someone tells the register being addressed what all the shouting is about—and does so *while* the shouting is still taking place—the register simply won't know what it's supposed to do. The control bus must therefore carry either a READ ("send your data to the CPU, please") or else a WRITE signal ("the CPU is sending you some data to store"). Nothing less definitive will end the confusion. If the signal placed on the control bus by the CPU is a READ, the register whose address is on the address bus responds by placing its contents on the data bus.

The analogy between buses and highways extends far enough so that it becomes reasonable to ask: What does a *crash* on this road look like? Fortunately such accidents are less common in modern microcomputers than they are on American highways, but they are just as lethal to the participants. How could a collision occur? Suppose that a READ signal from the CPU causes a memory register to place its contents on the data bus, and at the same time, a WRITE signal has caused the CPU to place a different word in the same data bus. The result is a crash, one that typically destroys not only both of the data words, but may seriously harm the CPU as well.

To make certain that this doesn't happen, READ and WRITE signals are arranged to be mutually exclusive, thanks to their ability to disable one another. Also, the control bus is usually held in the READ position. If nothing else, that prevents random signals or noise from entering the memory chip and accidentally altering the contents of any of its registers.

Communicating with a Distant Peripheral

The CPU isn't limited to shouting messages only to its own memory registers. If you've ever seen a computer print a message on a TV screen or teletype, you know that the CPU has the ability to address any number of devices. That is, somehow the microprocessor can communicate not just with its own memory chip, but with the outside world as well.

It is hardly surprising that these devices which exist on the periphery of the microprocessor's world are collectively called *peripherals*. Keep in mind that, as seen from the CPU's point of view, they are indeed "out there," somewhere. Nonetheless, they are as important to the effective functioning of the CPU as your sense organs and limbs are to your brain. Some of the peripherals (for instance, keyboards) are concerned solely with input. That is, their job is to collect or enter information into the system. Other peripherals (for instance, printers) are more like your mouth, arms, and legs. That is, they take information that is already in the system and make it available to (or produce a response in) the outside world.

Regardless of how powerful a particular microprocessor may be, it is useful to us as human beings precisely because it can accept messages from us and send some back as well. The television screen that accompanies most microcomputer installations is called a CRT, which is an abbreviation for cathode-ray tube—that is, the picture-tube part of a normal television set. You really don't need the rest of the set, especially the knobs and dials that come with a typical TV, since in this case you won't be changing channels constantly to see what's on the other stations or turning off the sound when an abrasive commercial suddenly appears on the screen.

What is fascinating is that in a recent nationwide survey we did of more than 4000 Americans who didn't own computers but would like to, more than half thought that a microcomputer consisted solely of an electric typewriter hooked up to a television. Where was the microprocessor? They neither knew nor cared. The vast majority didn't even know what the word meant; they assumed that, as one put it, "everything you need is in there [in the typewriter or CRT]." Since processors have shrunk drastically in size in recent decades, while keyboards and TVs have gotten larger if anything, their conclusion isn't quite as wild as it sounds at first. More important for our purposes, the comfort most people feel in front of a TV set, together with the knowledge they have of an ordinary typewriter keyboard, has made the microcomputer (as a typewriter-with-TV-attached) appear enormously more friendly to them than large mainframe computers used to seem. Now that the processor has shrunk to micro proportions, the intimidating part of the machine has just about vanished.

Be that as it may, there are two points here that should be emphasized. First, there is a wide range of other input and output devices besides keyboards and CRTs, the most important being disks, both the hard and the floppy variety (more on this later). Many peripherals are capable of doing double duty, that is, serving as both input *and* output devices. That's nothing new; so do your feet. When you use them to kick a can down the street if you're feeling glum or annoyed, they are acting as an output device. When your feet hurt, they are acting as an input device. Pain is the message they're sending.

The second key point here is that peripherals tend to be very much slower than microprocessors, and for good reason: Things that work electronically tend to be vastly faster than those that are mechanical. Electrons move at blinding velocities even relative to high-speed gears and precision ball bearings. Making a mechanical device partly electronic (and calling the resulting hybrid "electromechanical") may speed it up significantly, but it remains slow by any measure when compared to a purely electronic device. For instance, while modern microprocessors can perform millions of calculations per second, no keyboard or printer can begin to approach such speeds.

Format too plays a major role in reducing the rate at which a CPU can communicate with the outside world. When you yell to a friend in a crowd, you yell his entire name. It doesn't come out all at once, of course, even if the name is only one syllable long. No matter how fast you say it, the first "b" in Bob is still uttered before the second. Nevertheless, Bob is likely to hear the sounds as if they all arrived at once.

In the last chapter we called the simultaneous transmission of a group of signals along a common pathway *parallel* transmission. By contrast, yelling Bob's name to him one letter at a time would be an example of serial transmission. To aid Bob in hearing his name when it's shouted, people normally say it more quickly. The excitement of seeing someone they're eager to make contact with speeds up their speech. Yet beyond that, they subconsciously sense that parallel transmission of the letters will help Bob to hear his name in a crowd. So they say the name not only more loudly, but more quickly as well.

Computers can't do the same thing. We've stated that, in essence, the CPU shouts, yet the way it actually does so is by placing an address on the address bus that travels to every part of the system. Then it is up to the device being addressed to realize that it is indeed being addressed, and respond. Unlike what happens in a crowd, where anyone may butt in to the conversation since both you and your friend are to some extent broadcasting your words (unless you're whispering in one another's ear), in a computer the communication *switches* from broadcast to point-to-point once the CPU and memory register or input/output device being addressed establish contact. To prevent crashes, every other memory register and peripheral is shut out of the conversation for the time being.

Even with all the other devices temporarily eliminated from the picture except the two that are now in direct contact—a necessary first step—there is still a serious problem, one that must be solved. Namely, the CPU can use its address and data buses to carry a parallel message only so far. After that distance (usually 100 feet or more), serial transmission is more economical *and* reliable, since the bits in each word tend to travel at different speeds over long distances. Whether Bob is 2, 10, or 50 feet from you, your mode of communication remains the same: shout, and the further away he is, the louder. The adjustment you make is merely a quantitative change.

In a computer, after a certain distance, shouting no longer suffices. Something qualitatively different must normally be used with a distant peripheral. If the first step a computer takes to establish and maintain good contact with a peripheral is to get every other device out of the picture temporarily (step 1: the switch from broadcast to point-to-point), the second step is therefore the switch from parallel to serial communication.

That is easier than it sounds. In fact, many students at this point ask some very good questions. First, "How and where does the CPU convert messages from parallel to serial, and vice versa?" Second, "How does the CPU distinguish between peripherals and memory registers? Do they have different addresses?"

Types of Input/Output

These questions, and many others like them, all fit under an extremely important heading concerned with the *interface* between a computer and its peripherals.

Interface is a word that has attained such widespread use that it is now bandied about regularly by people who haven't the foggiest idea what terms such as accumulator, ALU, or bus mean in this context. They don't know what a microprocessor is, and they associate the word "register" with "a complaint" or else "to vote." Small wonder that when they make comments such as, "My boss and I really interface well," they are unwittingly stuffing one and often both feet in their mouths.

The fellow who made this remark with abundant self-assurance asked his boss for a raise a few days later. The boss's response was a blunt "no," followed by a hostile lecture. "Wow," said the stunned employee, "I've *never* seen him that mad before."

Why tell you about this in a computer book? Because one of the crucial features of every interface between a computer and its peripherals is predictability. The job of the interface is to help smooth, and at best, erase, the many differences that exist between the CPU and its internal memory chips, on the one hand, and input/output devices, on the other, which allow the machine to interact with the world. Where was that all-important predictability when the guy asked his boss for a raise? Maybe he was confused. Instead of "interface" he must have been talking about getting it "in the face."

Let's quickly review some of the key differences between the CPU and internal memory versus the most commonly used peripherals, then we'll see exactly how the interface makes possible an orderly and predictable flow of information between them:

1. The CPU and memory are electronic devices, whereas peripherals are electromechanical.
2. The CPU operates at enormously higher speeds than the peripherals, thanks to item 1.

3. The data format used by the CPU on its internal buses (namely, parallel) often differs from that used by a peripheral, particularly a distant one, which is likely to send and receive bits serially.
4. Since there is such a discrepancy in speed and style between the CPU and peripherals, it is essential that one not barge in on the other without first checking that it is all right.
5. Finally, since everything the CPU does is strictly according to the clock—that is, is synchronized by clock pulses—peripherals too have to find a way to operate in sync with the CPU and its internal memory chips.

Simply listing points 1 through 5 makes it clear that anything which is to be legitimately labeled an interface has a formidable set of tasks to perform. Let us take one pivotal job that every interface must handle and see precisely how it does it. Until now, we've concentrated on gaining an understanding of how a CPU gets information from, or stores information in, its memory chips. What we found is that the concept of addressing a register—worrying about its location, not contents—moved to the fore.

Rather than having to scrap that approach when we turn our attention to input/output devices, we find that there is a welcome bonus: The same approach can be used, unchanged. Why? When we speak of data being held in a computer peripheral or interface, we certainly don't mean that they are sitting in a brown paper bag, the way a sack of tomatos might. Instead, the data the peripheral wants to send to the CPU are held temporarily in one of the interface registers.

That may seem an underwhelming thought to you at first, but it actually provides real insight into not only the manner in which interfaces handle data, but also how the CPU might interact with that data. After all, if a CPU is good at nothing else, it knows how to address a register, and then, using READ or WRITE, obtain its contents or change them. Who cares, then, that the register is in an interface instead of being an internal memory register?

Some of the nation's top computer engineers have a wisecrack about an interface that is very illuminating here. "The whole idea of a good interface," they often say, "is to *trick* the CPU into thinking that there is no interface present, and that the peripheral is 'just like' the CPU in speed, format, etc." In other words, what you've learned in the previous three chapters should be sufficient to describe—at least from the CPU's point of view—everything that happens in a computer. The CPU should therefore think it is merely addressing a memory register, when in fact it is communicating with a register that is in an interface.

When the trick works, that is, when there are no separate input and output instructions for the CPU to worry about, the arrangement is called *memory-mapped input/output,* often abbreviated as memory-mapped IO. The CPU places an address on the address bus without knowing where that address is. Whether it is a memory register or CRT interface is not something that the CPU can determine on the basis of the instruction it has fetched from memory and is now executing.

The arrangement may be a simple and appealing one, but there is a penalty for using it. Namely, once an address represents a CRT interface register, it cannot also be used to represent a register in memory. Some memory addresses—more than most people expect—must be set aside, then, and reserved for interface registers of all sorts (we'll be discussing this topic in detail later).

Anything that reduces the available range of addresses strikes some computer designers as an arrangement to be avoided. Even though there are vastly more memory-reference instructions than those that refer to input/output, this group of designers doesn't mind having a separate procedure for the latter.

What does such an input/output instruction look like? The typical format is as follows:

op code	address code	command code

Here the op code tells the CPU immediately that it is dealing with an input/output instruction. As with any op code, it must also tell the CPU whether it has finished fetching the entire instruction, which may be one to four words long. The fact that an interface register is being referenced here doesn't alter the condition that, just as with ordinary memory-reference instructions, some are longer than others. Finally, although the op code tells the CPU that this is indeed an input/output instruction, it must in addition tell it *which one,* input or output.

The address code accomplishes the same thing here that it did before: It singles out one register in the interface, and hence allows the conversation in which the CPU subsequently takes part to be in point-to-point instead of broadcast mode. However, there is an important difference between memory-mapped input/output and what's taking place here, which is called *isolated input/output.* Why is it called that? Because this arrangement isolates (or separates) the addresses of all the input/output interface registers from the addresses of memory registers. For that reason, the range of memory addresses doesn't have to be reduced in any way as a result of giving each interface register a unique address for input/output operations. The two sets of addresses have indeed been isolated from one another.

The last part of a typical input/output instruction contains the command code. Students at this point sometimes say naively, "It doesn't seem that this part of the instruction should be necessary, since the CPU already knows what it wants to do."

That is all well and good, but who will tell the CRT, printer, magnetic tape, or disk memory what to do? Keep in mind that the CPU talks to the peripheral *through* the interface. Moreover, if the interface is successful, then, as we've seen, the CPU will barely even know that it's there. The command code must therefore contain bits that tell the peripheral such things as (1) input some information to the CPU, (2) receive some output from the CPU, and (3) if the peripheral is a magnetic tape player, say, to rewind or enter fast-forward mode in order to get to the right position. In short, the CPU, through the command code, takes charge of readying the peripheral either to input or output information, and then makes sure it does it.

Serial and Parallel Interfaces

None of the (CPU) register-to-(interface) register transfers we've been discussing can take place until the interface has organized its data correctly. In the beginning of this chapter we saw that buses may be thought of as multilane highways, ones that allow an entire address to travel in parallel on them (if they're address buses) and data words to travel in parallel on them (if they're data buses). A very important function of an interface is therefore to convert the information it receives in serial form from the outside world into parallel form for transmission on the data bus to the CPU.

Although most people imagine the conversion process to be difficult and the device that does the converting to be complex, the need for serial-to-parallel and parallel-to-serial conversion is so common that the converters have become standard. In fact, they are included as one of the handful of pieces of hardware that you get when you buy most microcomputers, even portable ones. Some of the newer, more expensive micros have even gone so far as to incorporate this interface (it's just a little chip containing an integrated circuit, or IC) right into the unit. The next time you see an advertisement in a newspaper or magazine for a computer, check to see if it includes, for example, the most common parallel-serial interconverter of all, the RS232.

This book is devoted to the fundamental principles that you need in order to understand computers now and in the foreseeable future, not individual pieces of hardware that the rapid pace of technological innovation may render obsolete tomorrow. Nevertheless, a brief examination of the way the RS232 works is warranted for two reasons: the extreme popularity of the unit, and the fact that any new unit that replaces it will still need to accomplish the same conversions it now does. To be precise, RS232 is actually a standard—RS stands for "recommended standard"—established by the Electronic Industries Association (EIA) for serial transmission. However, it is common for engineers as well as manufacturers of devices that meet the standard to call the device itself an RS232, even though products bearing the name come from dozens of different companies.

The first thing to note is that the RS232 has separate transmitter and receiver sections. The transmitter section accepts an 8-bit parallel word, say, from the data bus, and transmits the bits one at a time. The receiver section does exactly the reverse. It accepts data bits that arrive serially and, when it finally has enough of them, assembles them into a data word to be placed on the data bus.

It is worthwhile for you to think of the RS232 interface as being used in pairs. We've been discussing peripherals as though they were always relatively near the CPU to which they are sending data and from which they receive data. It's not so. There is no reason why the CPU and its peripherals couldn't be on opposite sides of the continent. In a growing number of instances, they are. What happens in that case is pictured in Figure 5-2.

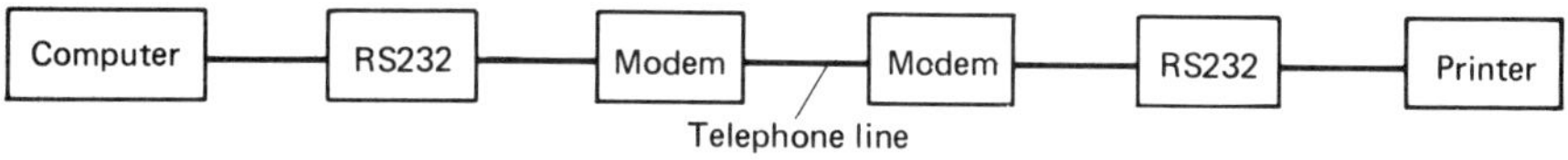

Figure 5-2 A computer communicating with a distant peripheral, a printer.

We'll be discussing modems later, but for the moment think of them as devices that facilitate the sending of serial data bits over telephone lines. How? The modem on the left starts the process by converting the serial stream of 0s and 1s it receives from the RS232 to its left into tones that can be distinguished from one another (that is, like musical notes you can tell apart because they have frequencies that are sufficiently different).

Just as you hear tones when you dial a number using a push-button phone, the modem at the other end (the one on the right) hears the tones and converts them back into 0s and 1s. What the first modem does is called *modulation*. The name is altogether appropriate, since in essence the unit is singing: producing musical notes as output when it receives 0s and 1s as input. What the second unit does is called *demodulation*. The word "modem" simply stands for a combination of the two actions: mo(dulation)-dem(odulation).

Reading this figure from left to right tells us that when an 8-bit data word appears in parallel on the computer's data bus, the RS232 converts it into a stream of data that is 8 bits long. When the stream of data arrives one bit at a time at the RS232 on the right-hand side of the figure, this RS232 assembles the serial bits. (How? By using a shift register that collects the incoming bits until the register is full.) The printer then uses ASCII code to determine what letter, number, or character it has been sent, and prints it.

What you should carry away from this picture is the idea that while two NOT gates in succession cancel each other out, a pair of RS232s can save you money. It would take eight telephone lines instead of the two that are normally present (one for input data, the other for output data), if the bits had to be transmitted in parallel form from the computer to the printer. Worse still, many of the newer micros are 16- or 32-bit machines and would therefore need 16 or 32 phone lines simultaneously. If the computer were in Texas or California and the printer in New York, that would make the message prohibitively expensive to send. Inserting the two RS232s (or any comparable devices) between the computer and the peripheral solves the problem and keeps the cost reasonable. Besides, neither the computer nor the printer really knows the two RS232s are there. Like any good interface, the RS232s succeed in making themselves largely invisible. The communication occurs at a slower speed, of course, than it would if bits were being sent in parallel packages. But other than that, the conversation takes place as if neither interface of the pair were present.

When speed *is* essential and distances are short, other devices are used instead of the RS232, whose top transmission rate is approximately 20,000 bits per second. The RS449 is capable of serially transmitting 2 million bits (2 megabits) per second. That is 100 times faster than the RS232's ceiling. However, the unit is more expensive and requires a more complex hookup to the computer. When the distance over which data have to be sent is 60 feet or less, there is also a parallel transmission bus that is becoming increasingly popular, the IEEE-488 ("the I triple-E," that is, the Institute of Electrical and Electronics Engineers), which was first developed by Hewlett-Packard. It has a top transmission rate of 2 million bytes (2 megabytes) per second. That's 16 million bits each second!

We've come a long way from Johnny and Fred and their state-of-the-art dedicated communications link. A final note: People usually think of the interface as working most closely with the peripheral, and that therefore the interface and the peripheral with which it is paired are housed together physically. After all, where else should your right arm be, if not attached to your body? However, the fact remains that both the RS232-C serial interface and IEEE-488 parallel interface are usually housed in "the box" you receive that contains the CPU, keyboard, and CRT. Rarely are these interfaces packaged together physically with the peripheral they serve. When you're buying or examining a microcomputer, you might want to ask what serial and parallel interfaces it has and check to see where they're located on the unit. As we'll see later when we discuss networks, both varieties of interface are becoming increasingly important.

chapter 6 the computer and its peripherals

In this chapter we'll look at some important connections between hardware and software. It is common for people who know a little programming to say, "Without software, a computer is just a useless pile of iron." Conversely, many computer engineers are convinced that the number of people who will eventually become expert programmers is miniscule. Their attitude leads them to the belief that "The public shouldn't be taught, much less expected to know, any computer languages; not BASIC, Pascal, nothing. Instead, sell them ROMs with the program already 'hard wired' into the chip. That way, you don't have to worry about people making a mess of the machine and frustrating themselves to boot."

The arguments between hardware and software freaks aren't about to disappear. Neither is the growing disagreement between those who want the public to have a good working knowledge of some computer languages *versus* those who want to sell software packages profitably to an ignorant public that buys them gratefully, and has no idea how to tailor them to suit personal purposes.

It is essential to get beyond the petty, self-serving rivalries that have sprung up in such abundance in this field. The arguments are as sensible as debates about which of the two you need more, your bones or your blood. The most fascinating aspect of the computer field is the continual interplay between hardware and software to solve problems that are difficult or impossible to tackle effectively in any other manner.

The computer's ability to do the same thing over and over again, millions of times each second if necessary, would bore human beings who had that ability to tears. Nonetheless, it is one of the machine's greatest sources of strength. There are a number of ways to maximize that strength, and in this chapter we'll see why the most frequently encountered ones have been chosen.

Remembering Where You Were

Suppose you are sitting in an armchair in the living room reading an interesting book, but one that occasionally uses a complicated word with which you aren't familiar. Across the room is a large, unabridged dictionary that happens to be the only one around. Instead of letting any strange words slip by without their meaning being understood, you make the trip to the other side of the room each time you need one defined.

There are two things worth noting about this situation. The first is that there is an action that takes place repeatedly: namely, your putting your book down, walking to the other side of the room, referring to the dictionary, then returning to your chair, finding your place once again in the book, and continuing your reading.

The second noteworthy feature of the situation is that the main action isn't the frequent visits to the dictionary. Instead, reading the book constitutes the principal focus; the trips to the dictionary are a (necessary) detour which aids that action. If you were keeping a running diary of the period during which you were doing the reading, it might look as follows:

⋮
196
197, line 23
WEBSTER
197, line 24
198
199, line 6
WEBSTER
199, line 7
200
201
⋮

The numbers are simply the page numbers of the book you are reading, and "line 23" refers to the twenty-third line on that page. WEBSTER, however, is different: It refers to the trips you've repeatedly had to take to the dictionary on the other side of the room. Writing the word WEBSTER and letting it stand for the complex five-part detour is doubly convenient. One word stands for what might otherwise have to be a lengthy description inserted into your diary, and even more important, the same word can be used to characterize each trip you have to take. Elsewhere in the diary, you would of course have to spell out what the term WEBSTER meant if you wanted someone else to understand what you'd written. In any event, if there were many trips to the dictionary while you were reading the book, your diary account of the period would be shortened considerably by using the shorthand we've just discussed.

Computer programmers do the same thing when writing a program, but it's not done merely as a convenience, in order to make the written description shorter. As we've already seen, right from the start computers have made use of the stored-program concept, meaning that the entire program is entered into the computer's memory chips, step by step, and then is run as a whole. Memory chips may be getting cheaper, but as a number of top experts have noted, the public's appetite for ever more memory capacity in the computers they use is growing even faster. For this and a variety of other reasons, it is still important to try to minimize the amount of space a program takes up. The shorthand conventions (like WEBSTER) adopted on the page, assuming they turn out to be the right kinds, allow similar savings on a memory chip.

It is therefore quite common to see computer programs which have been laid out in a manner comparable to that shown a few paragraphs back. Since reading the book—that is, following a numbered sequence of pages from beginning to end—was the main purpose of the activity, having to walk over to the dictionary and look up a word was considered a detour. You won't be surprised to hear, then, that a similar detour in a computer program is called a BRANCH. Another name for it is JUMP or JUMP TO ______. It is indeed a temporary branching or jumping away from the main line of the program being run, and the words BRANCH and JUMP are written in capital letters because the machine has to be *instructed* to do what you do automatically. That is, what made you get out of the armchair and walk over to the dictionary in the first place was an internal signal that told you you had encountered a word whose meaning was unfamiliar. In a computer program, there must be an explicit instruction to tell the machine to do the same; BRANCH or JUMP accomplishes that purpose.

Switching focus slightly for a moment, once you've decided to put your book down and look up a word, the same five-part procedure is put into motion every time:

1. Mark the place you'd gotten to in the book, and put the book down.
2. Walk to the other side of the room.
3. Refer to the dictionary.
4. Return to your chair.
5. Find your place once again in the book and continue on your merry way.

It is precisely because the five steps are the same each time that it makes sense simply to write the word WEBSTER in your diary. If it describes one event, it describes them all. Similarly, in a computer program, the five-step (or any other number, for that matter) detour that in general is called a BRANCH is called a *procedure* in this specific case. It is also called a *subroutine.* (After you've gotten out of your chair for the twentieth time to look up yet another word in the dictionary, you know precisely why). The main program is the routine of which this is the *sub-*.

Clearly, BRANCH is a more all-encompassing word, whereas procedure or subroutine refers to a piece of the program that will be run repeatedly throughout it. To save space in the program (and therefore in memory), the procedure is written once, placed in a separate set of locations in memory, and then, just as with WEBSTER, whenever the procedure is needed, the computer performs a BRANCH or JUMP to the first instruction in the procedure and runs through however many steps there are in it. After that, it returns to where it was originally.

Procedure Calls

There is some commonly used terminology here that is worth knowing and is quite illuminating as well. When a doctor is devoting a specific number of hours waiting to be of service to patients needing medical attention, we say that that physician is "on call." The meaning of the phrase is clear: If we ask for help, the doctor will respond immediately. Notice that the phrase contains the implication that the doctor isn't occupied with other matters, medical or otherwise, when the call arrives—or that the other matters will be dropped abruptly when the call comes. Inactivity, or at the very least a state of stand-by readiness, is an inherent part of being on call.

It is the same when you were reading the book and the dictionary sat across the room "on call," temporarily inactive but ready to be of service at any time. WEBSTER thus represents an activation of that readiness. In a computer, the procedure or subroutine that has been separated from the main program and stored elsewhere for ready (and repeated) reference occupies a similar position. It waits. For what? A CALL instruction. Hence CALL as a step in a computer program means "run the procedure at this point in the program."

But which procedure? Suppose there are many of them (that's usually the case). For this reason, programmers do the same thing with subroutines that paging operators do with doctors in a hospital. What you're likely to hear in the halls of a hospital is "Calling (or paging) Dr. So-and-so." Since a computer uses numbers instead of names and everything has an explicit location, the correct form for a CALL instruction therefore is the word CALL followed by an address. Which one? The address of the first instruction in the procedure being called.

Throughout this book we've been emphasizing the concept of register-to-register transfers. Often, these are data transfers. However, there is such a thing as a "transfer of control" too, and it is important to understand what the terminology refers to. As long as the main program is running, it is providing instructions to the CPU. Even though the CPU is the dynamic element which carries out those orders, it is fair to say that the main program is in charge. If the main program calls a procedure, however, the procedure then proceeds to take charge. A CALL therefore represents a transfer of control.

The situation is analogous to what happens when you have a medical emergency. Usually you're in charge of your behavior and well-being, but if a serious illness or accident befalls you, in a very real sense you then hand over control temporarily to a doctor. But it doesn't end there. Given the degree to which modern medicine has become highly specialized, it is common for one doctor to call in another. So control can pass from you to a doctor and then to another doctor, more specialized in the problem at hand.

It's the same in a computer program, where the main program may CALL a procedure right in the middle of the program, and that procedure may CALL a second one right in the middle of the first. In that case, they're called *nested* calls; one nests in the next. This double transfer of control is more easily understood if it is visualized in terms of the hardware involved—that is, the locations in memory that are utilized during the transfers. The memory chip pictured in Figure 6-1 may be assumed to be either a ROM or a RAM.

What the first box on the left tells us is that the program which has previously been fed into the computer's memory chip runs, step by step, until it comes to the place where a procedure CALL occurs. Then control is transferred to a second set of addresses in memory and the instructions there are fetched and executed one by one as if *they* were the main program. For the time being, they might as well be. Midway through the first procedure another CALL instruction occurs, and it results in the transfer of control to a second procedure. The second

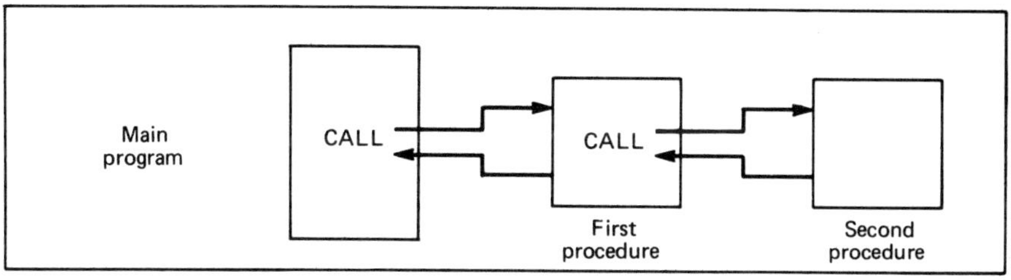

Figure 6-1 Nested CALLS.

procedure that is called in this case runs from first step to last without calling yet a third procedure (though in many programs it might) and then returns control to the second procedure.

We certainly wouldn't want there to be any slip-ups at this point, whether we're talking about patients or programs. Transfer of control from the second procedure back to the first and, eventually, from the first procedure to the main program must be done in a careful manner. The transfer is therefore formalized as an instruction: RETURN. That is, the last step of any procedure is an explicit instruction to return control to the part of the program that called it in the first place. Thus, CALL and RETURN instructions mark the beginning and end of each procedure's period of control.

It is all well and good to speak about a procedure returning control to the main program, say, that issued the CALL, but how does the procedure know precisely—that is, the exact address—to which control should be returned? Remember, the initial CALL instruction contained an address, so the CPU knew the location of the first instruction in the procedure being called. RETURN instructions, however, do not similarly contain an address. Where, then, is this crucial piece of information?

Both the hardware and software aspects of the matter are essential to an understanding of what occurs here, and why. In Chapter 4 we discussed the notion of a stack. To review briefly the most important concept involved, a stack should be thought of as a reserved part of memory (that is, a group of registers in RAM) that houses data temporarily on a LIFO (that is, last-in, first-out) basis. The stack pointer register (SP) allows us to keep track of items that have been pushed onto or popped from the stack.

In the beginning of this chapter we saw that when you were about to check the dictionary once again—or, in computer lingo, were about to CALL a procedure named WEBSTER—the first thing you did was mark where you were in your book when the need for the procedure arose. You didn't want to lose your place. A computer that invokes a procedure marks its place by temporarily storing somewhere the values in its CPU registers. Since the contents of these registers are an essential part of the definition of the state of the system at that time, putting them away in a safe place helps ensure that the machine will be able to resume where it left off, once the procedure is finished.

How are the registers that need to be saved actually saved, and which ones are? The first register we should consider is the program counter (PC). The function of this register, you'll recall, is to point to (that is, give the address of) the next instruction to be fetched. Obviously, that is a valuable piece of information where a detour from the main program as sizable as a procedure CALL is involved. The program counter is always one of the registers whose contents are automatically pushed onto the stack by the CPU.

When does that happen? As soon as the instruction register (IR) realizes that it has received a procedure CALL. (It comes to that realization by decoding the op code in the CALL step of the program.) Having just fetched an instruction, the CPU increments the program counter to the address of the next instruction, while it busies itself with executing the present one—in this case, transferring control to the procedure that has been called. How convenient it is to have the return address we need sitting right there in the program counter. Obviously, then, what needs to be done whenever a procedure is called is to push the contents of the program counter onto the stack, and then, as soon as the procedure is finished, pop the contents of the stack register holding the program counter back into the program counter register.

In short, the stack removes the burden of having each procedure specify the address to which control should be returned when the procedure is finished. Good thing too, since the stack does the job more simply and easily.

Other information usually has to be pushed onto the stack as well, namely, the contents of the flag register and some of the general-purpose registers. Why do these also have to be saved? For space reasons; the procedure may well have to perform some computations, and if it does, the general-purpose registers and flag register may be needed. If their contents are not stored somewhere else temporarily for safekeeping, the binary numbers in those registers will be written over and altered permanently by the procedure that was called. They too are therefore added to the stack—that is, pushed onto it—and popped back into their respective positions automatically by the CPU once the procedure is through.

Polling and Testing

It is time for us to see what happens when a peripheral wants the CPU's attention. Until now, we've been examining transactions that involve only the CPU and memory, both electronic and both neatly tucked away from the user's view. Input/output devices are the tools that users employ to make contact (through an interface) with the CPU and memory, and although these devices are more visible, their operations have some very important similarities with the procedure calls we've been discussing.

To begin with, we need to make a distinction between those peripherals that are under the control of the CPU and those that aren't. As long as we're talking about control, we might as well know who has it at any given moment. Many students at this point ask: "Why can't the CPU always have it? That is, can't all the input/output operations of a computer be simply reduced to a matter of good programming?"

The answer is no, for two key reasons. First, there is a flaw in the stored program concept. Namely, a program can be loaded into the computer's memory, so that the entire set of instructions it consists of can be run from beginning to end at high speed, but the same usually cannot be done with the data the program needs. To choose two frequently encountered examples, if the computer is being used to monitor a production line process in a manufacturing plant or a liquids-handling mixing operation at a chemical company, there is no way for the data to be fed in beforehand, when the program is being entered. In other examples, this information generally arrives weeks or months later, and more important, at slow speeds when it finally does.

You probably won't be surprised to hear that the name given to a data processing operation in which the needed data *can* be gathered and entered beforehand is called *batch*. That is, it is available in a batch or bunch prior to the processing run. We'll look at batch processing later, since a huge amount of it takes place daily.

In the two industrial examples, as with a space shot, the data are being generated continuously and monitored in real time, meaning moment to moment. The sensors that monitor these processes and are connected to the computer's peripheral devices are under only limited control of the CPU. In what way? The CPU can't make them gather and transmit the needed data any faster than they're now doing so. It's not up to them—they're only digital intermediaries.

The second reason the CPU and one of the programs it is running at that moment can't always be in charge is that other users, with other programs, may want access to the CPU. As computers have progressively shrunk in size and cost, and microprocessors have become available by the millions for individuals to use, there is much less jockeying for position among users than there used to be. In previous decades, when there was only one large mainframe—and nothing else smaller—available to an entire local community of users, it was common to hear "your time is up" just as you really got rolling, and someone else (and his or her program) took your place.

Even now, however, you may be running one routine and have questions arise that only another can answer for you. Or you may simply want to make a complicated calculation of some kind (for instance, the square root of 21,771) that has nothing to do with, say, the word processing program you are running at the time. You'd resent it mightily if the CPU prevented you at that moment from taking control briefly and pursuing what you at least consider a fruitful line of inquiry.

Getting into a wrestling match with the machine—with you shouting and the machine repeatedly printing, "Hey, who's in charge here, anyway?"—would be just a little bizarre.

However, the best possible reason for not allowing the CPU always to be in charge is that, odd as it may sound at first, that's an extremely wasteful route. What does it waste? Time, lots of it, and a good way to see why is to watch an anxious set of grandparents who are babysitting for the first time for a young child who is sleeping.

Wanting to do a good job, and deathly afraid that harm will come to the youngster if they're not watching, they look in on the child constantly. What they're doing (in terms of what goes on in a computer) is called *polling*. They are intent upon not missing any signals the child sends, so they keep checking every few minutes to see if there is anything at all to which they should respond. A computer in the same situation is even more restless than these two are; it doesn't do its checking every few minutes, it does it many thousands of times each second.

The CPU sends a message to the peripheral (by putting the address of an interface register on the address bus), asking if it has any data it wishes to send. In software terms, that is, in terms of the program used to accomplish this inquiry, the message is called a TEST. What is the CPU testing? We saw in the previous chapter that every interface, like every CPU, has a flag register. In a moment you'll not only see why it has one, but why that's a very good name for the device.

In rural settings, the mailbox usually sits on a post, right next to the road, instead of being attached to the house, the way it is in suburban settings. To make the mail carrier's job easier, rural mailboxes are often clustered together in one place by the side of the road, though the six to ten houses to which those mailboxes belong may not even be close enough to see one another. For our purposes, what's important to note here is that the person who delivers mail in rural settings normally picks it up as well. How does that person know which mailboxes along the road contain mail to be picked up? Having to look in every one each day, when less than 20%, say, receive mail on any given day, would be very inefficient and time-consuming.

The solution that is used most frequently is that a small flag is attached to each mailbox, and when its owner has something to send, he puts it in the mailbox and raises the flag. That alerts the passing mail carrier that there is a pickup to be made, even if there is no delivery to the box that day. After picking up the mail, the carrier then puts the flag down to prevent herself from stopping there accidentally for the same piece of mail the next time around.

In a computer, when one of the peripherals has a message to send, its interface acts similarly and raises a flag (that is, a specially designated flip-flop goes from 0 to 1, thus alerting the CPU). However, the CPU may be busy doing something else at the time. The situation is comparable to that of a student quietly raising his hand in class when the teacher is in the middle of an important thought or looking in another direction. In terms of the mail-route analogy, the flag could be raised but the carrier might be traveling on other roads at the moment and hasn't yet seen it.

What a CPU TEST therefore does is check whether there are any flags raised. If one is, the CPU knows that there is a message waiting, ready to be sent. After it is picked up, the CPU resets the flag (that is, the flip-flop) to 0, so that it won't try at a later time to obtain a message that it has already received. In short, when a CPU is polling, this is what it's polling: the flags attached to the interfaces between itself and its various input/output devices.

Again, the situation is quite comparable to what happens when a mail deliverer with nothing to deliver to a cluster of 10 mailboxes nevertheless scans them all as she passes, to make certain that no flags are raised. Note that in this instance the mailboxes act as both input and output buffer registers, temporarily holding messages that are going one way or the other.

Why It Is Desirable to Allow Interruptions

It may have occurred to you by now that polling isn't the most efficient method for grandparents, mail deliverers, *or* CPUs to determine whether their services are required at that moment. The best way for us to see the alternative, and why it's so frequently adopted, is to take another look at the situation of anxious grandparents who are babysitting. Instead of checking every two minutes to see it the child needs them, they could do what the child's parents would usually be doing at the time: Look in occasionally on the youngster, but for the most part watch television and count on the fact that they'll hear a howl or noise of some kind if the child wants something.

A CPU can busy itself with its normal activities and arrange things so that a peripheral that wants its attention must ask for it. As opposed to polling, this arrangement produces *interrupts*. Earlier in this chapter, and in Chapter 4, we discussed the idea of a stack. We saw that a program detour (in the case we examined it was a procedure CALL) requires the contents of the program counter, status, and scratchpad registers to be stored elsewhere temporarily so that these registers can be freed up to help handle the detour. At the time, we were discussing detours from the main program that were generated by the program itself (that is, they were written into the program before the program was even fed into the machine). In brief, a procedure CALL (or jump to a subroutine, JSR, as it is often labeled) is a *software* interrupt.

In contrast to that, when an input/output device sends an interrupt request (INT REQ), the equivalent of a child's howl, and the CPU responds with an interrupt acknowledge (INT ACK), the equivalent of the parents saying, "We're coming, sweetheart," the resulting detour from the main program is a *hardware* interrupt. It certainly wasn't planned for beforehand to occur at precisely this time; otherwise it could have been written into the program. It is unplanned, and more to the point, the peripheral's interface initiates this type of intrusion.

It is worthwhile to note that there are many important similarities between a procedure CALL or jump to a subroutine, on the one hand, and an interrupt initiated by an input/output device's interface, on the other. Where does the similarity lie? Both require a type of service that causes the flow of control to be transferred away from the main program to a subroutine stored somewhere else.

It makes perfect sense to students that a jump to a subroutine might result in a prolonged detour, but for some strange reason they're inclined to feel that servicing an interrupt takes virtually no time at all. In their view, program interrupts and procedure calls, whatever their similarities, differ significantly in this regard.

Let's back up for a moment, then, and see what happens in everyday settings should an interruption occur. When a student in class calls the teacher's name aloud as well as quietly raising a hand, the concepts of polling and interrupt both appear. In essence, the student doesn't trust the teacher to call on him quickly enough by using a polling procedure, so he takes matters into his own hands, switches to the opposite approach, and interrupts. The interrupt signifies the urgency of the situation; that is, either he has a brilliant idea or else he has to go to the bathroom.

In our other example, when junior let out a howl with his grandparents in the next room, we know which of the two it was. Finally, old farmer McCluskey just called the post office to make certain that the mail carrier stopped by to pick up a letter to the IRS (that's Internal Revenue, not some instruction register, IR) containing a check. "It has to be postmarked today," he said nervously. Servicing these three interrupts requires, respectively, talking to the restless student, changing a wet diaper, and if necessary, making a special trip to old man McCluskey's place.

If what goes on in a computer reflects to any extent what occurs in real life, and it does, there is no inherent reason why servicing an input/output interrupt should be a less significant matter and involve fewer complications than jumping to a subroutine. The principal contributor to this distorted view of input/output interrupts has to do with the keyboard and CRT. Most students believe that depressing a key on the keyboard results in that letter, number, or character (let's suppose that it is a "k") being printed on the screen. They've seen it occur so often, they assume it's automatic—and therefore instantaneous. But it's not so.

Pressing a key on a keyboard is an example of an *input* operation. Yet if you think about it for a moment, you'll realize that having the letter "k" appear on the screen is an example of an *output* operation. Far from being automatic, this "echo printing" requires not only that the correct hardware design be implemented at the factory, but also that a software subroutine be present in the machine's memory. Among other things, it will then *instruct* the CPU to echo-print each character when you depress that character's key.

(There is a bit of terminology that it is valuable for you to know: The subroutine is called an *input/output driver,* and it is part of the unit's operating system, as we'll discuss in greater detail in a later chapter. For now, envision that the low addresses of the computer's memory—the uppermost floors of the memory building on page 65—are filled with a collection of separate programs called "interrupt service subroutines," one for each peripheral.

In spite of the complexities involved, echo printing is a useful way for the operator to monitor what's being fed into the machine through the keyboard. It may look like it, but it is *not* mere typing, this time on a TV screen.

To sum up, the steps involved in an input/output interrupt are as follows:

1. A peripheral sends an interrupt request (INT REQ) to the CPU.
2. The CPU completes the instruction which it is currently fetching and executing.
3. The CPU acknowledges the interrupt request (with an INT ACK) and clears the interface flag (by resetting the flip-flop).
4. To make certain that it can "find its place" after servicing the request, the CPU saves the contents of certain counters and registers: the program counter, accumulator, flag, and scratchpad registers.
5. The CPU branches to the starting address of the particular subroutine that services the interrupting peripheral. The address is furnished either by the peripheral itself or else is stored in memory. (If the starting address of the service subroutine is furnished by the peripheral, it is called the *interrupt vector* of the peripheral.)
6. The input/output service subroutine is fetched and executed, step by step, until it completes the subroutine.

7. The status of the CPU, especially the incremented program counter, is restored.
8. The main program resumes running.

Establishing Priorities

Servicing an interrupt involves branching to a subroutine. However, there are many occasions when a CPU might be better left uninterrupted. What, specifically, determines whether or not it will stop what it's doing and switch to the subroutine? One of the bits in the status register that we haven't discussed before is called the *interrupt-mask bit*, abbreviated simply by an "I."

When the I-bit is a 1, say, interrupt requests from a peripheral are ignored by the CPU. If the I-bit switches to a 0, the request can be processed. How does the CPU know what this bit says? Because it checks it after every fetch-and-execute cycle. That is, when the CPU has finished executing the instruction it is currently processing, it checks the status of the I-bit. Then it fetches the next instruction.

As we've said, there are many occasions when we might not want the CPU to be interrupted. For instance, it may be running a piece of software that we'd like it to complete before turning its attention to handling any other tasks. We therefore should be able to override, or more accurately, veto temporarily, a request from a peripheral that wants to interrupt. In that sense, we want the CPU to be able to act very much as human beings normally would in similar circumstances. "Not right now, dear," a busy parent might say to a youngster who wants something that can easily wait a little while. When a CPU temporarily suppresses an interrupt request, we say that it has *masked* it; that makes it a *maskable interrupt.*

Modern microprocessors allow for the alternative as well, by providing a *nonmaskable interrupt* (NMI) terminal on the CPU. If a peripheral has been hooked up to this pin (or terminal) on the CPU, its interrupt request will always be honored just as soon as the current instruction on which the processor is working is completed. Clearly, peripherals attached in this manner are explicitly being given *priority* over the others. We'll have more to say about this shortly.

As mentioned previously, pitting hardware against software, and arguing emotionally about which is more important, is not only juvenile, it also gives a very lopsided view of what computers are and how they are designed to operate. It is simply not the way any of the first-class minds in the field view current achievements and hoped-for future innovations. There is a good example here of the way in which hardware and software have been intended right from the start to operate together. An experienced computer programmer can usually prevent large parts of a program from being interrupted. How? By using a special *disable interrupt* (DI) instruction. At the end of that sequence of instructions, the condition is no longer needed, so the programmer inserts an *enable interrupt* (EI) instruction, which once again allows the program to be interrupted.

Suppose that a sequence of 10 instructions has been safeguarded by a disable-interrupt instruction, and an interrupt is received after the first instruction of the 10 has been executed. Question: When will the interrupt request finally be processed? Answer: Only after the other nine have already been fetched and executed.

If the interrupt request is received on the nonmaskable interrupt terminal, however—that is, if the peripheral hooked up to that terminal has been accorded top priority (assume for the moment that it's the Hot Line from the White House)—then no software instruction is capable of disabling it. A hardware decision has been made in this case that deliberately prevents any piece of software that happens to be running at the moment from causing the interrupt request to be shelved temporarily.

The problem of assigning priorities is as important in a computer as it is in our everyday lives. The difference is that we usually do it subconsciously and often not at all, while in a computer it must be done and explicitly at that. Ignoring the matter can lead to real chaos. Why? Because not all peripherals are created equal. Some are decidedly more important than others to us, and we want those input/output devices to be able to interrupt the CPU, if any can at that moment.

A *priority interrupt* system is therefore implemented that allows us to determine which peripheral will be serviced first when two or more request attention at the same time. Often, but not always, high-speed peripherals are given priority over ones that operate at slower speed. But whatever the reason for the priority assignments finally settled upon, a peripheral that has been assigned the higher priority will always be serviced first in case of a tie.

Handling Multiple Interrupts

Assigning a higher priority to a peripheral gives it so much clout, that its interrupt requests will be serviced even if they arrive *after* those of a lower-priority peripheral. When we were discussing procedure calls, we saw that not only can the main program call a procedure, one procedure can call another. The second procedure can, in turn, call a third. When that happens, the collection of procedures involved is said to be *nested*—that is, each nests in the middle of the one before it.

The similarities between procedure calls and program interrupts emerge once again here. Assume that you are watching a television program that you're enjoying thoroughly but decide to make a quick trip to the kitchen for a snack. Just as you open the refrigerator door, however, the phone rings. What does this have to do with computers? It is an example of an interrupt interrupting an interrupt in the main program.

The first interrupt may be thought of as arising because your stomach was growling and making it hard to hear what the characters on the screen were saying. In that case, the main (TV) program was interrupted by the rattling sounds emanating from your plumbing—clearly, a hardware interrupt. The second interrupt was also a hardware interrupt, the ringing of the telephone. What's important for our purposes, though, is the fact that the second INT REQ (interrupt request) was honored while the first "interrupt service subroutine" was still in effect.

In short, the phone is obviously a higher-priority peripheral in our everyday lives than the 'fridge. Few people would ignore the ringing with a, "Not now, I'm gathering the fixings for a feast." That set of priorities is based on the fact that the food isn't likely to go bad if it has to wait a few minutes to be eaten, whereas the phone caller is likely to quit after seven rings. Also, people usually assume that they can dispose of the call more quickly than they can down a tuna on rye. But there is no way to know that in advance. At least with computer peripherals, one knows beforehand whether it's a high-speed or low-speed device that's doing the interrupting.

It would be nice to have a picture of what actually happens in a computer's memory when a higher-priority peripheral interrupts in the middle of a subroutine that is servicing a lower-priority interrupt.

We mentioned earlier that the interrupt service subroutines that the computer needs are stored with its operating system—that is, they occupy the lower addresses in memory—as in the following picture:

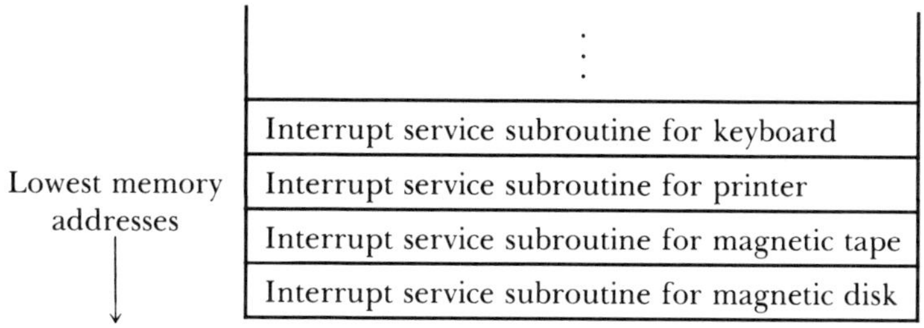

The program needed to service each peripheral occupies a separate floor in the building—that is, it takes up a certain number of registers which, grouped together, we are calling a floor. Suppose, then, that we're on the third floor, servicing an interrupt request from the printer for output. Right in the middle—that is, halfway between the top and bottom of that group of instructions—assume that an interrupt request is received from the magnetic disk, whose interrupt service subroutine is housed on the first floor. It wants to input some information into main memory. Modern disks, as we'll see in Chapters 9 and 10, can do this at a surprisingly high speed, and hence this peripheral in our system has been accorded a higher-priority than the printer.

The result: an abrupt move to the first floor—that is, a transfer of program control to the first instruction in the interrupt service subroutine that is housed there. Of course, the contents of the program counter and other registers connected with the printer's service program are saved—that is, stored on the stack—so that we'll remember which floor we were on when the higher-priority interrupt arrived.

Each interrupt service subroutine ends with a RETURN instruction, just as each procedure CALL does. Why? That pops whatever we'd previously pushed onto the stack to service that particular interrupt, and it therefore returns us to the prior piece of program we were working on. Here, that means we are catapulted back to the third floor as soon as we're finished on the first.

chapter

7

the difference between computers and calculators

One of the most interesting sets of questions that people ask about the subjects covered in this book are: "What's the connection between a computer and a calculator? Are they basically the same? If not, what does a computer do when it's acting as a calculator that's different from the way it acts when it's just being a normal computer?"

This is the appropriate place to answer those questions. What you've learned in the previous chapters can be used to provide real insight into the operations of both devices.

Playing Ping Pong with a Calculator

There are fancy, programmable calculators and simple ones; units that cost $10 and others that sell for nearly $1,000; some offer a variety of mathematical options, such as the trigonometric functions sine and cosine, while others just do basic arithmetic. What all these units have in common, though, are keys for the 10 numbers 0 through 9.

"So what?" you might reply. "Every computer does too."

True enough, but the 10 numerical keys are vastly less important in a computer, particularly if your main interest is word and not data processing. In a calculator, however, the numerical keys are the hub of the wheel. They are the center around which everything else revolves.

When we discussed ASCII code in Chapter 3, we said that it had attained prominence because it allowed every decimal number, letter of the alphabet, and many common symbols (such as $ and @) to be represented by an internationally standardized 7-bit sequence of 0s and 1s. Notice that in this code, the decimal numbers 0 through 9 don't occupy any special place, nor do they stand at the center of the proceedings. They are merely 10 out of 128 maximum possible characters ($2^7=128$) that are transformed, or more precisely, encoded, into a 7-bit string of binary digits. Once that's done, they can be housed comfortably in a computer's registers and manipulated according to a program by its microprocessor.

There is an illuminating rule here that computer engineers have used for years, and it goes as follows: "The *longer* a piece of information is scheduled to bounce around inside a computer, the more essential it is that the information be in standard binary form." What makes the rule so interesting is that it sets computers and calculators apart right from the start.

The numbers you punch into a calculator aren't intended to stay there for any length of time. Quite the contrary, the sum of a column of figures is to be returned to you just as soon as you've finished entering it. Similarly, you want the result immediately of dividing some dollar amount by 12, say, to see what the monthly payments would be. In short, nothing you put into a calculator is supposed to stay there any longer than is absolutely necessary to complete the calculation on which you are working.

Contrast that with the situation in which a large and diverse inventory of products is being monitored by a computer. Information entered isn't expected to be coughed back out seconds later in an arithmetically revised form. In fact, it may stay in the computer—or more accurately, its internal and supplementary external (that is, mass storage devices such as magnetic tape and disk) memory—for months and even years. Of course, the manufacturer who has produced this inventory in the first place dearly hopes that it will soon be sold, and hence that the figures will have to be revised downward. Even in that fortunate circumstance, though, new products would have to be manufactured and inventoried to fill orders from impatient customers.

In either case, it is clear that "the data in the machine" almost have a life of their own. The many people whose job it now is to keep the figures in such machines current often joke that they would feel right at home if their next job involved feeding animals in the zoo. As one put it, "There I'd be tossing meat into cages, here it's data into files; the zoo would be less taxing mentally, I guess, but otherwise not all that different." That makes this situation almost the polar opposite of the one involving a calculator. The computer in this instance is being used as a constantly updated numerical snapshot of a physical reality. Next to that, doing a computation with a calculator is much like playing Ping Pong, the numbers remain inside so briefly.

In the beginning of the chapter we said that this was the appropriate place to discuss the differences between calculators and computers, yet we haven't made much use thus far of the material in the preceding chapters. Let's do so. If we look at the two devices in terms of the amount of input/output they do, something startling emerges. A calculator is oriented totally toward input/output. When we say that the numbers you punch in are supposed to bounce back out almost immediately in arithmetically revised from, we are saying that the machine does little else but input/ouput. In the first few chapters of this book, we saw the reason why. If a device consists solely of logic gates, it can do arithmetic for us but doesn't remember the results. Circuits containing these gates are said to be *combinational*, meaning that their inputs at that moment determine their output at that moment. The past isn't involved. When it is (which happens thanks to flip-flops), the circuit is said to be *sequential*. In short, computers make extensive use of memory, calculators don't.

It is precisely because of that difference, however, that calculators are vastly more oriented toward input/output. Computers make frequent use of input/output operations too, but thanks to their memories, they have a much richer "inner existence." In that regard they reflect something of crucial importance about human beings. The fact that we have a stomach makes it possible for us not to have to eat constantly. One large input operation (usually called a "meal") from time to time is all we need. After that, the physiological equivalent of a ROM—the metabolic program we call digestion—handles the input. Similarly, thanks to our brain, we don't have to keep staring at, for instance, the car we're interested in buying. Having seen it a few times and made a mental note of certain data about it (year, number of doors, price) and how it looks, we can continue to think about the matter from afar, as if the car were still present. In essence, thanks to our stomach and brain, one input operation may last us quite a while before another is needed.

Calculators Nibble, Computers Eat

When a computer is acting like a calculator, its input/output operations predominate. In that case, there are good reasons for considering a temporary change in the way the computer normally functions. Under ordinary circumstances, every character that is fed into a computer is encoded as a 7-bit sequence; letters, numbers, symbols—everything—undergo a standardized transformation into a string of seven 0s and 1s. Then, in order for the output to be recognizable to human beings, it has to be transformed back from 0s and 1s to letters, numbers, and symbols. That seems like a particularly inefficient way of doing things if all we're dealing with is numbers, not letters or symbols.

Especially when the computer is being used as a calculator, then, we recognize the need for an easier method of handling simple arithmetic problems, a method that involves less "overhead" as computer engineers are fond of calling the excessive number of back-and-forth transformations going on here.

Once you know it, the solution is so obvious you'll wonder why you didn't think of it yourself. (Sentences like that one are often obnoxious, but this time it just might be true.) The first 10 decimal numbers are 0 through 9. We start at 0 since almost everything that is counted in a computer—including memory registers—has 0 as its first one. Let's write these 10 numbers as a 4-bit sequence as shown in Table 7-1.

TABLE 7-1 *Decimal Numbers Written in 4-bit Binary Form*

Decimal	*Binary*
0	0000
1	0001
2	0010
3	0011
4	0100
5	0101
6	0110
7	0111
8	1000
9	1001

In other words, 4-bit sequences, not 7-bit, are sufficient to describe the 10 numerical keys on a calculator. It's only because of the numbers 8 and 9 that we even had to use a 4-bit sequence to handle them all. If we'd been counting only from 0 to 7, a 3-bit sequence would have been enough. Make a point of noting that there are a handful of 4-bit sequences we haven't used. How many? Well, the largest 4-bit number we can write is 1111, that is, 8+4+2+1=15. So there are *six* unused 4-bit sequences:

Decimal	Binary
10	1010
11	1011
12	1100
13	1101
14	1110
15	1111

Key question: How would these numbers be represented if we *had to* use only the 4-bit sequences in Table 7-1. The answer might not occur to you immediately, but as we said earlier, after you'd wrestled with the problem and it did, you'd probably wonder why it hadn't done so earlier. Take the number 12, for instance. Viewed in positional terms, it's just two decimal numbers, a 1 and a 2, side by side. We could therefore represent it by

0001	0010
1; that is, line 2 of Table 7-1	2; that is, line 3 of Table 7-1

Let's try a different, much bigger number, and you'll see how easy it is to use Table 7-1 to represent any decimal number, no matter how large. Say the number is 6853.

0110	1000	0101	0011	4-bit binary
6	8	5	3	Decimal

The result of transforming a decimal number into a 4-bit number using this process is called a *binary-coded decimal* (BCD). It has to be one of the worst names that could have been chosen.

As you've probably noticed by now, most of the names used in the computer field may not be fancy, but they're good. They capture something unique about the process or device being described. For instance, calling the CPU's general-purpose register in which results are placed the "accumulator" is sensible, since what sets this register apart from the rest is that after two numbers are combined in some fashion in the ALU, this register, not the others in the scratchpad, normally houses the result. However, a name like "binary-coded decimal" usually confuses more than three-fourths of the students who hear it for the first time because, as they rightly protest, "I thought decimals *and* letters and symbols were already being converted into binary form using standard ASCII code."

They are indeed, and that's the main reason for you to become comfortable with ASCII and the idea of converting characters into 7-bit sequences, and vice versa. What sets the concept of a binary-coded decimal apart from ASCII—and this is what's worth remembering—is that it uses only 4 bits, not 7, to represent every number in terms of the first 10 decimal numbers, the single-digit ones, 0 through 9. Longer decimal numbers such as 6853, aren't converted directly, but are done one number at a time, as we've just seen. A better name for the process would therefore be *4-bit BCD*. When you see the letters BCD in the future, you might want to think of it as an abbreviation for the useful and accurate name, "4-bit binary-coded decimal."

(Some useful terminology you may already know: An 8-bit number is called a byte, and amusingly, a number only half that length, that is, 4 bits long, is called a *nibble*.)

Since not all 4-bit sequences (nibble numbers) were used, an interesting problem arises almost immediately when we try to do arithmetic. The number 9 in decimal becomes 1001 in BCD, and the number 5 is 0101. Adding the two together gives:

Decimal	*BCD*
9	1001
+5	+0101
14	1110

The sum 1110 is certainly correct, since 8+4+2=14. However, 1110 is not one of the ten 4-bit sequences we've agreed to use in BCD. In other words, a simple piece of arithmetic is capable of taking us outside our system. Some system. That's as ridiculous as adding 84 to 83 and ending up with 6 (though that might well be the result if we were trying to complete a 167-story, two-tier building, and the thing collapsed into a pile of rubble six stories high).

The only way for us to stay within the agreed-upon confines of our simple BCD system is to make an adjustment whenever the sum of two BCD numbers exceeds the largest BCD number we have, which is 9—that is, 1001. What is the adjustment? Add a 6—that is, 0110—to cover the six numbers we omitted (that is, the six 4-bit sequences we're not using). It's easy, and making a computer do it at the right moment, through a *decimal adjust* instruction, is even easier:

	1001	9	in BCD
	+0101	+5	in BCD
	1110	14	which is more than 9 in BCD, so add
	+0110	+6	
0001	0100	20	which is 14 in BCD
1	4		

Let's do another example involving larger numbers, and you'll see how straightforward the process is. This time, we want to add 78 and 54:

78 in BCD is 0111 1000

54 in BCD is 0101 0100

To find the sum, we first add the 4-bit numbers on the right (we're working on the lower-order nibble, as it's called): 8+4=12, which exceeds 9, so we have to add 6—that is, 0110. Our first column therefore becomes

	1000	which is 8 in BCD
	0100	which is 4 in BCD
	+0110	which is the adjustment factor
0001	0010	

Clearly, we have a 1 to carry from the first nibble to the second, and we've written it here as 0001. Remember, in BCD, every single-digit number is written as a 4-bit number; 1 isn't a BCD number, but 0001 is.

The second column now becomes

0001	which is the carry from the first nibble
0111	which is 7 in BCD
+0101	which is 5 in BCD
1101	

Since this is 7+5+1=13, which exceeds 9, we have to add 0110 to this sum too to get into the correct BCD form:

	1101	
	+0110	which is the adjustment factor
0001	0011	

So our final answer is 0001 0011 0010, which you can easily translate from BCD back to the decimal numbers we're all used to. It is 132, which is the right decimal answer to the problem we were given. BCD addition, using the adjustment when necessary, clearly works.

A similar adjustment is needed when doing subtraction (6—that is, 0110—must be subtracted if the resulting nibble is larger than 9), but we won't go into the details because they are available if you need them in hundreds of standard texts. The bibliography lists a number of readable ones. What we wanted to accomplish in this chapter is to familiarize you with the BCD concept, and especially, to have you realize that BCD is a nice, middle route when there is a high level of input/output operations involving numbers. Converting the decimal number 165 into standard binary numerical form would have produced 1010 0101. Later it, or whatever happened to it, would have to be converted back again. That may be too much overhead for the simple computations one wants to do. Converting 165 into 001 0110 0101 instead in BCD makes it easier to convert back to decimal 165 as part of an output operation, so that humans can read it more comfortably.

Summing up, thanks to their much greater orientation toward input/

output, calculators *always* use BCD in their arithmetic operations. Computers, on the other hand, can use either full binary or BCD operations. It all depends on whether the calculations are simple and the degree of input/output is high. The user gets to decide which is the better method, and embodies that decision in the program written to perform the calculation.

chapter 8 direct memory access

There may be less input/output going on at any given moment in a computer than in a calculator, but what there is of it needs special attention. Thanks to the great disparity in speed between the CPU and its peripherals, the peripherals constitute what is, in essence, a separate world.

The best way for us to get a handle on that world is to compare a computer and a large company. The structure that is normally imposed on the collection of input/output devices in a computer parallels remarkably the organizational features of a sizable firm.

Moving Air and Electrons Is Easy

The CPU is a purely electronic device. What does that correspond to in a firm? First of all, the CPU corresponds to the firm's chief executive officer (CEO). Second, the fact that the device is purely electronic corresponds to the fact that the chief makes decisions, not products. That is, as the firm's top decision maker, Hank, as we'll call him, does a lot of thinking and talking, yet doesn't do anything physical. He doesn't drive nails or a truck. His job is mental, not manual.

The plans that Hank comes up with, however, cannot remain mere thoughts and words. They have to be converted into actions. The company he heads manufactures products, not hot air. So others must be given instructions which, note well, they can't carry out as quickly as the CPU—oops, make that CEO—can issue them.

We're all used to seeing pictures, either in movies, magazines, or novels, of bosses who bark orders impatiently and can't possibly imagine why the orders aren't executed instantly. It doesn't seem to have occurred to them that what occurs in a computer also occurs in a firm: A profound difference exists between the all-electronic CPU and the electromechanical input/output devices that have to do what the CPU wants them to. That is, talk is not only cheap, as the old cliché goes, it's also quick. Converting the words into action takes a little longer. To do its work, the CPU only has to move electrons; the peripherals and the firm's employees have to contend with a larger-scale material reality. A slower speed of execution is therefore inherent in the nature of the tasks that have to be performed.

What does this have to do with modern computers, small and large, micro and mainframe? The activity of a typical input/output device has been changing over the years and no longer requires the attention of the CPU for each input or output step to take place. On the contrary, the trend is accelerating and now favors ever-greater independence for the peripherals. In fact, much of what used to be handled by the CPU has become decentralized (remember, the C in CPU stands for central). Another, simpler computer called the *input/output processor* has relieved the CPU of many of its former chores.

To see how and why, let's look briefly at large firms again. As a company increases in size, more responsibility and authority is delegated to subordinates and subsidiaries. The chief executive may have previously played a personal role in every decision, big and little, but after a certain point in the growth of the company, that is nearly impossible. Instead, contact with the CEO becomes less frequent for the overwhelming majority of the firm's employees, and more important, the contact they do have must be structured. Why? So that the limited amount of time each gets to spend with the CEO can be used to the maximum advantage of both. The old way of communicating ideas to the CEO ("Hey, Hank, can I talk to you for a second") is replaced by a more formal procedure for passing information back and forth ("I have the report on project XYZ ready for your review," a note might say). Size affects almost every interaction in the firm.

One final point about large companies needs to be mentioned before we see how all this is reflected in the design of computers. When all is said and done, what is it that forces each employee to make good use of any of the CEO's time in a major corporation? The answer is: other employees. It is true that too much is happening at any given moment for the CEO to be involved personally with all of it, and therefore authority is delegated to others. However, each of those others wishes and usually needs to make regular contact with the CEO to coordinate policies, suggest and then implement changes, and check results.

What does that correspond to in a computer? Odd as it may sound, it's worthwhile to think of the collection of input/output devices attached to a computer as being in *competition* with one another for the CPU's time. If you own your own microcomputer, that may not be evident at first.

The keyboard on which you type input messages, say, and the CRT on which they are echo-printed, certainly don't appear to be in contention. Similarly, the secondary, memory storage units—usually floppy disks—and the printer, which makes hard copies (on paper) instead of soft copies (shown on the CRT), don't seem to be vying with one another either.

However, not only is there a great difference in speed between the average peripheral, on the one hand, and the CPU, on the other, there are important differences in speed among the various peripherals. Why is that? And why do those differences have to be taken into account even in small computer systems? The answer is crucial to your understanding of the underlying principles that apply to the design of all systems, large and small.

As human beings, we are limited in the rate which we can input information into, or receive output from, a computer. For instance, although many people can type more than 100 words per minute, none can type 1000 words in a minute. Yet a microprocessor can easily handle more than a million instructions per *second.* Similarly, the words, numbers, and symbols that appear on a CRT have to (1) be of a certain minimum size if we're to be able to read them, and (2) stay on the screen long enough for us to grasp their meaning, individually and in context.

In a very real sense, then, the keyboard and CRT are "for us." Since the two are naturally paired, they are often referred to in a single breath as being the "console." To repeat: The keyboard as an input device and the CRT as an ouput device are deliberately designed to be slow enough so that we humans can make effective contact with them.

Other peripherals, which are usually thought of as being "in the back," while the console is "in the front," are more like the CPU in terms of speed, though the difference is still substantial. That makes these peripherals, particularly tape and disk, enormously more important than they seem at first glance. What do these input/output devices that are in the background have as features that make them so valuable? First and foremost, since they don't have to be read by the unaided human eye, the form in which information is stored on them may be very dense—and tiny. Looking at them, even through a magnifying glass, doesn't allow one to appreciate the fact that there may be a billion bytes of information, for instance, on a disk pack.

The Advantage of Being Quick

The very fact that a peripheral is a high-speed device opens up certain possibilities that are denied slower-speed devices. For instance, the peripheral may be allowed to communicate *directly* with main memory and not have to go through the CPU to do it. We need a picture here of how that can be arranged.

Ordinarily, the CPU and main memory are in regular contact, since both the instructions and data the CPU needs are stored there. By putting an address on the address bus and sending the right control signal, the CPU causes the contents of a memory register to be copied into a CPU register (READ), or vice versa (WRITE). However, there are times when the CPU doesn't make use of additional data or already has the data it needs; for example, it may be doing an addition of the data in two of its scratchpad registers, R3 and R5. In that case, it can execute an

ADD	R3	R5

instruction without making any further reference to main memory (see Figure 8-1).

A high-speed peripheral such as disk can therefore be allowed to take advantage of the situation to transfer information directly between itself and main memory. The process is called, naturally enough, *direct memory access* (DMA), and it is permitted to continue as long as the CPU is busy performing operations that don't require it to make any references to memory. Since peripherals always communicate with the computer through a peripheral interface, the picture of DMA we've been discussing is illustrated in Figure 8-2.

What should be striking to you about this picture is that the CPU is no longer at the center of the action; instead, main memory now is. In some ways that is appropriate, because main memory is very important in its own right: It is the place where the stored program the CPU will execute resides. In fact, one of the most crucial—and most frequent—transfers from disk to main memory is just that: another program, or other parts of the same program (main memory might be too small to hold the whole thing).

The picture in Figure 8-2 is deceptive in one major respect. Namely, the single line that connects the CPU and main memory really stands for

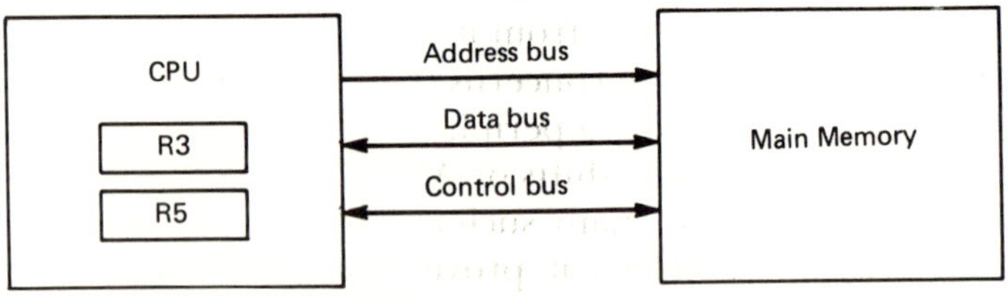

Figure 8-1 ADD R3 R5, an example of an instruction whose execution doesn't require a memory reference.

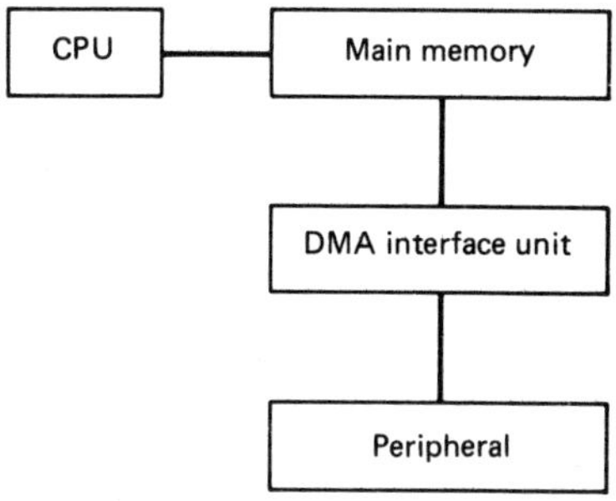

Figure 8-2 Main memory communicates with both the CPU and the DMA interface.

three buses, as we know by looking at Figure 8-1. The single line connecting the DMA interface and main memory could also stand for three other, separate buses, of course, but do we really want to duplicate these electronic pathways? That is, isn't there some way to allow the DMA interface unit to make use of the already existing address and data buses?

There is. What we must do is make certain that the CPU relinquishes control of these buses whenever a DMA transfer of instructions or data is to take place. Once that happens, the lines become available for an input/output device to make use of them. There are two important observations that should be made about this arrangement.

First, since the CPU is essentially being momentarily elbowed out of the picture here, the DMA interface will need addressing facilities of its own. Previously we saw that when the CPU wants to communicate with a particular memory register, it shouts that register's name—that is, it places the address of the register on the address bus and, simultaneously, sends either a READ or WRITE signal on the control bus to let the memory register know what all the shouting is about. Now, the DMA interface will have to carry out those tasks itself. Not surprisingly, then, the DMA interface has a memory address register (MAR) of its own, in which the address of the memory register to which it wishes to have access is held, and it has a buffer register as well, in which the word it is sending to main memory or receiving from it is temporarily held.

The second noteworthy issue here concerns the CPU. We began our discussion of direct memory access by a peripheral by assuming that the CPU was busy doing something, say, shifts or ADDs, that didn't require any memory references. There are many such moments in the ordinary functioning of a CPU. Nevertheless, it provides a very halting and uncertain way for a peripheral to pass data or instructions directly to main memory, or receive them from it.

If the point hasn't struck you forcibly before, let it do so now: The *only* instructions that the CPU can execute and data it can manipulate are those that are housed in its main memory or scratchpad registers. The fact that a computer program is comfortably ensconced on a tape or disk in the system's secondary memory storage units does the CPU no good *unless* the program or data can quickly find its way into the CPU's main memory when needed. In saying that computers are, and always have been, stored-program machines, we mean that the machine will only run a program that is stored in its main memory, not one that is sitting in a peripheral memory device.

For that reason, rather than have a peripheral that wants to pass information to (or receive information from) main memory act essentially as a beggar, it can be made to intervene more aggressively. That is, it can switch from being a beggar to being a thief. What is this method of DMA called? *Cycle stealing.*

Under this arrangement, the DMA interface doesn't wait patiently for the CPU to become involved only with itself and its scratchpad registers before initiating a transfer; instead, it barges in. First, it sends the CPU a request-to-intervene signal, a DMA REQ. That causes the CPU to complete the instruction it is currently working on and suspend operation during the next machine cycle. During that brief period of idleness, the DMA interface transfers one word between main memory and the peripheral to which it is attached.

It will help you understand what's going on here if you keep in mind that we said the DMA intervenes rather than interrupts. Why? Because it does not in fact interrupt. Remember, in the world of computers, the word has a technical meaning: In an interrupt, some or all of the CPU's program counter, scratchpad registers, status flag, and accumulator may wind up being stored temporarily on a stack while the interrupt is being handled. Not here. These registers and counters are simply left undisturbed while the DMA interface goes about its business. After that, the CPU resumes the program it was running at the time. The CPU has really been delayed rather than interrupted, since it never did turn its attention to handling any other task.

Larceny on a Grand Scale

So far, we've been considering what is essentially "finders keepers"—that is, "you're not using main memory just now, so I will"—and petty theft (that is, cycle stealing). It is time for us to look at the equivalent of grand larceny.

Almost all the programs you see in programming textbooks are short. The BASIC, COBOL, FORTRAN, or Pascal program, say, that is shown is kept brief for the purposes of illustration. Nonetheless, most of the programs that you actually utilize to accomplish something worthwhile with a computer are likely to be long. Instead of a few dozen lines at most, the best and most effective software you buy or use will probably be many thousands of instructions long. Cycle stealing is simply too slow a way for programs of that length to be transferred from the disk or tape on which they are stored into main memory, the only place from which the program can be executed.

The solution is to use DMA *block transfer*. Thanks to the high-speed nature of peripherals such as tape and especially disk, the transfer is carried out under the supervision of the peripheral interface, not the CPU. That doesn't mean the CPU plays no role; it does. But that role is limited to initiating the transfer of a block of information in the first place, usually instructions or data from disk or tape, and also specifying the number of words in the block.

More precisely, we saw that the DMA interface contains its own addressing facilities—that is, memory address register as well as buffer register, to hold briefly the word it is sending or receiving. In addition, the DMA interface contains a word counter register. Why? Because block transfers *always* involve a previously agreed-upon size of block. The machine doesn't operate the way a real grand larcenist might, with an attitude of, "While we're here, we might as well take everything we can." Instead, in its role as a thief, the DMA interface transfers only blocks of a fixed size, rather than "all it can in the allotted time." Note well that the word-count register is also necessary because the data or instructions that are transferred are stored one right after the other in consecutive locations in memory. This is a neat—as well as sneak—thief. It is the word-count register in the DMA interface that keeps careful track of the movement of words, one at a time, between the interface and main memory.

In sum, DMA block transfers take place in a well-defined series of steps. Ordinarily, when a program is being run, only the CPU and main memory are involved. That is the reason they are shaded in Figure 8-3a. However, the CPU has been designed to respond to signals from peripherals. It operates so much faster than they do that it goes about its business at top speed until it hears from one. Suppose in this case that it is a memory peripheral, a magnetic disk or tape drive, that is ready to take a block of data from main memory, as part of a WRITE operation. It therefore sends a DMA REQ to the CPU.

The CPU acknowledges the request with a DMA ACK, completes the instruction on which it is currently working, and enters a wait state. Before entering this temporary state of idleness, the CPU sends the DMA interface the address of the location of the first word in the block

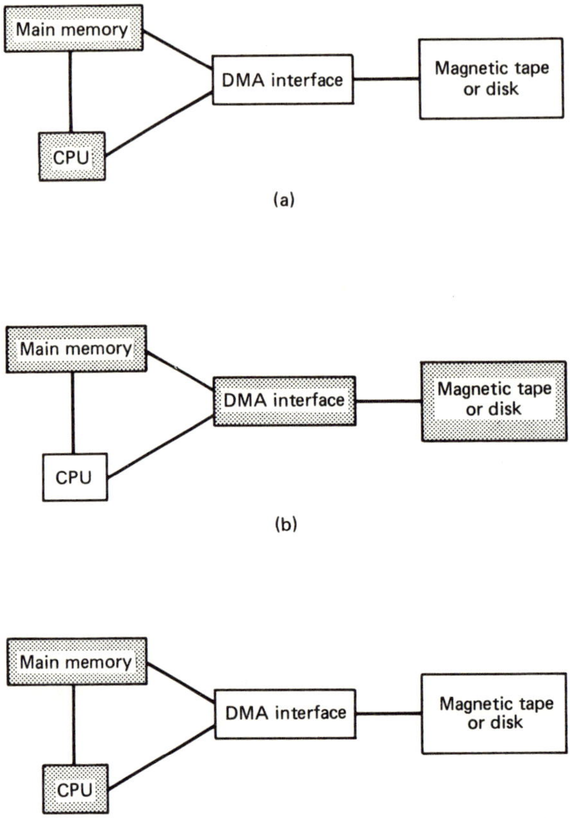

Figure 8-3 (a) Program is running. (b) DMA transfer; CPU waits. (c) Program resumes.

and the direction of data transfer (input or output). That is, the CPU acts like a homeowner telling the movers where to put the incoming or outgoing pieces of furniture; the CPU instructs the DMA interface where to park (or get) the first word it is sending (or receiving), and hence, thanks to the word-counter register, where to park (or get) the rest of the words in the block. At this point, the CPU stops communicating with the DMA interface and lets it take over (see Figure 8-3b). Once the DMA operation is finished, control returns to the main program, which continues where it left off (Figure 8-3c).

That is easier than it seems at first glance. Why? Because the same rules apply here that applied to cycle stealing. Since the state of the CPU—that is, the contents of its program counter, accumulator, scratchpad register, and status flag—is left undisturbed by a DMA, the CPU has no difficulty whatever in resuming where it left off. It has merely been delayed, perhaps considerably. During this time, the CPU could have been busy only with calculations or operations that did not involve any memory references. Remember, the address and data buses it would have needed in order to make a memory reference had been borrowed temporarily by the DMA interface for addressing and data transfers involving the peripheral.

chapter

9

input/output processors

As firms grow bigger, certain subsidiaries and subordinates are granted an increasing amount of authority. Their area of responsibility inevitably widens. The same thing happens to cities, where the surrounding suburbs increasingly come to reflect the structure and operation of the hub on which they were once merely the periphery. Ditto for computers—with a twist.

As computer systems have grown in size and sophistication, the peripherals attached to each system have become more in need of being managed, not less. There is a limit to how independent each may be allowed to become. A microcomputer may make use of a CPU that is vastly smaller than those used decades ago, but keyboards have, if anything, gotten larger and more complex, and disk packs are now capable of holding previously unimagined quantities of information. Each peripheral may seem simple and easy enough to use and understand when viewed in isolation, yet the system's collection of them is even more important than are all the suburbs of a major city to its central business district.

Coordination of the peripherals is a problem of paramount importance. There are a large number of students who feel that this is one difficulty that should always be able to be managed by hand, if necessary. They are right. It is possible to make certain that no two peripherals are actively competing for either the CPU's or main memory's attention at the same time. How? By disconnecting every other input/output device except the one you intend to use at the moment. This used to be done in inadequately wired houses; turning on the air conditioner meant not using the toaster during that time, lest the fuses blow.

At first glance that might seem to be a simple and workable solution in a computer system too, but there are two key reasons why it isn't. First, it would make remarkably little sense to store a program in a computer (so that it could run from start to finish at breakneck speed without external assistance) and then have to run around the machine like a frenetic, silent movie Charlie Chaplin trying to hook up and disconnect the devices needed at the moment, such as tape, disk, or teletype—all the while trying to prevent a crash on the buses. Second, and more important, modern computer design stresses ease of interaction of the CPU, main memory, and mass storage devices, particularly disk. In the past it was acceptable to do the job "quick and dirty," if that was the only way it could be done. However, it is a sign of the growing maturity of the computer field that users and computer pros expect to see a certain polish in the way major problems are confronted. Spit, glue, and Scotch tape not only don't work very well to hold the system together, they're no longer viewed as signs of an admirable attempt by a valiant engineer who had little else to work with. Now, there are plenty of wonderful hardware and software solutions available, often in integrated circuit (IC) or "firmware" form. In fact, operating systems, the subject of the next chapter, would lose a great deal of their effectiveness and enormous value if peripherals were continually being unhooked and reconnected.

Strange as it may sound at first, the best solution to the problem of coordination and competition among a computer's peripherals is a special-purpose microprocessor, *one with direct memory access.* These units started out being simple; each was merely a central clearing point for input/output operations. Like many suburbs of major cities, though, peripheral coordinating units have become increasingly complex—and for good reason, as we'll see in the final two chapters of the book.

Before we examine the additional tasks that an *input/output processor* (IOP) can manage so well, we should note that any unit capable of handling even the problems we've already discussed is worth its weight in gold. Until now, we've been assuming that each peripheral must have its own DMA interface. Not only does that represent a needless duplication of expensive hardware, it contributes mightily to the problem at hand because the interfaces cannot readily be made to work well together without adding yet another hardware *and* software layer to the system. Why is that? Because the interfaces must be made to operate in sync not only with one another, but with the program that happens to be running at the time as well.

Using one input/output processor instead, to which all the peripherals are connected, allows a significant simplification of the system. It also makes input/output operations easier to coordinate with the program that is running, because—and this is what's crucial—the CPU has much less difficulty making effective contact with its collection of competing peripherals if it does so *through* an input/output processor. Keep in mind that the CPU still initiates input/output transfers, but once they are initiated, the input/output processor takes over from there. It moves data and instructions into and out of main memory without any further assistance from the CPU. As soon as the input/output processor is finished with its operations, it allows the CPU to resume the program it was running and once again make memory references. Remember, the CPU needs to do this if for no other purpose than to fetch the next instruction.

A picture of the new arrangement is shown in Figure 9-1.

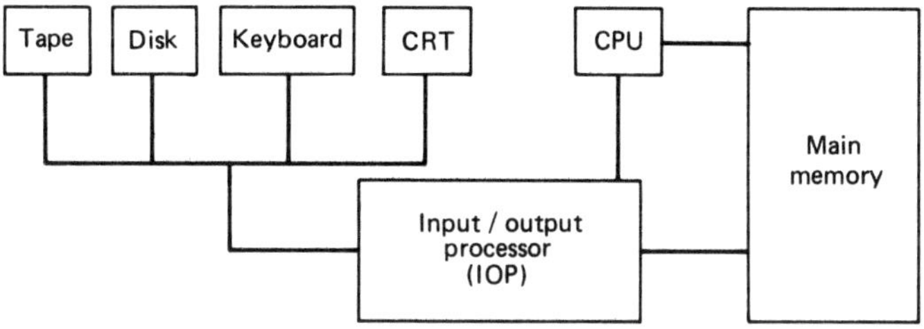

Figure 9-1 Peripherals attached to CPU and main memory through an input/output processor (IOP).

In order to be clear about which unit is communicating with which, some simple terminology has been developed that you should know. An instruction from the CPU to the input/output processor is still called an instruction, but one that the input/output processor gets from main memory (it was stored there expressly for the purpose) is called a *command*. That is, the CPU may instruct the input/output processor to obtain a command that had previously been written into memory regarding an input/output processor.

Students who recall that every peripheral attached to a computer was described as having an interface (see Chapter 6) are often puzzled by the above picture. Their question, "Does the new input/output processor do everything the old interface it replaces previously did?" is an excellent one. The answer is yes—and then some. To see why, it is illuminating to think for a moment about a good stereo system instead of a computer. We'll assume that the stereo is an expensive one, with all the parts of the system existing as separate components (see Figure 9-2).

Let's look at the turntable. The (musical) information that it inputs to the system is in the form of variations in the grooves of a record instead of binary digits. That is, there are continually varying physical differences in the record (which are translated into continually varying voltages) as opposed to two-state, 0 and 1, magnetic difference on a computer disk or tape. However, what we want to focus on here is the turntable itself. It is only when people buy a component stereo that they

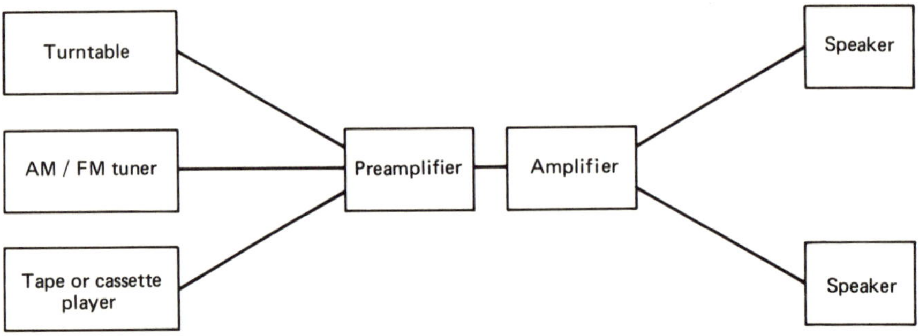

Figure 9-2 A component stereo.

get a chance to see just what each unit, in isolation, really does. Inexpensive systems usually cluster components in one package to save money and space, which makes many devices serve double duty and often masks the main function of each. Here, all the important decisions that correspond to what an input/output processor does in a computer are made by the preamplifier. It has bass and treble controls, as well as such things as high-/and low-frequency filters and equalizers.

What the turntable does in a stereo system—and a disk or tape *drive* does in a computer—is spin the information-bearing object (the record, or respectively, tape or disk) when it's told to, and does so at the right speed. It must also position the needle (or read/write head) over the desired cut on the album, or track on the tape or disk. The terminology used to describe the device that helps the tape or disk drive do this is the *controller*. The drive and controller are usually packaged together, and a reference to the one generally should be taken to mean that the author is talking about both.

In short, in most computers, large or small, peripherals are likely to be connected to the CPU through a controller and drive that handle important mechanical functions. In Figure 9-1 there should therefore be some additional units between the peripherals and the input/output processor. For instance, see Figure 9-3.

To sum up, the information-bearing object, the disk, is read from or written into by the disk drive (the equivalent of the tone arm and cartridge in a turntable), and the disk drive is run by the disk controller, a straightforward piece of hardware in the system.

If all this seems to you to be much ado about nothing, and that all we're doing here is splitting hairs and creating excess terminology, it would be well to keep in mind the large and rapidly growing number of input/output devices now attached for everyday use to computers large and small—everything from joy sticks and light pens to fuel-injected carburetors and ink-jet printers. Also, many peripherals that can act as either input or output devices, such as tape and disk, must in fact be treated electronically as though they were two separate units, if a crash is to be avoided. The hardware in the interface is actually arranged as if there *were* two separate peripherals present, one for input, the other for output. What it boils down to is that the hardware and software requirements of the input/output transfers of even a small computer system are usually quite formidable if the system is to function smoothly and with a minimum of operator inconvenience.

Streams That Take Turns Flowing

You probably won't be surprised to hear that in systems which use an input/output processor it is common for the high-speed peripherals to be separated in some way from those of lower speed. Seeing how that is done will tell you much, not only about present-day computer systems, but the probable structure of future ones as well. Before going further, we need to discuss multiplexing to understand what input/output processors do with low-speed input/output transfers.

When people first hear the word "multiplex," most report that it sounds much to them like "multiply." Multiplex in Latin does indeed mean multiple. Yet at least as the term is used regarding computers and electronics, it indicates exactly the opposite: A multiplexer has many inputs but only *one* output. "So what," you might reply, "so do most major rivers."

However, a multiplexer is very different from a bunch of streams flowing together to form a river. The crucial difference is that the streams truly merge, while in a multiplexer, only one stream can flow into the river at any one time; the others must wait. Then it is another stream's turn to flow, and so on. That is an extremely important feature of multiplexers, one to keep in mind when you hear the term, for it means that each input gets to maintain its original identity—and hence can easily be recovered later. For that reason, we can use a multiplexer to

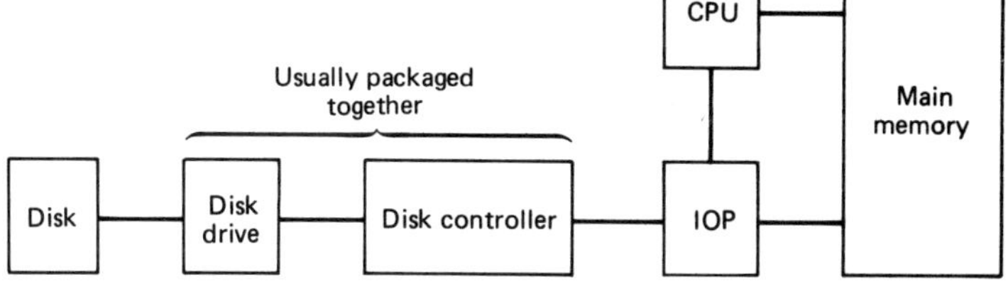

Figure 9-3 Between the disk and the IOP are the disk drive and disk controller.

choose which one of the inputs will become the output at any given moment.

If we look at a very simple computer system, one with only two low-speed peripherals, A and B, we'll be able to see immediately why a multiplexer is useful even in this situation. By the way, A and B could both be input devices, output devices, or one of each; it doesn't matter. (See Figure 9-4)

Thanks to the fact that A and B are slow, the CPU to which they're attached has no trouble whatever in keeping up with both of them. It doesn't handle both of them simultaneously—no CPU ever does—but it operates at a speed so much higher than either A's or B's that it *looks* as though it is dealing with both devices at exactly the same moment. For instance, if A is a keyboard and B is a CRT, then as you type on the keyboard, it may seem as though the letters appear on the screen simultaneously. But it's not so. The keyboard is an input device, the CRT an output device. No matter how fast a human being types on that keyboard, it's still pathetically slow relative to the speed of a central processor. The CPU has more than enough time between keyboard strokes to output to the CRT the letter that was just typed. And so it goes, letter after letter. The CPU operates so fast, in fact, that it can do this not just with two peripherals such as the keyboard and CRT, but with *hundreds*.

What the multiplexer does—and it's essential—is to make certain that multiple input/output operations are handled in an orderly manner. Thanks to its presence, peripherals that want the CPU's attention take turns instead of compete. No two ever send messages that are received at the CPU at precisely the same time, even though it may appear that way to the naked eye. In short, peripherals that operate at slow speed are usually connected to a computer through a multiplexer. Since the input/output processor is also at times called a *channel*, what we have

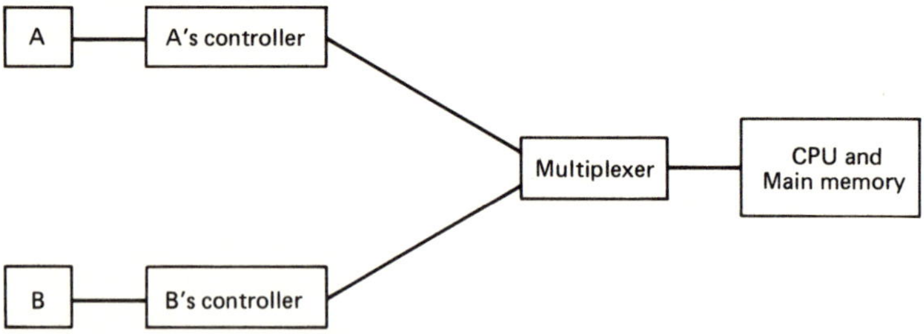

Figure 9-4 Two peripherals, A and B, attached to the CPU and main memory through a multiplexer.

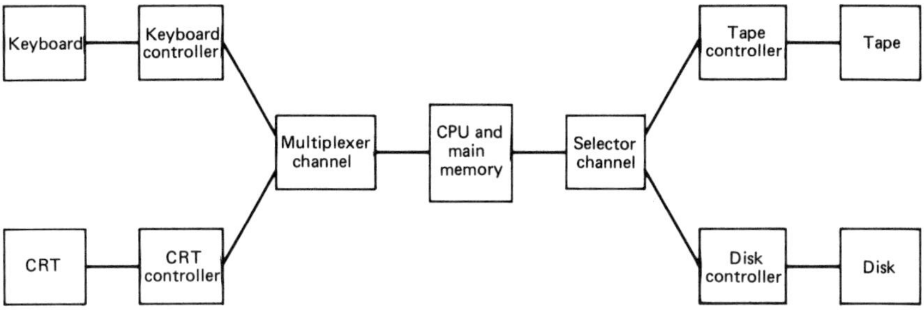

Figure 9-5 Peripherals and input/output processors arranged according to speed.

here would be termed a *multiplexer channel.* It allows 1 byte at a time to be input or output from a peripheral; then it switches, and allows another peripheral to do the same.

High-speed peripherals, on the other hand, aren't suited to this round-robin, one-byte-from-each-peripheral style of operation. They do better to operate in *burst mode.* Meaning that once they've been selected by the input/output processor (which is sometimes called a selector channel for that reason), they transfer an entire block, not just a single byte of information. The overall arrangement of the system, with both low- and high-speed peripherals now included, is shown in Figure 9-5.

A useful way to think about the difference between the left- and right-hand sides of this figure is in terms of a casino at Las Vegas. Assume that there is an automated dealer at a card table where poker is being played. When the machine goes round the table, asking first one player, then another, whether each is in or out of the hand, it is acting as a multiplexer channel. For it prevents everyone from shouting simultaneously, "I'm in" or "I'm out," and having all the replies lost in the din. If one of the players then says, "I'll take three cards, " and keeps two of the five she'd been dealt, the input (as well as subsequent output) operation switches to burst mode.

The card game analogy should alert us to an important point, one we've mentioned before and will develop here. Namely, input/output operations that involve more than 1 byte per peripheral (that is, burst mode) always specify exactly how many bytes beyond the first will be transferred. None of this is left to chance. Students often ask: "How is the number determined? And when? Does it ever change, so that many bytes are transferred in one burst and a smaller number in the next?"

Answering these questions affords us a glimpse of the inner workings of an increasingly important peripheral: disk. This is one input-and-output device about which the more you know, the better.

A Guided Tour of Disks

People who have formed their impression of what a large computer installation looks like from watching Hollywood movies usually recognize that tapes are part of the system. A hundred years from now, tapes will probably still be used in the movies, even if they're no longer used in reality. How else will the people in the theater know that the Giant Brain is "thinking" if they don't see blinking lights and spinning tapes? In that sense, advances in microelectronic technology that reduced large mainframes to tiny microprocessors have wreaked comic mayhem upon the image of the Giant Brain. It would be nice to see a sci-fi movie that catches up with current engineering realities and allows a pea-sized brain to rule the Earth. (I know, some think that that's already happened.)

Tapes may provide an unmistakable visual sign of activity when they spin, but they suffer a severe handicap: They are sequential access devices. Getting to the middle of the tape means having to reel though the earlier or later part of it, depending on whether it's in fast-forward or rewind. Disk is a tremendous improvement in that regard. Most students think of disk as being another world entirely from tape, yet it's important to see how the two are related. A reel of tape could be cut up into small snips and glued onto a platter, as in Figure 9-6.

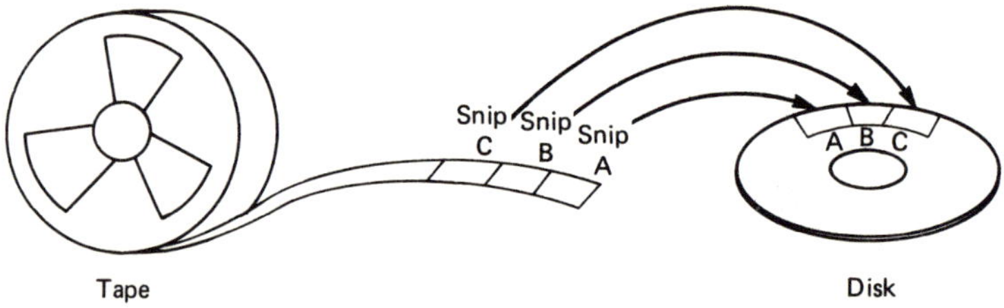

Figure 9-6 The correspondence between data formats on tape and disk.

The advantage of having the information on a disk instead of a tape becomes immediately apparent if you think about how easily the tone arm on a record player swings to the appropriate song you want to hear—say, the third cut. As far as most people are concerned, that makes disk a random-access memory device, because the read/write head on the disk (instead of a cartridge needle on a record) can be positioned anywhere on the disk, at random. However, many computer professionals prefer to call this a direct- (instead of random-) access device, since the word random in silicon semiconductor solid-state RAMs means that every memory cell in the chip can be accessed in the same time. That's obviously not so on a disk, where certain locations take longer to get to than others.

Disks can be either *hard* (made of an aluminum alloy) or *soft* (made of plastic), and therefore also called floppy, since they're flexible. Hard disks come in three standard sizes, 14, 8, and 5¼ inch. Soft disks come in two standard sizes, 8 inch and 5¼ inch; the latter is also called a minifloppy disk to distinguish it from the 8-inch disk. The 3½-inch floppy is also gaining wider acceptance. Hard and soft disks are both covered with a iron oxide coating that can be magnetized in one direction or the other at any spot (think of north versus south poles) to indicate a 0 or a 1. Floppy and minifloppy disks are presently the chief form of direct-access secondary memory storage in microcomputer systems. Information is stored on them using the same layout that would result if tape were actually cut into snips and pasted on the disk in rings (or *tracks*, as they're usually called), starting from the outermost track on the disk and working toward the center.

For the purposes of our discussion, assume that the disk we're using has 77 tracks, numbered from 0 through 76 (since that is standard on 8-inch floppy disks). Let's continue with our analogy of making each track by cutting up a reel of tape and pasting the snips along the track until we've covered it, then moving to the next inner track and doing the same. If each snip of tape is the same size as all the others, we say that the disk is *hard-sectored.* If the snips are of varying size, depending on the information each snip contains, we call the resulting disk *soft-sectored.* Keep in mind that hard and soft here modify the word "sector" and have nothing to do with aluminum versus plastic. And what's a sector? All 77 of the tracks are divided up into them as shown in Figure 9-7. It is

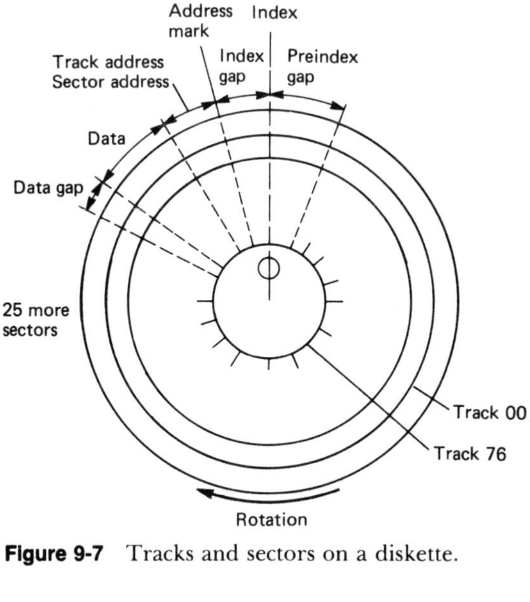

Figure 9-7 Tracks and sectors on a diskette.

common for each sector in a hard-sectored disk to contain 128 bytes, and for there to be 26 sectors in each track. Key question: How many bytes can such a floppy disk hold? The answer is: 77 tracks × 26 sectors/track × 128 bytes/sector = 256,256 bytes.

Once people have seen and perhaps used a floppy disk a few times, they often come up with some interesting questions. To begin with, they ask: "Where does a circle begin? By that I mean, what is the first sector on any given disk? How will I know it when I see it?" Figure 9-7 shows that the sectors that make up a track are arranged on it like pearls on a string. "What, then," people want to know, "corresponds to the clasp on that string of pearls?"

The answer is: a hole. In fact, the holes on a floppy disk tell you a great deal about what kind of disk it is. If there is just one hole, then when it comes around and light shines through it, that point in the disk's rotation is earmarked as the beginning of the track. A photocell which picks up the sudden flash of light makes certain of that (see Figure 9-8). When the disk is hard-sectored, on the other hand, there is a series of holes to mark the beginning and end of the various sectors. In fact, there is a one-to-one correspondence between the number of holes and the number of sectors. The situation is represented by Figure 9-9.

What takes the place of all these holes on a soft-sectored disk? Lots of headers and gaps. A header is used to identify each sector, and there is at least one gap connected with each sector so that it can clearly be seen to be a thing apart from the others, even without reference to the header which explicitly identifies it.

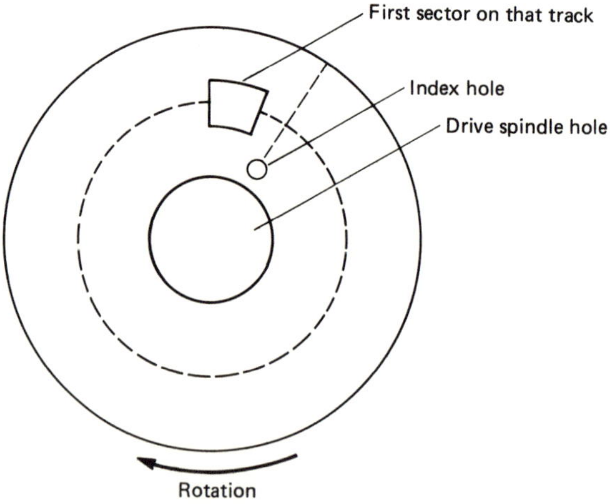

Figure 9-8 An index hole is used to mark the beginning of a track on soft-sectored disks.

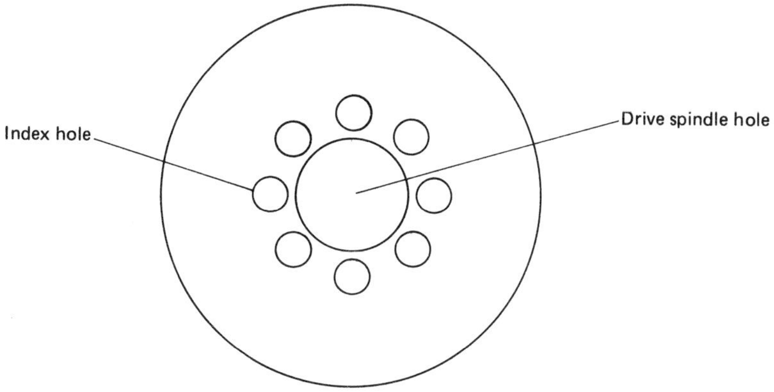

Figure 9-9 A hard-sectored disk. Holes and sectors are in one-to-one correspondence.

There is much else of interest to say about disks, both hard and soft (the bibliography provides some readable and informative references), but instead of discussing the topic further, we should look briefly at the equivalent of the tone arm in a record player. The needle cartridge at the end of a tone arm performs read operations only. That is, it retrieves whatever musical information has been embedded in the record during its manufacture. Disks, however, would be vastly less useful than they now are if we could only read what is on them. Information can readily be written into their surface as well, so a read/write head on a disk is what takes the place of the read-only diamond needle on a record player.

The process of positioning the read/write head over the right track takes a certain amount of time, called the *seek time*. It can vary by quite an amount. The head may have to move across only a few tracks to get to the right one, and that can be done very quickly (in about 5 milliseconds—that is, 5/1000 of a second). On the other hand, on 14-inch hard disks, the read/write head may have to traverse over 800 tracks to position itself correctly for the next read or write. Once the read/write head has been moved to the right track, the disk has to rotate enough for the particular location it is looking for to come under the head. That too takes a certain amount of time, called the *rotational delay*. At worse, that might entail having to wait almost an entire rotation. The picture of the combined search times is shown in Figure 9-10.

You probably won't be surprised to hear that in certain computer systems that typically have to stand a great deal of vibration and/or abuse, such as those used on jet planes, space ships, and high-tech military equipment, a slightly different arrangement is called for. Instead of a single read/write head that constantly has to be reposi-

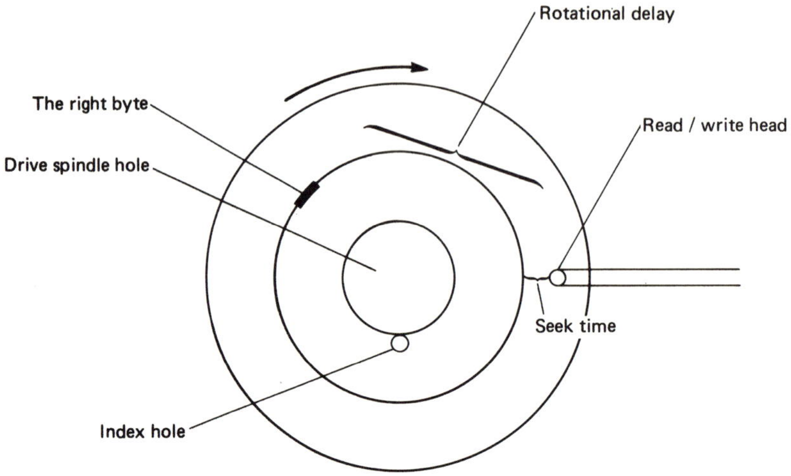

Figure 9-10 Search time consists of seek time plus rotational delay.

tioned, and which doesn't function effectively once it has been until it stops vibrating, there are many heads. In fact, in these disk memory storage units there is one read/write head for each track. Not only does that reduce significantly the vibration associated with moving the head from track to track, it also eliminates seek time altogether. Each track already has a read/write head in position to read it. Rotational delay still exists, though, in these rugged, very fast, and very expensive memory peripherals.

A few final notes about disks before we discuss how they fit into the operations of a typical computer system. First, floppy disks are often called *diskettes* to distinguish them from their big brother, the hard disk. It is usually clear from the context which type is meant, even though it is unnecessary to make the distinction in many cases because of the many similarities between the two. Second, hard disks often come in packs called *disk packs*—that is, they are stacked together and bound that way, like a pile of plates that have been glued together as a package.

Third, some hard disks are deliberately made to be not removable. The manufacturing and operating tolerances of the disk and disk driver into which they fit are minute, and as you know if you've ever slid something into and out of its holder many times, it usually starts to loosen. Here, that could cause real trouble. A disk that isn't removable and hence is always part of the system is said to be *on-line*. More precisely, that means it is always accessible by the CPU. Other disks, however, especially floppies, are made to be removed. One pays a price for that convenience: The disks and disk drive aren't manufactured to the same high standards and therefore can't hold quite as much data. That is, the *density* with which information can be placed on the disk is decreased.

Many users whose memory storage needs are huge (for instance, banks and insurance companies) view the density reduction per disk as a small price to pay for the ability to remove the disk pack and replace it with a fresh one. Disks or disk packs, when they are removed from the disk drive, are said to be *off-line*—that is, not accessible by the CPU and therefore not really a part of the system at that time. A growing number of microcomputer systems now use a mixture of a fixed hard disk and a removable floppy. You'll see the name *Winchester* applied to the nonremovable 5¼-inch hard disk in micros. What is delightful about this unit is that it is sealed, and hence safeguarded against the appalling damage that even a small amount of dust can do to your data.

chapter

10

the disk operating system (DOS)

As the title indicates, the subject of this chapter is operating systems. What are they, and why bother studying them? Because they are what gives a computer its magic.

Learning about the hardware in a system, everything from the microelectronic circuitry to the electromechanical peripherals, will make you appreciate why a computer can operate at such phenomenal speeds. And learning about the programs the machine runs to accomplish specific tasks that the user wants done will allow you to understand how software brings the hardware to life. Yet anyone who sits down to operate a modern computer will immediately realize that an enormous amount is going on that remains hidden from view. No picture of a computer that portrays it as consisting merely of two parts, the hardware that's sitting there and the programs you put into it like bread into a toaster, is adequate. Why? Because unlike what happens in a simple toaster, the computer is clearly providing a wide range of additional services that make the machine easier to use. Each year there are more of them, making it still easier to use.

In fact, computers have undergone an evolution in the past two decades that parallels the one cars have gone through in the past 60 years. If you've ever watched a silent movie, an early talkie or a Laurel and Hardy film, you've seen someone on the screen have to "cold start" a car by inserting a handle into the front of the engine and manually cranking it until it began firing by itself. Getting such a car to leave a tight parking space was no problem either, assuming that you had the arms of a King Kong. There was no power steering to assist you, and hence there was little difference in the amount of effort it took to pilot a car versus a small truck. Rolling down the road with no shock absorbers made the difference seem small later as well.

Finally, getting the car to go from one gear to the next was a feat unto itself. People who get behind the wheel of a present-day sports car and say that they enjoy shifting manually from gear to gear, think that it was always this easy. But it wasn't. A manual transmission of early decades installed in a current car would infuriate its owners. Among other things, it required the car to come to a complete halt before first gear could even be engaged. Also, as the frequent sound of grinding gears attested, there was no guarantee that you could find and then engage the next gear you wanted. Automatic transmissions, particularly in city traffic, struck most drivers as a boon when the option was finally introduced.

Starting, steering, shocks, and getting a computer to shift "gears" smoothly has also become progressively easier in recent years. Most of the credit for the enormous expansion of public interest in computers has been given to size and price, both of which have shrunk drastically. That's valid in part, but only in part. The more you learn about computers, the more you'll realize that the advent and development of operating systems—the computer equivalent of "all that extra stuff under the hood"—has been equally, if not more, instrumental. Who wants a small and cheap but constantly balky electronic box? Early computer systems were definitely not "user friendly," and it is only because of operating systems that the phrase applies to today's computers at all.

To gain a clear picture of operating systems, we need a few definitions. A computer program intended to accomplish a specific purpose for the user, such as payroll, inventory, word processing, or statistical analysis, is called an *application program.* The user of such a program is well aware of its supposed area of application. By contrast, the many programs the user knows little or nothing about but which serve to coordinate the programs run by and peripherals attached to the computer are called *systems programs.* The package of all the systems programs being used in a particular installation is its *operating system.* It helps make the system function more smoothly by making internal conflict much less likely.

Computer engineers have an illuminating way of describing a systems program: They call it "overhead." What makes the description revealing is that it highlights the fact that operating systems don't benefit the user *directly.* They are intended for the machine more than the operator. Make no mistake about it, though: The user derives substantial and continuing benefit from systems programs, though they remain unseen. The word overhead is valid anyway, since they aren't applications programs which embody the specific tasks the user wants the computer to accomplish at that moment. In short, if a computer has only systems programs to run, it gets nothing done for the people using it. Only when an application program is also run on the machine, and the systems programs help it to run smoothly, is real work accomplished.

How Data Are Stored on a Disk

It is time for us to look at a concrete example of how the operating system assists an application program to run smoothly. Let's assume that we need to do some data or word processing on a computer that has a disk drive (either hard or soft) as its main form of external storage. Readers who wonder why we call the unit a disk drive instead of a disk should keep in mind that we say a stereo system has a turntable, not a record, as one of its components.

To see exactly how the disk drive fits into the system, we should quickly review what happens when there is no external memory in the system, such as tape or disk. In that case, all it has is its internal memory (you might want to imagine that it's one of the growing number of portable computers), in which the programs and data are housed in a standard way—namely, separately, as shown in Figure 10-1. This is a mandatory division because each instruction in a computer program is housed in the memory's registers as a string of 0s and 1s, and each piece of data is stored in the same form. These 8-, 16-, or 32-bit words look too much like one another to the CPU. So one way to tell them apart is to keep them apart. Therefore, instructions are stored in one set of locations, and the data the instructions will manipulate are kept in another.

Now let's move up a notch or two on the price scale and assume that our system is a little more elaborate; in particular, it has a disk drive as a memory peripheral. Question: How should we arrange the data we want to store on the disk? This seemingly innocuous question is one of the most crucial that it is possible to ask about current computers. Why? Because there is no sense in making disk drives an important component

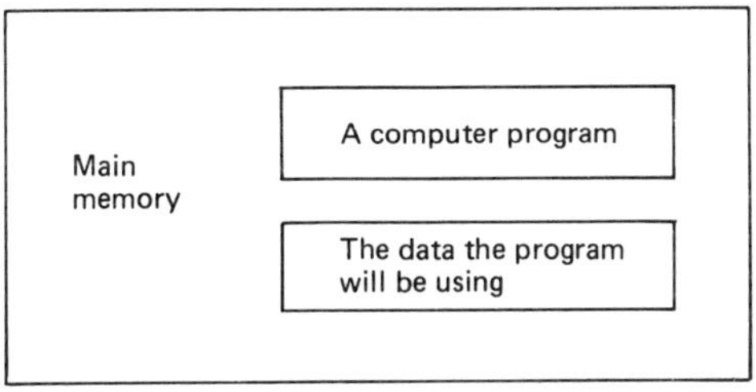

Figure 10-1 Physical separation of data and instructions in main memory.

in sophisticated and expensive microcomputer systems, proceeding to store lots of data on the disk, and then not be able to retrieve the data whenever it's needed—and quickly, at that. It would be frustrating indeed to have to sit at the keyboard and scratch our heads while the machine did the equivalent of saying: "Now, let's see. I know it's in here somewhere. Hmm, if only I could remember where I put it."

One thing that would definitely help is for the disk to have an index. An index on a disk isn't like an index at the back of a book; it's more like a detailed table of contents, and is normally called a *directory*. Each entry in the directory should tell us where that particular clump of information is located on the disk. One problem that has to be resolved before we go further concerns where to put the directory. There are a variety of possible locations, but the nearly universal solution is to place it on the disk itself, on one of the disk's outermost tracks.

As for data, most people have a mistaken impression of how three pieces of unrelated data, say, are stored on a disk. (From here on, when we say data, we mean either data or instructions—any kind of information, really, in binary, codified form.) The prevailing general impression is that the three data words could be placed in three arbitrary locations, just as they might be in main memory. Main memory isn't physically broken up into sectors, though, and as we saw in Chapter 9, disks usually are. Normally, each sector is 128 bytes, but the number could just as easily have been chosen to be 256, 512, or 1024 (1K) bytes, if that is deemed more suitable. Similarly, a hard disk might well use 2K or 4K fixed-length sectors. The point, and it's a very important one, is this: Data are never stored at random on a direct-access medium such as hard or soft disk.

Instead, every piece of data is assigned to its own sector, or to a sector that has already been assigned. It is always in a bin of some kind, rather than on its own somewhere, as the general impression would have us believe. A picture that brings us much closer to the truth here is that of a well-organized home workshop in someone's basement. One conspicuous feature of such a shop is a large cluster of small drawers. Even if one of the drawers contains only a single item, the item nevertheless is in a bin of some kind, not sitting around somewhere. In case it seems wasteful to you to give an entire drawer to one item when there is room in it for seven more, look at the bright side: Carefully labeling each drawer and then keeping a directory of where the individual drawers are located in the two-dimensional array (third one in from the left, and four down from the top), allows you to locate it readily when you need it. In computers, as in basement workshops, that doesn't have to mean that every item gets a separate drawer. The three pieces of random data might find themselves in the same bin, one with the entirely valid label, "miscellaneous."

We are now in a position to say something of great importance about those bins on a disk, or sectors, as they're called. In Chapter 9, when we were examining the physical characteristics of disks (aluminum versus plastic, 5- versus 14-inch, etc.), a sector merely seemed like a nice, neat unit that resulted from dividing up each track into so-and-so many pieces. (In our case it was 26.) However, it is enormously more than that when looked at from a dynamic instead of a static angle. Above all, a sector is the *smallest* quantity of data that can be transferred when a step in a computer program contains a READ or WRITE instruction—that is, READ (from) or WRITE (to) a disk.

What makes that so important is the obvious fact that the information stored on a disk isn't there for the purposes of decoration; it's put there to be retrieved at some later time. Don't forget that in a computer system which is actively processing words or data, say, there is a great deal of movement of information from main memory to disk and, conversely, from disk to main memory. But to repeat: It's not isolated pieces of data that are ferried back and forth. Rather, an entire bin—a sector, and maybe many of them—is brought in during a READ (which is an input operation) or sent out during a WRITE (which is an output operation).

The CPU Finally Meets Its Match

How quickly does that happen? The answer is a delight to behold. Instead of just giving a numerical value and leaving it at that, let's look at the underlying principle first so that we can fully understand what the number means.

We tend to think of the read/write head on a disk drive as floating near the disk, only a small fraction of an inch from the surface. For the moment, suppose that we think of it as a U-shaped shovel instead. What do we want it to scoop up? Information from the disk's surface.

If we were using the shovel to dig a long, shallow trench on a piece of land, and wanted to increase our speed, we'd make it a point to cover more ground in the same time. *We'd* have to move faster, since the earth beneath our feet isn't about to. With a disk in a disk drive, the situation is different. If the read/write head is acting as a shovel, we can get it to scoop information faster in a very simple manner: just make the disk spin more quickly.

Now you know why the rotational speed of a disk drive is so important. The knowledge goes a long way toward explaining why disks are becoming an increasingly significant medium for external storage. To be specific, while floppy disks normally rotate at 300 to 360 revolutions per minute (rpm), hard disks rotate at 10 times that speed: 3000 to 3600 revolutions per minute. Even apart from the greater density with which information can be stored on a hard disk (particularly if it's a sealed, Winchester unit), that would set the two types of disk drive worlds apart.

In sum, don't be surprised if you find a smile coming to your face as your knowledge of disks and disk drives expands. For at some point you may well find yourself saying, "Aha, at last the superfast CPU has met its match. Together these two can really make music." A disk pack can easily hold more than 650 million bytes, and its disk drive can transfer them at rates in excess of 3 million bytes (24 million bits) per *second.*

Names Instead of Numbers

Once a machine with such incredible capabilities has been developed, it can be made to do extremely useful things for you. Such as? One of the most onerous and difficult tasks in dealing with large quantities of data is filing them correctly so that they can later be retrieved in a flash.

A disk may have a shape that looks very different from the large chest of small drawers in a home workshop, but the two make use of the same principles in deciding where to store things. In the chest of drawers we say that the item we're looking for is in the bin that is at row 3, column 4 (that is, three rows down; fourth drawer in that row, counting from the left). On a disk, we say that the data we need are in a sector that is located on track 3, the fourth sector in, counting from the index hole. Figure 10-2 shows the correspondence.

Don't let the shape of the disk throw you when you're trying to think about how data are stored on it. Many systems programmers and data pros cut the disk mentally along a line that extends radially from the spindle hole through the index hole to the edge of the disk. Once that's done, the disk is not only easier to think about for storage purposes, it ends up looking like the chest of small drawers on the left in Figure 10-2. In this case, the disk-as-a-chest-of-drawers would have 77 rows (one for each track on the disk) and 26 columns of bins (one for each sector).

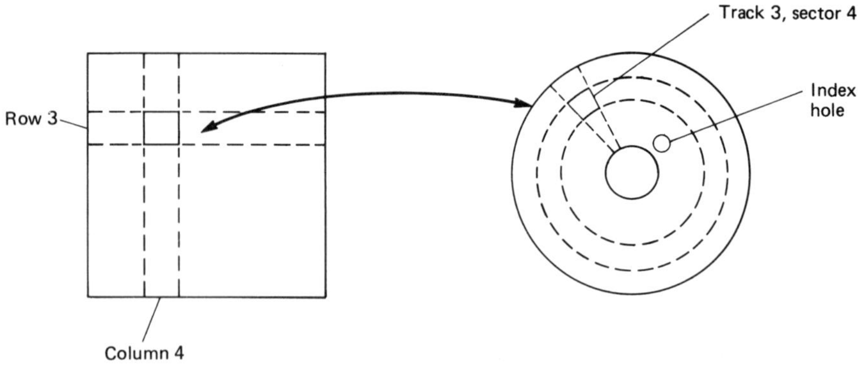

Figure 10-2 Correspondence between square and circular data storage formats.

The most useful chest of drawers for a home workshop is made out of clear plastic so that the owner can see into each bin without even opening it. Unfortunately, one can't do the same with a disk. The electronic signals on it (stored in magnetic-direction form) are invisible to the naked eye, and would make little sense even if they could be seen. Whether a particular string of 0s and 1s were data or instructions, or both, would by no means be obvious from the numbers alone. Therefore, just as with the mob of identical murderers in our hypothetical prison who helped us understand how main memory is organized and addressed, here too each sector on the disk must be carefully—that is, consecutively—numbered so that it can be correctly addressed.

It wasn't until our disk started spinning that we saw why this object had become such a valuable medium in a modern computer. Looking at the static physical product didn't reveal its many merits. Similarly, it's only when we've set our disk spinning and are actually making use of it that we begin to realize just how difficult it will be to keep track of all the data on it. It's not that the spinning motion of the disk moves the data around. However, if we're using the disk for word processing, say, data representing the words, spaces, punctuation, and formatting instructions will be shuffled around repeatedly, especially if the report we're working on will be edited and revised on a number of subsequent occasions. Keeping track of the sometimes extremely high degree of sector-to-sector movement promises to be a real pain. We could easily wind up spending more time monitoring the constantly changing location of our data than using it productively. Compared to the complexity of that task, people with a balky old manual transmission on their Model T had it easy.

The stuff that is stored in the clear plastic drawers of a workshop chest would never be moved around so repeatedly and fast; nor would it serve a useful purpose even if they could. Assuming they were, though, it would certainly be easier to keep track of what's where, because we can *see* into each bin. A moment's reflection on what "seeing" means in this case produces an interesting result: It means that we are able to bypass the number on each bin (for instance, row 3, column 4), yet know what the item is anyway. In short, the ultimate goal we should be working toward in arranging data on our disk is the same, natural one as this: to use *names* instead of numbers for the contents of each sector. When all is said and done, that's what makes using a clear plastic set of drawers so much easier to use than our disk.

The File Manager

What will allow us to use so convenient a method of describing the information we want to store on the disk? The answer is: the disk operating system (DOS). It radically reduces the amount of attention and effort the computer user must devote to playing file clerk, and thereby encourages the time to be spent on more productive and creative work instead.

That sounds wonderful, but how in the world does the disk operating system turn a bookkeeping task this complicated into one that seems simple and natural to human beings? The underlying principle isn't at all difficult actually, and is one we've encountered before. In Chapter 4 we saw that most of the instructions in a computer program have a standard form:

op code	address

You'll recall that "op code" means the kind of operation to be performed, say, ADD, LOAD, or STORE. The "address" portion of the instruction gives the location in memory where the data the CPU needs are temporarily stored or where data are to *be* stored as a result of the instruction. Typically, then, in this most common form of instruction we have an English word in the box to the left and a numerical address in the box to the right.

When the disk operating system acts as a file manager, it makes use of a similar, standard form. This time, the box to the left contains the name you give to that particular file, say, MYFILE. (Read this as "my file"; spaces are omitted in such labels because they waste space and, as we'll soon see, also confuse the machine.) The box to the right contains the address—that is, the location on the disk—of that particular sector. For instance,

MYFILE	TRACK 3, SECTOR 4

means that the information you've designated as MYFILE is located in the fourth sector of the third track.

Forget computers for a moment; you've been using a very similar filing system ever since you were a kid, if you've taken books out of a major library. The card catalog there allows you to know only the author's name or title of the work and yet locate the book in the building. In essence, the catalog acts as a map between everyday names and titles, on the one hand, and physical locations, on the other. The directory on a disk does the same thing. The entries in the directory that correspond to cards in the card catalog are called *file control blocks* (FCBs), but they're basically the same thing.

Books on a library's bookshelves and the items contained in a home workshop's chest of drawers are similar, and both are markedly different from the data that are stored on a disk. In what way? The information that is stored on a disk is normally in a constant state of flux, and therefore the disk operating system must actively play the role of file manager and allocate space whenever it's needed. It must also take note of space that was being used but now no longer is. That is, it manages both filled and empty space on the disk.

We saw earlier that the best place to put the disk's directory turned out to be right on the disk itself, typically on track 2. Where do you imagine is the best place to put the disk operating system? Once again the answer is: on the disk itself, this time on tracks 0 and 1. For a variety of reasons, not every disk has to have a disk operating system on it. (Briefly, one DOS can take care of a number of disks.) The overall arrangement of our disk is shown in Figure 10-3.

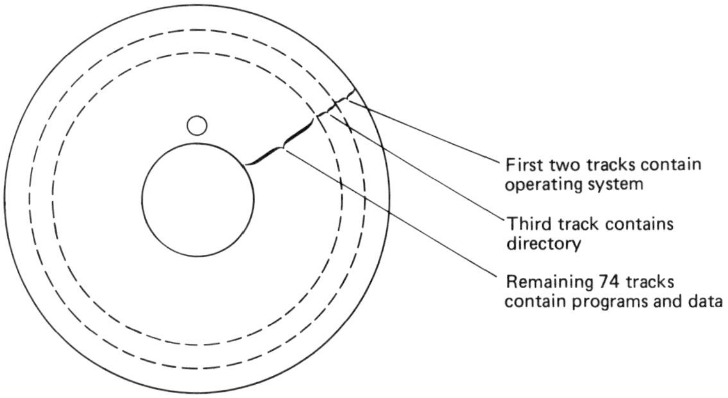

Figure 10-3 How disk space is utilized.

How to Handle a Large Program—or Many Small Ones

We've been discussing what's on our disk, but it is important to keep in mind that none of the programs stored on the disk's tracks can run until it is brought from the disk into main memory. Only instructions that have first been transferred from external to internal memory can be executed.

Since external storage (or *mass storage*, as it's often called) is usually so much bigger than main memory, some students become puzzled here and ask: "If a disk pack can easily hold more than 500 million bytes and main memory's capacity is only 64K (65,536 bytes), how can it run any programs that are larger than 64K?" It is true that the instructions have to be brought from the disk pack to main memory to be executed, but instructions are executed only one at a time. That is, a program is a numbered sequence of instructions which are processed one after the other by the CPU.

That being the case, there is no reason for *all* the instructions in the program to be sitting in main memory at the same time. Here we see a perfect example of how useful it is for information to be transferable from main memory to disk, and vice versa, at extremely high speeds. You'll recall we mentioned a few sections back that hard disks can transfer more than 3 million bytes per second; floppies can transfer between 500,000 and 1 million bytes per second. Thanks to that fact, we can bring in a new block of instructions as soon as the old ones have been executed—and the CPU never need know that they weren't there all along. In short, we can make excellent use of disk as a high-speed peripheral. If the CPU has to have an instruction housed in memory before it can be executed, we'll get it there pronto, and the entire process will go unnoticed by the CPU.

What applies to one large program applies even better to a number of smaller ones. Before we see what that means, let's note that having more than one application program in our computer's memory is a definite advantage. It may not take very long to run most user programs, but entering them into the system (usually through the console—that is, the keyboard and CRT) can be quite time-consuming. There is no question that having a good quantity of them already on disk makes it easier to switch from one job to the next. However, the same question that arose before arises here as well: "What happens if we can't fit all those programs at once into the computer's internal memory?"

As you may have guessed by now, we don't have to. Just as we brought in pieces of a very large program, so too we can bring in first one program and then another to main memory and run them. As before, the CPU will be fooled; it will think that those programs were simultaneously in residence all along.

If you own a microcomputer, the exact number of instructions it executes per day may not be of any great importance to you. When you need the machine, you use it; when you don't, you don't, and it just sits there. However, in a large, commercial computer installation, the *throughput*, the number of application program instructions it runs per hour or per day, is often the measure used to judge whether the machine was worth the intitial—and continuing—cost of having it. Great effort is expended by the firm's staff to make certain that the CPU is kept busy almost constantly. Job scheduling, for instance, receives special attention, with certain tasks being given clear priority over others. It is standard in such systems for there to be many application programs, all ready to run, housed in the system's internal and external storage units.

The process is called *multiprogramming*. It should be apparent to you by now why disk has come to occupy so prominent a place in large computer systems.

Since the high-speed disks we've been discussing can place a variety of programs in main memory almost instantaneously (but not simultaneously), it is appropriate for us to ask: "Which programs, if any, *have* to be there? In particular, does the operating system need to be brought in from the disk for application programs to run smoothly?" The answer is: not all of it. Thanks to the speed with which parts of the operating system can be "rolled in" and "rolled out," as the quick, smooth process is often described, we can bring in exactly the parts we need, and only when we need them. Then they can be sent back to the disk to make room for other application or operating system programs.

There is a related term that is commonly used in this connection. It's called *spooling*, and there are two kinds. *Input spooling* means putting program after program (or one large one) into main memory which, because of its limited size, outputs them onto disk instead of executing them. Then, as soon as they actually need the CPU, back into main memory they come. *Output spooling* takes programs or data out of main memory and buffers them (that is, stores them temporarily) on disk for a different reason: Namely, it wants to send them to an output device, such as a printer. When the printer is free and the CPU isn't busy with something else, back into main memory from disk the program comes, and it is then output to the printer. In short, spooling helps distribute more evenly the various input/output and processing demands made on the system. A final note: Although the word "spool" brings to mind tape, and that is indeed the peripheral that was previously used, it is testimony to disk's growing importance that it, not tape, is now typically involved in spooling.

Making Hardware Friendly

Well, what part of the operating system *does* have to be resident—that is, residing steadily in main memory—while a variety of application programs are brought in and run? The first one is the control program. Before we describe what the phrase "control program" designates, let us note that CP/M, one of the most popular operating systems for 8-bit microcomputers, stands for *c*ontrol *p*rogram for *m*icroprocessors. However, as we'll soon see, CP/M, like every other operating system, contains more than just a control program. And what *is* a control program? It is nothing more than a collection of systems programs that process the commands entered by the user on the keyboard.

Not every instruction is a valid command. In fact, the number of commands that CP/M, for instance, allows is just six. They include some you're already familiar with, such as DIR. That stands for directory, and typing the command DIR therefore permits you to see the contents of the disk's directory. Since, as we've seen, one of the most useful parts of the disk operating system is its file-managing capability—you type in a name and it handles the physical part of filing—DIR is a frequently used command.

Another typical command is SAVE, but you're probably more used to thinking of this one as STORE. What it instructs the system to do is copy the contents of a file in main memory out onto the disk. In that sense, it does indeed differ from STORE, since we were using the term earlier as the opposite of LOAD. Namely, STORE represented a word (that is, data and/or an instruction) being moved from the CPU to main memory ("store in main memory"), and LOAD was the reverse. It still is. Finally, ERA means erase a file that is on the disk and TYPE means display the contents of a file on the CRT.

These primitive commands allow the user to just sit down at the computer, turn the machine on, and proceed immediately to do some useful work. Data or word processing can begin without delay. Why? Because nearly every application program will require data to be input and the program or results to be displayed on the CRT or output to the printer. In addition to the control program, the file manager program and some programs to handle input/operations are also resident. That is enough for the interface between the user and the application program, on the one hand, and all that cold and complex hardware, on the other, to begin to appear "soft and friendly." Other parts of the operating system are also needed to help convey that impression convincingly, but as we're about to see, they can be brought in from the disk as they're needed.

Translating Higher-level Languages into Machine Language

A look at a concrete example will show how all the parts and pieces of an operating system—*modules,* as the parts are often called—function together as a whole. Suppose that you sit down at a computer and turn it on. Strictly speaking, nothing should happen. Why? Because main memory is volatile—that is, as we discussed in Chapter 3, when it loses power, it loses its memory. Since there is nothing in main memory (you've just turned the machine on), and a program has to be there or else it can't be executed (and you haven't yet entered any), presumably the machine should be unable to operate.

Without your being aware of it, though, the most basic parts of the operating system were moved into main memory right after the machine was turned on, a process called *cold boot*. It's a good thing that the most frequently used parts of an operating system can get themselves moved into main memory by themselves, that is, can pull themselves in by their own bootstraps, so to speak. Most people would find that entering these modules into main memory manually was every bit as onerous a chore as having to start a car's engine on a cold morning using a hand crank.

Now that the machine is on, what next? The majority of users attempt to communicate with their computer by employing a packaged program that is written in one of the four most popular programming languages: BASIC, Pascal, COBOL, or FORTRAN. Since the computer doesn't contain any application programs at this point, users might try to put some into the system by making use of a program written in one of these languages, which are usually referred to as *higher-level languages*. (By contrast, the sequence of 0s and 1s that actually make the machine perform correctly is called *machine language*, and it is obviously as low on the language scale as one can go.) Diskettes and books containing useful application programs, for instance, are available in bookstores, by mail, or in many cases come with the machine.

Wherever the program comes from, be it one that you enter yourself or buy in cassette or disk form, it should be apparent to you that there is no way the machine will understand even the simplest statement in BASIC, say, much less an entire program written in this language. The reason is that computers understand only 0s and 1s. A statement in a programming language, BASIC or any other, isn't 0s and 1s. It's mostly words. Something or someone has to translate the *source program*, which is the name given to the sequence of statements written in a programming language, into an *object program*, which is the same sequence converted into the appropriate strings of binary digits. These the computer does understand.

Not surprisingly, then, the operating system brings into main memory another of its parts, in this case a BASIC interpreter if you're programming in BASIC. Until then, this interpreter program (yes, it's also a program) had been sitting on disk. We're assuming, of course, that your system has such a module available. It may not, since this is usually an extra-cost option. The interpreter provides the translation service the user needs—without the user even being aware that it's doing so.

The idea of languages being interpreted may not strike you as particularly novel, since it goes on all the time at the United Nations. Nevertheless, what should strike you as fascinating about the translator in a computer is this: *Its input is a program* (here, written in BASIC) *and so is its output* (the correct sequence of strings of 0s and 1s). There are exceptions to this rule, and we'll look at them later. The general picture is shown in Figure 10-4.

Some people have difficulty with the concept primarily because they still think of computers as electronic data processors—in essense, glorified calculating machines. Its input would therefore consist merely of a collection of numbers, and its output would be just one number, say, their average or their total. Quite clearly, then, any programs that are stored in such a machine handle only data, not other programs.

Once you've grasped the important idea that a computer can have programs in it—maybe many of them—that have programs as their input and output, there is nothing about operating systems that will seem strange to you for long. It's only a matter of finding out in each case precisely *what* that particular operating system module does to the programs it processes. For instance, suppose you change your mind and decide to do some simple word processing tasks as your first job. This is usually a nice way to ease yourself into contact with the machine, since it doesn't—or at least shouldn't—require any knowledge of programming languages. All you're going to do is move some natural language (in this case, English) text around, and for that, you merely have to know which keys to push.

This is one task your machine can handle readily because it probably has an editor. A great mystique surrounds word processing in the minds of people who know little about what actually goes on inside a computer. Yet the fact remains that the editor is just another program. It is an operating system module that responds to simple commands, such as INSERT and DELETE. Let's assume, then, that you begin by typing into the system a moderate amount of text, say, 15 pages. (That's more than most microcomputers can handle in main memory, since 1300 words—about six pages—would typically use up 64K of RAM.) While you work,

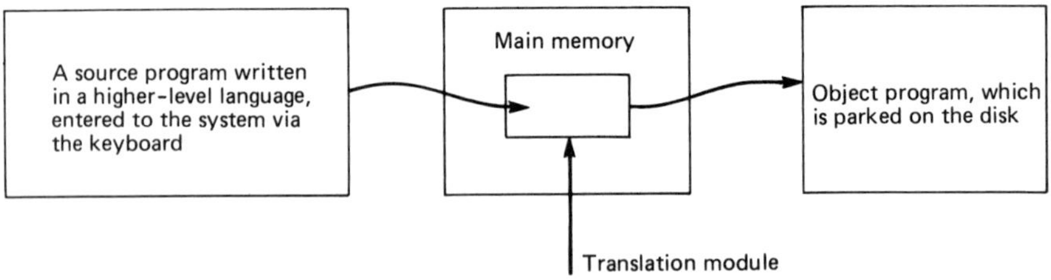

Figure 10-4 Both the input and output of the translation module are computer programs.

the disk operating system plays file manager and quietly parks this material for you on the disk.

To do your editing, you have to call in the editor. Depending on the system, you'd generally have to type E, ED, or EDIT to make that happen. What does the editor do? It reads a text file from the disk into main memory, displays it on the screen, and then asks you whether you want to make any changes in it. If not, you move forward or backward in the text until something appears on the screen that you'd like to modify. The process of moving through the text this way has been given the colorful name *scrolling*. We're used to thinking of text as being organized in page form, yet the world of high technology has in some ways taken us backward as well as forward in time. Ancient texts were written on continuous rolls of papyrus (for instance, the Dead Sea scrolls), and that is how computers handle the 15-page word flow as well. Once you've finished making revisions in the text, you send the modified text file back to the disk.

Resident Modules

It is worthwhile to summarize some of the key features of the material we've covered thus far and put in a few details that were deliberately overlooked. They would have been confusing if discussed earlier, but once you've gotten a good view of the forest, noting the fine points of some of the trees is rewarding too.

To begin with, every peripheral you attach to a CPU and main memory is unique. Some are high-speed, while others are low-speed. Many are serial-access storage devices (such as tape), while others are direct-access (such as disk). Each requires a separate and distinct small program—called a *driver*—to make certain that its input/output requirements are handled properly. Thus, a keyboard has a keyboard driver. A CRT has a display driver. A disk has a disk driver—that is, a piece of software, as opposed to a disk drive, which is definitely a piece of hardware. All these drivers are part of the operating system.

Not only are they operating system modules, *they* are the part of the operating system that must be modified when you change a peripheral, even to another of the same type. For that reason, peripheral device drivers are said to be *machine-dependent*. The rest of the operating system is usually *machine-independent*, and hence can be used without modification on other systems or configurations. Small system owners frequently ask, "Why can't I move from one printer to another?" Or, "I'm only changing from one size disk to a bigger one, why should that present any problems?" The problem presented in these cases and almost every other may or may not involve hardware, but the software—the absolutely essential driver subroutine—will indeed have to be modified.

The alert reader may have noticed that we used the word "subroutine" to describe the driver program for each peripheral. It is just that, and it fits into the overall functioning of the operating system in much the same way that the "jump to a subroutine" (JSR) instruction did in the ordinary programs we discussed in Chapter 6. What that means is this: When you type on a keyboard, for instance, the operating system jumps to the subroutine that handles input from the keyboard. Then, other parts of the operating system or the applications program handle the actual request you are making through the keyboard (INSERT and DELETE, or LOAD and SAVE). The reason users rarely notice that a number of different operating system modules are normally busy during this time is that all the transactions take place so fast. The speed of the CPU and disk (on which the operating system is stored) allow the machine to be seen as enormously more "user friendly" than it would otherwise be.

Disk may be the fastest peripheral, but there are certain operating system modules that are used so often, they are moved into main memory when the computer is first turned on, and that's where they stay. These are the *resident* modules. The drivers are part of the input/output system (IOS). They are always resident, and deservedly so, since they are needed whenever a command is typed. In CP/M this collection of modules is called the *basic input/output system* (BIOS), but the word "basic" here has nothing whatever to do with BASIC, the programming language.

There are only two other parts of the operating system that are normally resident. First, the file manager, which handles the disk's files. It is called the *basic disk operating system* (BDOS) in CP/M. Second, the control program, which validates and executes the rudimentary commands the user enters at the keyboard. It is called the *console command processor* (CCP) in CP/M. Typical BDOS operations would involve OPENing, READing from, WRITing to, and CLOSing a file. A typical CCP command would be DIR, to examine the disk's directory.

Finally, let us note that there are a number of very useful operating system modules that simply don't need to be resident in main memory. They can be brought in when needed, used temporarily, and returned to disk until they're needed again. It probably won't surprise you to hear that the place in memory to which they are brought is called the *temporary program area* (TPA). We've already seen a common use of this area, when the BASIC interpreter was brought from disk, where it's usually stored, and placed here. More accurately, it was *copied* into main memory, since nothing has happened to disturb the original on the disk.

Two Types of Translators: Interpreters and Compilers

Many owners of microcomputers, and people who've had only a little programming experience using BASIC, think that an interpreter is present in every system. It strikes them as a natural way of doing things. Moreover, they are of the belief that interpreters do the bulk of program translation—that is, convert each statement in the program into machine language, 0s and 1s—even in mid- and large-sized systems. However, there is a very good reason why that isn't so, and you should know what it is.

Suppose that you receive a letter written in a foreign language with which you're not familiar. You could give it to someone who is fluent in the language and have the person translate the *entire* letter, then give you the version written in English. On the other hand, you could have the translator physically present and have the person read the translation aloud as she reads the letter herself for the first time. Question: If your time is extremely valuable, because you have a number of other, pressing matters to attend to, which translation method will consume less of it? Obviously, the former.

The first way, giving it to someone to translate completely before she gives it back to you, is essentially an example of batch processing. That is, all the words are processed (translated) before you get a chance to interact with the results. The second route, in which you are present and the letter is translated a little bit at a time, is much closer to interactive processing. That is, you can stop the translator if something strikes you as odd and try right then and there to straighten out the discrepancy.

The batch-type method of translating a source program into an object program is called *compiling* it. The program that does the translating is called a *compiler*. How does it actually work as part of our computer's operations? The compiler, like the interpreter, is an operating system module. Since it's not resident, when it is needed it is brought in from the disk and placed in main memory in the temporary program area (TPA), which is specifically set aside for such use. Its input consists of BASIC, COBOL, Pascal, FORTRAN, or other language statements (each language requires a different compiler), and its output is the machine-language equivalent of those statements. The output—that is, the object program—is almost always longer than the input, because each line of the source program is generally equal to several lines of object program.

For instance, to tell a human being to add two numbers, A and B, and let the letter C designate the sum, takes one line: "A + B = C." But to tell that to a computer usually takes five machine-language statements. Only when the compiler has finished its work completely does the program run.

That is both an advantage and a disadvantage. It's an advantage for the same reason that having someone translate a letter completely for you in your absence is one: namely, once you have the translation in front of you, you can read through it at high speed. Similarly, once the compiler has finished its work, the object program it produces can be run, and quickly at that. We're assuming that it's correct, of course. If it isn't, it has to be sent back to the compiler to be recompiled in the same way that you'd have to send the letter back to the translator. Since errors in a program can arise from a variety of sources, the program may have to be recompiled a fair number of times. Some of the bugs—that is, errors—may prove particularly intractable.

An interpreter, on the other hand, doesn't produce an object program. It simply translates a statement and then executes it immediately. In that way it's much like a chef who consumes each dish as soon as he finishes preparing it. No meal is ever produced. People using an interpreter have the same attitude: "Why bother to produce a program?" they might well ask. "The interpreter *executes* each statement as soon as it's finished translating it into machine language. Since it has already been executed, what do I need the translation for?"

There is more reality in this situation than it might seem at first glance. A translator we interviewed at the United Nations told us, "No, I don't remember a thing I translated today. It came in as words and phrases in one language and went out the same way [in another], and that's that." This translation mode is definitely slower than using a compiler, as we'll see in a minute. However, for development work, where you're looking to locate and remove bugs before they are incorporated into what is supposed to be an error-free program, it definitely has its place.

A final and often important difference between interpreters and compilers concerns the amount of valuable space they each, respectively, take up in main memory. A compiler for the particular programming language you are using, say, Pascal, would be moved from disk to main memory and compile your program. Then its usefulness comes to an end temporarily, at least as far as that particular program is concerned. (We're assuming that no errors were found and that the program runs smoothly.) The compiler can therefore be removed from main memory and the space used for other purposes—that is, other programs and data. An interpreter, however, *cannot* be absent from main memory when the program runs. Remember, no object-language program is produced by an interpreter. It merely translates and then executes whatever it has just translated. The interpreter thus has to be present in main memory whenever the instructions that you want executed also are.

When all is said and done, interpreters provide a remarkably inefficient way of translating programs. For example, we discussed in Chapter 6 that one of the great strengths of a computer is its willingness to do the same thing a nearly endless number of times, whereas a human being in the same situation would be bored silly and increasingly error-prone. One instruction that makes the computer repeat an act or computation again and again is the repeated use of a jump to a subroutine. Loops and subroutines are very commonly encountered in programs.

A compiler translates a subroutine instruction just once. An interpreter, however, translates the entire subroutine again, every time it encounters it. You may recall that the principal reason for structuring a subroutine in the first place was to save space in the program and avoid needless repetition of our programming effort. (Keep in mind that repeatedly writing WEBSTER in a record of a reading session produced a considerable saving of space early in Chapter 6.) An interpreter, by translating each and every statement as though it had never seen it before, undoes much of the work that went into structuring subroutines.

Linkers and Loaders

Two other operating system modules whose names you'll frequently encounter are concerned with getting a translated program ready for execution. A major change has taken place in the world of applications programming. It used to be common for one person to be assigned the task of writing an entire program, and then making certain that it worked. That is no longer feasible in many instances. The programs needed today in business, government, and scientific research have become increasingly large and complex.

As a result, they have grown more structured—that is, more likely to make use of subprograms, procedures, and subroutines—each year. Not only does that make it easier to write the program in the first place, since one is essentially using a "building block" approach, it also makes the process of finding errors and correcting them easier. These reasons would have been sufficiently compelling to force adoption of the structured approach in any event, but it has helped (and been helped by) *teams* of programmers working on the same application or operating system program. Each can be given a well-structured miniprogram to work on—that is, a self-contained piece of software—which should fit neatly into the whole when it's finished.

Nevertheless, something in the machine itself must make certain that these parts and pieces are hooked together at execution time so that they can run as a seamless unit. The operating system has a module whose job it is to guarantee that outcome: the *linker*. The name of this important module tells the whole story, but a picture here is also useful (see Figure 10-5).

The trouble with Figure 10-5 is the same one that we experienced when we first discussed disks. There was only so much we could learn about them by examining their characteristics as physical objects that were static. Once they were put into a disk drive and we had a chance to watch them in action, then and only then did we see what astonishing things they can do for the user, and ever so quietly, since they do it ever so fast. The same goes for the linker. Students often ask at this point: "If all the linker does is glue pieces of a program together, why couldn't that be done—and done better—by an 'external' linker, so that the pieces are already glued together in the right way before the program is even put into the machine?"

It's a very good question, but it is based on too static a picture of what a computer can do for you, thanks to its operating system. Let's call the collection of subroutines that the user of the system has available its *library*. Many of the students who use a city or school library to write a report, say, make use of more than one book at a time. To make the analogy appropriate, let's assume that each student has to use six books. If that were always the case, why couldn't we, as managers of the library, simply package the books in clumps of six and hand them to the users as they came in? We too would be acting as "external linkers." The answer is clear: It is not at all certain *which* six books any given student will choose for his or her report. The linker in the computer's operating system allows the user the same freedom of choice. The library is there; how you use it is up to you.

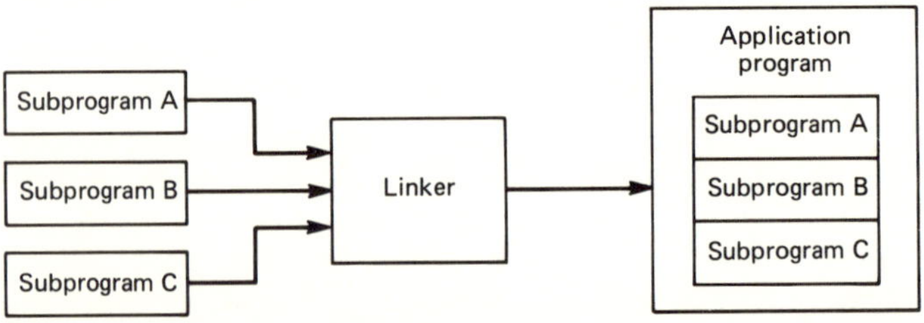

Figure 10-5 The operation of a linker module.

The name of the last operating system module we'll look at is called the *loader*. It's an unfortunate name. Linkers do in fact link together electronically subprograms and/or subroutines so that they can run as a unit, but loaders do something else of equal importance besides loading into main memory the final, linked version of an object program. They also relocate any addresses that need it.

What does that mean? And when is such an operation called for? The answer will be easier to grasp if we forget computers for a moment and look at what might happen to you at work. Suppose you're an avid reader and over the years have accumulated a valuable collection of clippings from various newspapers, articles from journals, and quotes from books. All this material is sitting in a host of boxes on your book shelves, arranged according to subject matter. At some point, you decide to make use of this extensive library to do a report for your firm. The report is well received, so much so that your firm decides to publish it in book form. A publisher agrees that that's a good idea and assigns you a research assistant to make sure that the quotes and references are accurate.

Just before that happens, however, your office is moved while you are on vacation. Much to your chagrin, you find that you now have three other office mates and—this is the key point—your library has been merged with theirs along one wall of the new, large office that has been earmarked for that purpose. When you take a closer look, you realize that your files have been dispersed randomly among those already there, and all are housed in the same green cardboard boxes.

You may be miffed, but your research assistant is lost. He hasn't the foggiest idea how to locate the quotes and references that lent so much weight to your report in the first place. What to do? Draw a map, one that gives the new address of each file in terms of its old address. Knowing where each document used to be allows you to determine immediately where it is now. In essence, the address of each statement (in your report) will be relocated so that the program can run—that is, your report can be checked and published.

In computer programming, it is common and even necessary for the programmer to assume that the program will start at memory location 0. These are called *0-origin programs*. Since it isn't known at the time precisely where this particular piece of software will be located in main memory at run time, a simplifying assumption of some kind is necessary. The vast majority of instructions in a program consist of an op code and a memory reference, that is,

op code	address

and this may have to be changed later when the program is moved. Updating the addresses is an operation performed by the loader, and is called *relocation.*

How do you know which statements need to be modified—that is, which instructions and memory references the loader should relocate? The answer will be clear if we return for a moment to the office analogy we were just using. The report you've written now has an appendix, a "translation—or relocation—code," that tells your diligent assistant where any references that are needed can be found. Loaders obviously resemble compilers in that regard, since both function as translators. For that reason, you may not be surprised to hear that the loader finds out from the compiler which instructions have to have their memory reference addresses changed.

Summing up, the last two operating system modules we've looked at—linkers and loaders—perform quite distinct functions yet are usually lumped together and referred to simply as *linking loaders* or *linker-loaders.* The overwhelming majority of programs that you enter into a computer undergo a standard three-step sequence—compile, link, and run—that seems to the programmer like only one step. And that's how it should be; that's what a good operating system is for. The loader is what guarantees the third step, since it hands over control to the final, linked version of the program.

UNIX, XENIX, and the IBM Personal Computer

CP/M was the most popular operating system for 8-bit micros, but there is another operating system, UNIX, that is quickly becoming the de facto standard for 16-bit micros and minis, and it seems certain to attain even greater popularity in the future. Those of us who used UNIX when it was available to the public primarily on computer installations at universities (as it was implemented on Digital Equipment's PDP-11 series) are happy to see it finding its way onto systems for personal and small business users. It's a pleasure to use.

UNIX is the result mainly of the work in 1969–1972 of two Bell Laboratories computer scientists, Ken Thompson and Dennis Ritchie, and it was designated largely to be used for in-house programming development purposes. The system is relatively small, but it is so flexible that by the mid-1970s there were already a number of variants of the system around. What they all had in common, among other things, was portability—that is, instead of being dependent on any one machine or product line from a single manufacturer, which was usually the case with operating systems of this period, UNIX could be used on almost any computer that had enough main memory and a high-speed disk drive (we'll see why these things are needed in a moment).

This is one operating system whose origins are still reflected in the major capabilities it possesses. Unlike CP/M, which was designated for stand-alone or single-user systems—that is, one microcomputer operating independently of and not connected to other micros or a large (mainframe) computer—UNIX was designed right from the start to be a *multiuser* and *multitasking* system.

Having more than one user on a system creates a host of potential problems whose solution makes UNIX more complicated than it would otherwise be. For one thing, UNIX incorporates a supervisor (a "superuser"), someone in an administrative capacity who makes certain that the people using the system have the right to, and, equally important, that they don't make a mess of anyone else's programs or data while they work with their own. *The operating system itself takes care of parceling out space in main memory*, where each program must find a spot first before it can run. But the superuser is still left with the general job of administering the system's resources.

The word "task" in "multitasking" really means "program." So the statement that UNIX was designed to be a "multitasking operating system" means that it was designed to handle more than one program at a time. For that reason, some people call this feature "multiprogramming" instead of "multitasking." In the next chapter we will see a concrete and everyday example of multitasking, in which an executive at one of the nation's largest firms did some financial planning on a computer equipped with UNIX at the same time that the machine was running a word processing task. In UNIX terminology, the word processing was put in the "foreground," while the financial planning calculations ran in the "background" whenever the CPU wasn't busy with the foreground task.

The first part of UNIX with which the user has contact is the *shell*. This is a program that *interprets commands* made by the user. This part of UNIX is frequently customized to suit the requirements of individual customers. Some users want a simple system that demands little prior knowledge and experience, while others are less naive and like a more direct, technical approach, one that offers a wider variety of commands.

The names that have been given to two of the three most important components of the UNIX system are drawn, by analogy, from a nut. A nut is surrounded by a shell, inside of which is a kernel. It's the same with UNIX: The shell interprets the commands you type at the keyboard and then turns them over to the *kernel* of the system for validation and execution. As with an edible nut, the kernel is the real meat of the matter. For that reason, the kernel of UNIX—and not the shell—is permanently resident in main memory. The shell is brought in from disk whenever you type a command. (That is the reason implementing the system—that is, making it fit and run smoothly on a particular collection of hardware—requires a high-speed disk drive. If the shell were brought in too slowly each time you needed it, you'd notice the delays.) In short, when you're using UNIX, you might want to think of yourself as typing on a walnut.

The kernel is the *resource manager*, where the word "resource" refers to the various pieces of hardware that constitute the system—the CRT, keyboard, main memory, printer, memory peripherals, and so on. The kernel makes certain that each resource functions as it is supposed to, in accordance with the particular applications program it is running at the moment, while avoiding conflict among the resources that are currently part of the system. In that sense, the kernel is the *co*operating system of the UNIX operating system—that is, it ensures cooperation among the system's resources.

Of paramount importance is the third major component of UNIX, the file system, one that is easy to learn and to work with. Like CP/M, UNIX makes use of directories to provide a mapping between the name of each file and its physical location on disk. Since there are many directories, just as there are usually many users of a system equipped with UNIX, there is one, most comprehensive directory, called a *root* directory, just as there is one user who is earmarked as being the superuser. The root directory contains all the other important directories.

Understanding the delightful and unique design of the UNIX file system requires the reader to have some familiarity with data structures such as trees and graphs. This is knowledge that the interested reader can easily acquire from the readable titles listed in the annotated bibliography. Even without assuming this background, however, we can briefly describe the key idea of a *pipeline* in UNIX, a major contribution of this particular operating system.

Earlier we stated that the reader could become more comfortable with how an operating system works by realizing that certain operating system modules have one program as their input and another program (or a different version of the first) as their output. (See Figure 10-4.) In similar fashion, a pipeline connects up a number of commands—that is, programs—by taking the *output* of the first and using it as the *input* for the next, and so on.

Let's look at a concrete and straightforward example. In UNIX, the simple command **who** results in a list of current users of the system being displayed on the screen. Suppose that Tom, Dick, and Harry are. Then, in simplified form (since other information would also be displayed, for instance, which terminal or port each is using and the time they each logged in), the screen would show:

Tom
Dick
Harry

In UNIX, **wc** stands for "word count," and the command is used not only to count words, but also to count lines and characters in a file, depending on which option you choose. Options are specified by simply typing in **-l**, **-w**, or **-c** to count, respectively, the number of lines, words, or characters in the file being named. (In this case, the file is the names of the people using that system at that moment.)

Since a vertical bar, **|**, is used to create a pipeline from two separate commands, the complete instruction is simply typed onto the system as: **who | wc -l**. Note that the screen will merely show the number "3" and not the names Tom, Dick, and Harry. The reason is that these three names became the input to the word-count command, **wc -l**, whose pipelined output is therefore 3.

What should be striking to you about all this is that we mentioned previously that one of the most important trends in recent years in the computer programming field has been the move toward structured programming. UNIX takes the trend a step further, since it is nothing if not modular. Its many separate and relatively independent modules give it a remarkably high degree of flexibility. That characteristic is evident in the example of pipelining cited above. In fact, it is fair to say that UNIX's whole approach centers on the construction of complex programs out of much simpler ones already in existence, rather than having to start on so formidable a project each time from scratch.

One reason that UNIX is likely to be much more widely known in the near future is because of its little brother, XENIX. Bell Labs, as a wholly owned subsidiary of AT&T, a regulated monopoly at the time, was unable to develop a viable commercial product based on UNIX and market it aggressively, even though a number of executives at Bell Labs were well aware of its economic potential. A company named Microsoft, in Bellevue, Washington, did it instead in 1980, calling their version of UNIX the XENIX system.

Major developments in 1983, involving AT&T and IBM, are now bringing both UNIX and the UNIX-based XENIX to a broader audience. In 1984 AT&T put into effect a Department of Justice plan that the firm be broken up into a number of independent companies—in exchange for which those companies, especially AT&T Information Systems, can now compete on an equal footing with commercial firms in the computer field. UNIX-based hardware and software, as well as continued growth in telecommunications revenues, are prime goals of the new, lean-and-mean American Telephone.

The antitrust suit that AT&T lost, IBM won. That has allowed the company to be even more competitive in the marketplace than it has been traditionally; the aggressive pricing of its products, as well as its purchase of a significant portion of the shares both of Intel, an important semiconductor manufacturer that makes the microprocessor in IBM's personal computers, and of Rolm, a telecommunications equipment maker, in 1983 give clear testimony to its expanded confidence. In addition, the success of its personal computer line surprised even veteran marketers at IBM and its rivals.

As we've seen in this chapter, every one of these computers has—indeed, has to have—an operating system. And which one is it? According to a senior executive at IBM, the *large majority* of the operating systems in the more than 10,000 personal computers the company is selling each week are the XENIX-related MS DOS, not CP/M. Neither the company's ads nor its salespeople mention the UNIX/XENIX origin of the system, and simply call the best-selling operating system MS DOS 2.0, which stands for Microsoft's Disk Operating System, version 2.0. It was preceded by a less powerful version, the 1.1. This style of numbering is often used: The number before the decimal is the version of the program, and the number after it represents enhancements—i.e., improvements to that version: 2.1 is an enhancement of 2.0.

(If you own, or are thinking of buying, an IBM Personal Computer, it is worthwhile to note a few technical details that will be important in upcoming years. MS DOS works only with Intel's 8086 and 8088 microprocessors, the latter of which is the CPU in the IBM PC. The XENIX operating system, on the other hand, isn't limited just to the 8086/8088 and can also be used with 16- and 32-bit microprocessors that are becoming increasingly popular, such as the Motorola 68000, the Zilog Z8000, and the National Semiconductor 16032.

(However, officials at Microsoft Corporation have stated that their intention is to upgrade MS DOS slowly but surely until, eventually, it and XENIX become nearly indistinguishable, as far as single-user systems are concerned. It might be useful for the reader, therefore, to think of the most popular operating systems for microcomputers as falling into three standard families: MS DOS, or if you prefer, XENIX; its big brother, UNIX; and CP/M.)

In short, you'll be hearing more in the near future about UNIX and UNIX-based products such as XENIX, though you may have to do a little digging to discover that you already know each of these roses by another name.

chapter

11

office automation and telecommunications

The subject of telecommunications is vast, and is important in its own right, but it is so essential to an understanding of the popularity and effectiveness of computers in personal and business settings that it has to be included. This chapter briefly discusses some of the key concepts, especially as they apply to the increasingly electronic office. Also, it gives the reader a chance to apply the topics presented earlier.

The material covered in the previous 10 chapters, in conjunction with the area to be introduced here, will make it clear how and why computers are permanently changing not only the physical appearance of the work setting, but also the very nature of work itself.

Collaborating via Computer

Before we take a closer look at what the phrase "office automation" means, we need to spend a minute examining what the word "office" used by itself means. To most people, the word has had the same definition for decades: "a place to work, consisting of a desk, a chair, and a phone." If it is the office of a high-level executive, people might add carpeting, a window, a higher-floor location, some extra square footage, and perhaps a private rest room, to their description, but the definition they give remains centered around a desk and a chair. It is now safe to say that this characterization will soon be as dated as spats and Hula Hoops.

The best way to see why that is already well on its way to happening is to glance at the results of a series of surveys that asked people who work in offices what they wanted in their own office.* They still asked for a

*The data are drawn from a six-year study (1978–1984) done by the author and his staff of the preferences of middle managerial business people between the ages of 25 and 50, these individuals having been selected at random annually from among the readers of a national business publication.

desk, a chair, and a phone, but the most important change during the past half-dozen years has been in the number of workers who want a computer terminal. Whereas in 1978 less than 1% included one in their list of ideal features, by early 1984 at least 20% did. A cynic might say, "Perhaps it's just a fad. They want one because it is the new 'in thing,' like owning a Rolex watch or a Mercedes."

That is always a possibility, so we asked workers what they would do with a sophisticated terminal of their own if they had one. The five most frequently encountered replies, in descending order, were:

1. Word processing (of letters and documents)
2. Accounting and financial planning ("spread sheet") applications, as well as statistical analyses
3. Graphic display ("pie charts, bar graphs, and data maps")
4. Communication, interoffice as well as international (via private and public networks)
5. Engineering calculations, involving data and equations, as well as modeling (simulation, computer-aided design and computer-aided modeling—CAD/CAM)

Since many of the respondents in our survey who wanted a computer of their own in the office were able to convince their employer to buy them one, or being self-employed, bought it themselves, we didn't have to wait long to see whether this was merely a faddish infatuation or a tool that in time became an integral part of the way they conduct their business. Desktop units seemed to be finding favor in the 1980s just as typewriters had earlier in the century and copying machines did in the 1960s and 1970s, only this time the rate of adoption proved much higher. Also, as we will see in the remainder of this chapter, these electronic marvels can do things typists a few decades ago would have considered science fiction.

People who got the right unit for their particular needs (no easy matter, as it turns out) and spent some months becoming familiar with its hardware and software, usually upgrading both to suit their purposes, started using it for tasks large and small. To begin with a simple but very common instance, Frank Lambert and Ron Evans, who work for the same company but have offices on different floors, were asked to give their assessment of an expensive new product (more than $10 million) their firm was thinking of buying. The two have different areas of expertise and hence were assigned to work on this project together, submitting their final recommendations—in written form—to a management committee.

Frank and Ron both had other work to do in addition, and the problem of communication between them arose almost immediately.

Frank often tried to get in touch with Ron when Ron was out of the office, and by the time Ron returned the call, Frank was busy or himself out of the office. The face-to-face meetings they were able to arrange on the spot were fine, but as Frank complained, "They don't result in any pages; *those* we each have to produce on our own."

One of the main reasons so many business people have developed a fondness for the computer is that it seems to them a friendly extension of the typewriter, one that allows them to generate soft copy (on the CRT), where they can see and easily correct it, *before* turning out hard copy (printed permanently on paper). That possibility became especially appealing to Frank and Ron, who began to employ (1) the word processing feature of their desktop units, and (2) the communications link that tied all the firm's units together.

Since both computers used the UNIX operating system, Frank would use UNIX's extensive text formatting and document preparation features to develop a few pages of written text, which he then sent to Ron via UNIX's electronic mail system. When Ron got back to the office, sometimes after 5 p.m., turned on his machine, and identified himself ("logged in"), he found the following message on his screen: You have mail. Ron then read the rough draft on his screen, added his own thoughts and findings to it, and sent the slowly expanding report back to Frank.

Shared Resources

Let's define some of the technical terms that are widely used to characterize what these two diligent workers were doing. When the computer era was in its early stages, large—that is, room-sized—mainframe computers were all there were, usually from companies such as Sperry and IBM. What was most desirable about these machines was their CPU, central processing unit, which could be used to do lengthy calculations quickly. Thanks to the CPU's speed, it could handle dozens of users simultaneously by giving each one of them a *slice* of time (see Figure 11-1).

Each user was usually unaware of the others, since delays were minimal. The arrangement was, and still is, called *timesharing*. It was popular at the time, even necessary, because of the great expense of large computers. The terminals through which each of the dozens of users made contact with the mainframe's CPU were "dumb"—that is, they had no CPU of their own. They were simply teletype machines, slow and loud, and without a CRT attached.

With the invention of the microprocessor by the Intel Corporation in 1969, the entire CPU was reduced to the size of the letter "o" on this

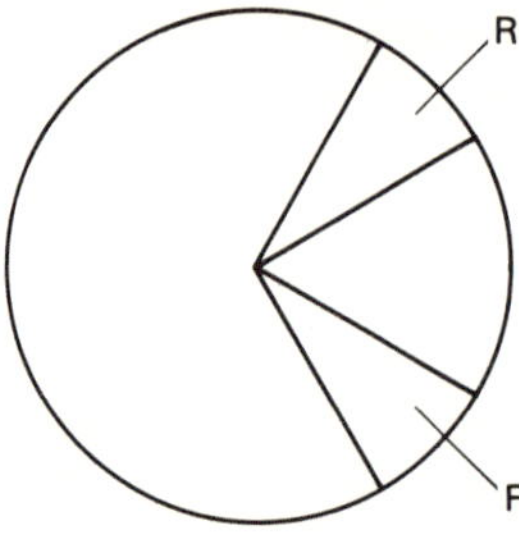

Figure 11-1 Timesharing. Each unit of time is divided into slices and given sequentially to users, clockwise.

page. The price of microprocessors plummeted during the 1970s from hundreds of dollars and limited availability to under $5 and mail-order availability from dozens of suppliers. It had finally become reasonable to equip each user's terminal with its own CPU. That allowed many functions that had previously been the sole province of mainframes to "migrate in an outward direction" and be handled by desktop units in other locations. (The same process is being repeated now with personal computers, where additional microprocessors are being added to the CPU to handle such things as input/output, as we saw in Chapter 9.) The end of the period of total dependence on mainframes can aptly be described as ushering in an era of computer democracy.

Frank and Ron made good use of the independence their desktop units afforded them. Since the mainframe at their firm was kept busy night and day with other data processing tasks, the independence was convenient for all concerned. A computer system in which CPUs are available as part of a number of terminals, not all of them necessarily located even in the same building, is said to be an example of *distributed* data processing. Needless to say, there is no reason for CPUs at different locations to be working on the same or even related problems.

That doesn't mean that Frank and Ron never made use of the firm's mainframe. They did, but mainly to access the billions of bytes of information stored on its tapes and hard disks. This was the firm's *data base*, which is defined as any collection of mutually related data, and contained the firm's vast records. The information it contained was important at various stages in the preparation of Frank and Ron's report. In fact, thanks to the multitasking feature of UNIX—that is, its ability to run more than one program at a time (as described in Chapter 10)—Frank on more than one occasion did some financial planning at the same time that he was doing the text editing.

The peripherals attached to each man's desktop unit were also used—

by the other man—regularly during the period. Specifically, Frank's computer had a dot matrix printer, while the printer attached to Ron's unit was of letter quality. If you've been in a restaurant lately that produces computerized checks for customers at the end of the meal (it does this primarily for bookkeeping purposes; the machine is keeping track of how many of each item were served), you have seen what dot matrix printing looks like. With rare exceptions, that is what all the systems being sold to restaurants, and supermarkets as well, use for printing output. Letter-quality printers produce a result that more closely resembles the pages in this book, and that was the look both men felt was appropriate for their final written report to the management committee.

The letter-quality printer attached to Ron's desktop was therefore a *shared resource*. So was the Winchester (5¼-inch, sealed, hard disk) memory peripheral attached to Ron's system. It has a capacity of 10 megabytes, which is 20 times the capacity of Frank's floppy disks, and its transfer rate is 10 times that of floppies. Frank and Ron's report, or sections of it, could therefore be brought into main memory much faster on Ron's system than on Frank's.

The phrase "shared resource" has become increasingly popular as distributed processing and microcomputer systems have gained prominence. In our example, one computer was able to use the peripherals—particularly printers and memory storage devices—attached to another computer elsewhere. The same applied to the firm's data base, which is really a pool of "shared data." That is not only an economical, but also an efficient way to make use of both hardware and software. An idle resource is shared and thus put to better use.

Frank and Ron both made extensive use of computers, computer peripherals, and data bases in distant locations while preparing their report. In order to understand what they were doing and, more important, *how* they were able to do it, we need to spend some time talking about how computers actually communicate. We start with a number of key definitions.

The Public Telephone and Data Communications

The first piece of telecommunications terminology we need concerns the direction of data flow. If data can flow in only one direction, from device A to device B, the pathway is called a *simplex* channel (see Figure 11-2). In Figure 11-2, A acts as a transmitter, while B acts as as a receiver. Their roles are fixed. The most frequently encountered example in everyday life is an electronic buzzer or doorbell in your apartment or house.

Figure 11-2 Simplex transmission. A is a transmitter, B a receiver.

Pressing the button causes the bell to ring, but nothing you do to the bell will cause the button to act like one. Simplex channels aren't used for data communications.

When A can be a receiver as well as a transmitter, and the same applies to B, the pathway between them is called a *duplex* channel. However, there are two kinds of duplex channels. If A must play *either* the role of transmitter or receiver, while B acts as the reverse, then the channel is called *half-duplex*. A good example of half-duplex is a lecture. The speaker transmits and the audience receives, but the reverse is usually the case once the lecture has concluded and the lecturer accepts questions from the audience (see Figure 11-3).

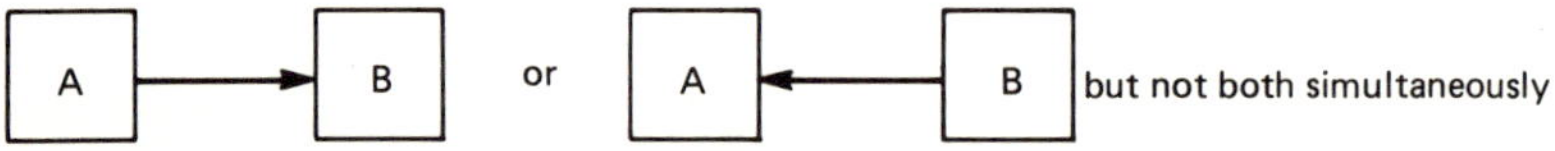

Figure 11-3 Half-duplex transmission. A and B must be able both to receive and transmit.

The final possibility is *full duplex*, in which A and B are able to act simultaneously as senders and receivers. The most commonly encountered example of full duplex transmission in everyday life is a shouting match. In the midst of an argument two people can usually still hear one another, even though they are talking simultaneously. A commonly encountered example of full duplex transmission in a computer system is called *echo printing*. Recall that a microcomputer console consists of a keyboard and CRT. The keyboard of the console acts as a transmitter, sending a stream of characters to the CPU and main memory; simultaneously, the CPU and main memory constitute a transmitting unit, sending the same characters back to the console, to be displayed on the CRT (or printed by the printer). The picture of full duplex transmission therefore looks like Figure 11-4.

Full duplex is clearly the most desirable arrangement, but when the telephone network was originally being installed, voice and not data transmission was on the minds of the network's designers. The consequences of that priority are being felt more each year by both the businesspeople and hobbyists, who find remedying it on their own to be

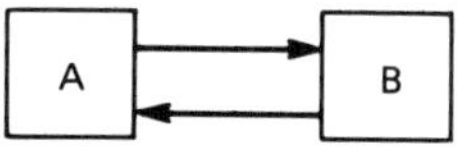

Figure 11-4 Full duplex transmission. A and B are receiver/transmitters.

costly. The chief consequence of the early emphasis on voice is that data communications equipment that now makes use of the ordinary (or *public*, as it's called) telephone network must transmit in half-duplex. Full duplex is available, but it either has to be leased from the phone company or installed by the user. In both cases, the line would then be termed a *dedicated* communications link. As we'll soon see, given the many advantages that accrue to this type of arrangement, particularly if the right kind of cable is being used for it, a wide variety of companies have found it worth the additional expense of installing or leasing one.

We've been talking throughout the book about digital electronics and digital computers. The word digital should be thought of as standing in contrast to *analog*. (There's no -ue at the end, though the word that sounds the same in ordinary English ends that way.) When a phenomenon or device is described as being digital, it means that it can exist in only one of a few states. If there are just two possibilities, we say that it is binary. A light switch that can be either on or off (but nothing in between) is binary, and so is a red-or-green traffic light. The 0s and 1s that have been with us explicitly or implicitly on nearly every page really represent the (voltage) output of two-state electronic devices.

However, most things in everyday life are analog. The range of light we see in the sky varies continually from morning to evening, even on a cloudy day. The music we hear isn't only two notes; if it were, we'd quickly be bored or irritated. In particular, the human voice isn't digital or binary, it is analog. We may describe certain people as speaking in a monotone ("one tone"), yet when it's measured carefully, the range of tones used still turns out to be wide. In short, when the nation's telephone network was being put in place, an analog signal—the human voice—was what it was designed to carry.

As soon as we start to discuss analog signals being carried over communications networks, we run into a very important question: How wide a range of frequencies should the lines in our network be expected to carry? Originally, the answer was left up to the human ear. At best, we can only hear frequencies that range from 20 cycles per second (cps) to 20,000 cps. (Instead of cps, many authors write Hz, for *hertz*, after the German physicist, Heinrich Hertz, 1857–1894. Thus, the voice band would be said to extend from 300 to 3300 Hz. From now on we'll say hertz instead of cycles per second when we're discussing frequencies.)

In case you have little feel at this point for what a range of frequencies "looks like," think of each frequency as a musical note. In that case, a ship's fog horn—a long, low note if ever there was one—would typically be in the 70- to 300-hertz range. So would the lowest note on a large church organ. On the other hand, a soprano on stage at the opera or a violin in the orchestra might easily reach notes that involve frequencies of 14,000 hertz or more. A picture of how different frequencies look on paper is worth having in mind. Let's take an interval of 1 second. If we say that something is vibrating at a frequency of 2 cycles per second (or 2 hertz), it would go back and forth two times (make two complete vibrations) in 1 second (see Figure 11-5).

We could show a 14,000-hertz musical note too, but you'd need a magnifying glass to distinguish each cycle, since so many of them would be crammed into one small space, side by side.

Although 20 to 20,000 hertz represents the range of human hearing, and then some, few human voices sound like violins or sopranos reaching for their highest possible note. So the decision was made, before millions of miles of telephone cable were strung overhead and buried in the ground, to lop off most of the spectrum. The result is that the range of frequencies that can be sent over the public telephone network is only 300 to 3300 hertz. The difference between the highest frequency and the lowest is the standard way of characterizing a carrier,

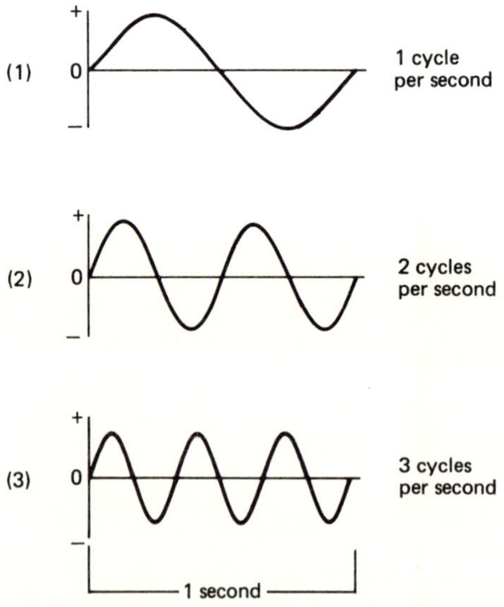

Figure 11-5 The number of cycles in a second.

and is called its *bandwidth*. Well, 3300 minus 300 = 3000. So the telephone network has a bandwidth of approximately 3000 hertz.

Multiplexing, by Frequency and Time

It takes a bit of familiarity with computers for the user to realize just how valuable it is to have a fair amount of memory capacity in the system, whether it be on-line or off-, in main memory or on disk. Similarly, as people gain an understanding of telecommunications principles, they realize the fundamental importance of bandwidth.

Bandwidths fall into three principal categories. The *voice band*, as we've seen, extends from 300 to 3300 hertz. Frequency bands that have a wider range than the voice band are called *wide band*. Communications channels with a bandwidth that is narrower than the voice band are called *narrow band*.

Before we see what can be accomplished with a dedicated communications channel, one tailored to our specific needs, let's see what we have to put up with in the public telephone network to get our data communications work done. If nothing else, the system is already there, a major national asset that was installed at enormous cost. As it turns out, we can make substantial improvements in the system's information transmission capability, and can do so with a minimum of effort and expense. How? By using a multiplexer. In fact, it is thanks to the presence of multiplexers and similar devices that people in the field often say that 65% of the cost of a communications network is for the transmission medium (coaxial cable, optical fiber, etc.) and 35% is for the communications equipment.

We first encountered multiplexers in Chapter 9, when we were discussing low-speed peripherals. A multiplexer prevents the various input/output devices attached to the system from competing with one another destructively for the CPU's attention. By forcing the peripherals to take turns, the multiplexer uses the CPU's capabilities more efficiently. The same applies to the multiplexer in a communications network. It is usually paired with a demultiplexer, which does exactly the reverse of a multiplexer: Signals come in on one line and are distributed to a number of receivers. The resulting arrangement is shown in Figure 11-6.

In Figure 11-6, A and B are both trying to transmit information to receiver C. Why do we need a multiplexer at all in this situation? Because an important characteristic of data communications is that they are "bursty"—that is, they tend to occur in bursts. This is true of voice communications too, where people use the phone to make a call for 8 minutes, say, and then don't use it again for a while. The same goes for letters; few people make trips to the post office every 10 minutes or so.

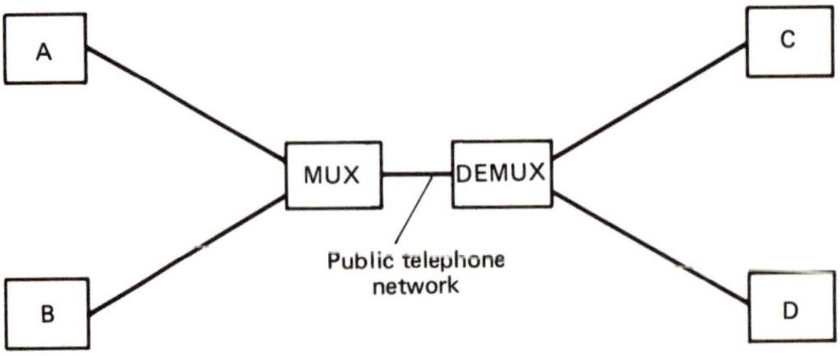

Figure 11-6 A multiplexed communications network. MUX stands for multiplexer; DEMUX stands for demultiplexer.

Data communications typically carries this process a step further, since there is nothing "casual" about most transmissions. Considerable attention is devoted to making certain that the data package being sent will be received. That, in and of itself, would prevent most people from sending a large number of small pieces—"Here are 6 bits, I'll send 15 more in a few minutes." As we'll soon see, a fair number of bits in each message must be devoted merely to format, identification, and error checking. That makes long messages substantially more efficient. The multiplexer takes these bursty communications which arrive at unpredictable times and places them on the same line. The line is already there and hence, just like the CPU, it might as well be put to maximum use. The situation is quite analogous to what happens when two lanes of cars, both traveling in the same direction, try to enter a one-lane tunnel. A cop at the entranceway, directing traffic, plays the role of multiplexer. One at the other end, sending certain cars into the left lane and others into the lane to the right, serves as a demultiplexer. This kind of multiplexing has a commonly encountered name and abbreviation: *time-division multiplexing* (TDM).

The other widely used type of multiplexing is called *frequency-division multiplexing* (FDM). Time is easier for most people to understand than frequency, so time-division multiplexing is easier for them to grasp. Yet the fact remains that frequency-division multiplexing is not only older than time-division multiplexing, it is also more commonly used. Why? The telephone's bandwidth may seem quite narrow at first glance—a mere 3000 hertz—but it is broad enough to accommodate a number of different low-speed data communications channels.

Before we proceed to divide up the frequency range available to us on the public telephone network, let's make certain we understand the central point here, namely, that different frequencies can be used to send different messages in opposite directions, simultaneously. A number of students have told us that the main reason the concept is hard for them to grasp is that they keep wondering what will *detect* the different signals. It may be helpful, then, to forget electronic sensing devices for a moment. Animals can detect a variety of signals that human beings can't. For instance, dogs can hear a much wider range of frequencies than we can. Many people tell us that the first time they realized that fact was when they watched a dog's owner blow into a whistle that seemed to be making no sound whatever, yet moments later, the dog came running. Now if only that dog had been carrying a data package. . . .

There is one very illuminating difference between the way a dog reacts to a whistle and what we expect from an electronic frequency-sensing device. To get the dog to come, the owner merely had to send one note, say, 100,000 hertz. That is far beyond the range of human hearing and explains why we think the whistle is "silent." However, a note—any note—in the voice band doesn't carry any information if all it does is just go on and on at that frequency. What we'd hear on the phone would merely be a steady hum.

Making Data Sing

Something has to *modify* the frequency if it is to carry any information. The carrier frequency therefore is temporarily shifted either up or down to a higher or lower frequency, and then returns to the original one. If you know how to whistle, you can do this easily: Start whistling one note, go up a higher one briefly, then return to the original. Figure 11-7 shows how that looks on paper.

Not surprisingly, this is called *frequency shifting*, and the kind of signal transmission that uses it is called *frequency-shift keying* (FSK). It is very widely used. The word "keying" is a now-meaningless leftover from the days when nineteenth-century telegraph operators sent all messages by pressing a single key. When you see the word "key" used in this context, it might be worthwhile to substitute mentally the phrase "coding (for data communications)" and read FSK as "frequency-shift coding (for data communications)."

A pair of tones actually serves quite nicely to communicate *binary* information. You probably didn't realize that when you started whistling one tone, then shifted to another and finally returned to the original, you sent a bit—that is, a binary digit, How? Let the original carrier tone represent a 0. When you shifted up and then back again, you produced a 1, as in Figure 11-7c. The same principle allows you to send *any* binary number (see Figure 11-8).

Figure 11-8b is very revealing. What it tells us is that the longer you hold the higher tone, the more 1s you produce. Once you know exactly how long to hold each tone, you can therefore produce any byte, say—

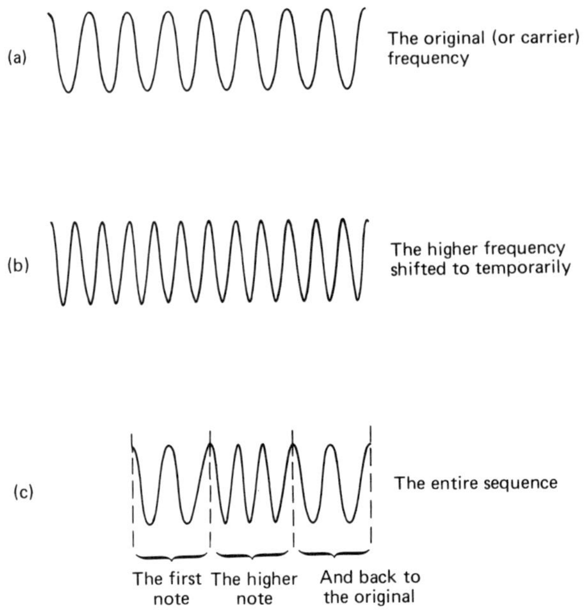

Figure 11-7 Frequency shifting. (a) The original tone. (b) Shifting to a higher one. (c) Shifting first up and then back.

that is, string of eight 0s and 1s—for transmission purposes. For example, 1001 1011 would look like Figure 11-9 (you might want to whistle it). That's what a modem does.

It is time for an interim summary, since you've gotten further into the process of data communications than you might suspect. To begin with,

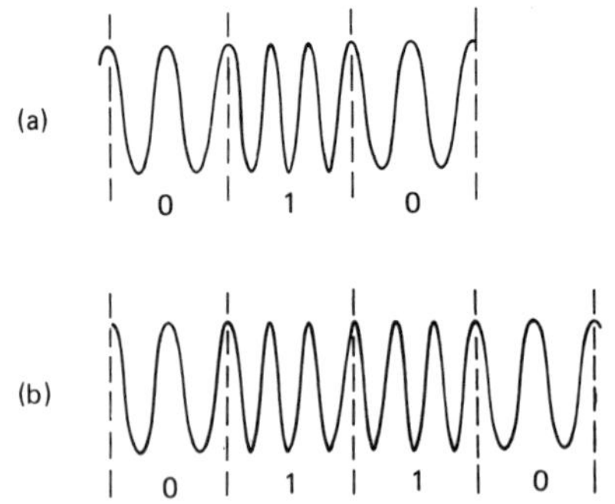

Figure 11-8 The longer a tone is held, the more bits of that kind are sent. (a) Only one 1 is sent. (b) Two 1s are sent.

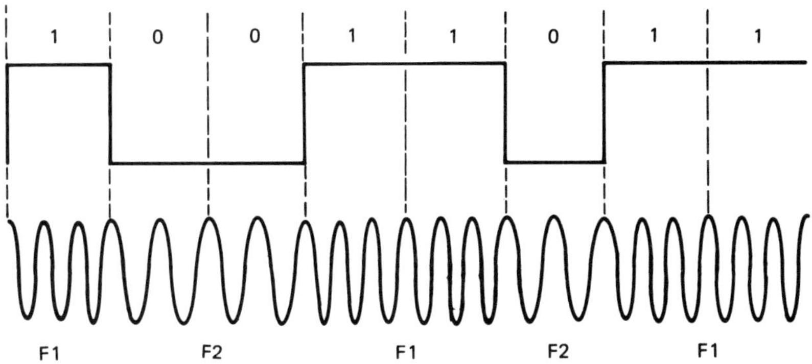

Figure 11-9 A sequence of bits converted into two frequencies, F1 and F2.

the public telephone network was designed with voice in mind, and hence is good at handling analog signals—that is, those whose frequencies can vary continuously. However, if we don't want to use each and every frequency, we don't have to, and therefore we can use this analog-oriented network to send digital signals. We pick one frequency, call it the carrier frequency, and then modify it (the technical name is *modulate* it) at the right time to produce another, higher frequency. That way, a sequence of binary digits can be sent over the phone. In short, thanks to frequency-shift keying, an analog signal can be made to carry binary information.

Full Duplex Operation

Since the voice band is narrow, we want to make good use of as much of it as we can. Multiplexing, as we now know, helps. But we should also do whatever we can to shrink the distance between the carrier frequency and the modulated frequency. That way, we can stuff more of these pairs into the voice band. We want at least two of them to be available, so that we can make use of full duplex operation in our data communications. Let's see precisely how that is achieved.

It is standard in the United States for 1070 hertz to be taken as the 0-reference carrier frequency for one of the two pairs. Well, if 1070 is the 0, what is the 1? That is, how much of a frequency shift must we make to produce a tone that is sufficiently distinct for detection equipment at the receiving end always to be able to tell the two signals apart? The answer is: 200 hertz. Therefore, the 1 in our first pair of tones is 1270 hertz. In short, imagine that 1070 hertz is the 0 in Figure 11-8 and that 1270 is the 1. Thus by whistling first one tone and then the other, and holding each for exactly the right length of time, we can send a stream of binary digits over the phone.

We want full duplex transmission, though, so we need one more pair of tones than can represent 0 and 1, respectively. It is standard in the United States to choose 2025 hertz for the 0 and (adding 200 hertz to that number) 2225 hertz for the 1. The two pairs look like Figure 11-10, given the voice band available to us on the public telephone network.

Many students tell us that they like to think of Figure 11-10 as a mountain, one that has two tunnels bored through it. The tunnel to the left is for traffic that is leaving this side of the hill (that's the reason the frequencies are labeled "originate"), while the tunnel to the right is for arriving traffic (which is therefore labeled "answer").

Figure 11-10 makes it easier to see why a communications medium that affords us a vastly wider bandwidth than the public phone network does is valuable. We can bore many more tunnels through it, so to speak. In fact, instead of having only two, as we have here, we might find that we were able to create thousands. As we'll see shortly, this is what explains the accelerating shift not only toward dedicated communications links, but also to telecommunications media other than standard, copper-core telephone wires. Satellites, microwaves, and optical fibers are more suitable.

You may recall that modem means "modulate-demodulate." Modems are the devices that actually convert binary signals into analog ones by using frequency-shift keying (FSK). The physical arrangement as you're likely to see it on any computer you own or use is simple. Before we draw the diagram, you may want to remind yourself that data are handled inside the computer in parallel form, with the size of the data bus determining the width of each data word it handles; an 8-bit-wide data bus carries byte-sized words, while a 16- or 32-bit data bus handles 16- or 32-bit words. Whatever its size, once the word emerges from the computer it is typically converted to serial format for data transmission. There are other parallel-to-serial interfaces, but the RS232-C is currently the most popular, so the overall picture looks like the one in Figure 11-11.

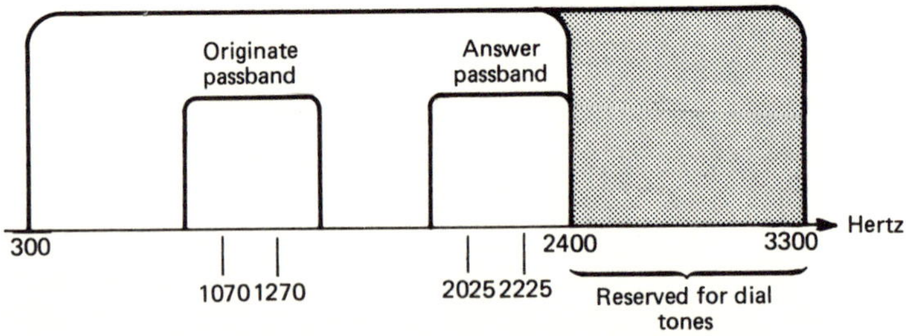

Figure 11-10 Full duplex data communication via the public telephone network.

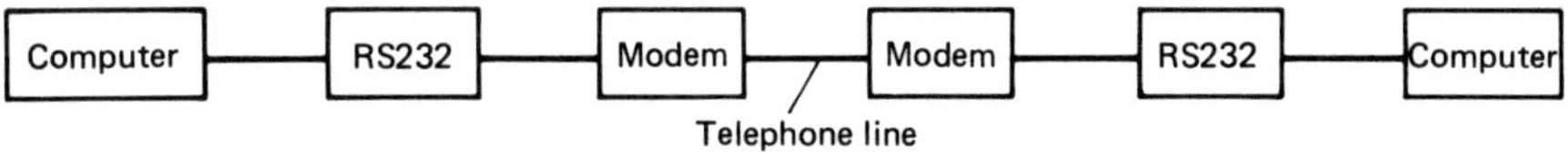

Figure 11-11 Computer communicating with a distant computer using parallel-to-serial interfaces, modems, and a telephone line.

What we should take a closer look at here is the connection between the modem and the phone line. The two most popular types are called the *data access arrangement* (DAA) and the *acoustic coupler*.

You may have seen home phones that can be unplugged from one location in the house and plugged into another. The jacks—that is, the outlets—that are provided for the purpose allow you to hook the phone up directly into the existing network. A data access arrangement is comparable in that it couples the modem to the phone line with a direct *electrical* connection, one that protects the network from voltage surges and other harmful effects.

Acoustic couplers, on the other hand, are just that. They are no more connected to the telephone network than you are, and instead, like you, they send their message acoustically by making the right sounds. Since those sounds (tones of different frequencies—1070 and 1270, or 2025 and 2225 hertz) are easily disrupted or masked entirely by surrounding noise, the acoustic coupler must make a tight connection with the ordinary telephone receiver it uses to send and receive messages.

For that reason, the acoustic coupler has a pair of rubber cups into which the handset of a (standard) telephone is placed. The rubber cups are angled to better match the phone's mouth and earpiece, and to do a reasonable job of insulating the handset from noise in the immediate environment (that is, there's no need to whisper around this device). The arrangement looks like the one pictured in Figure 11-12.

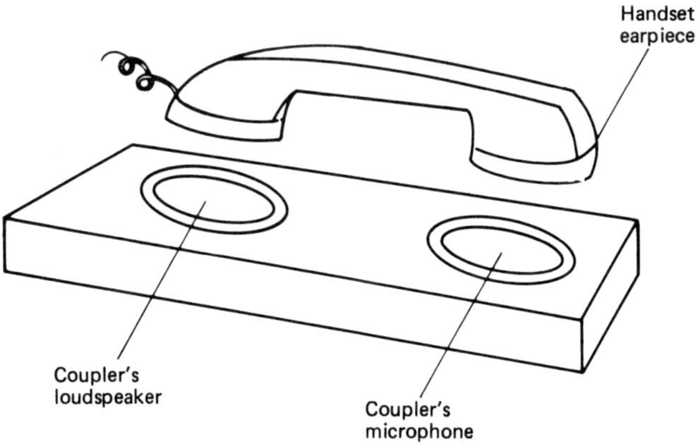

Figure 11-12 An acoustic coupler. The telephone handset fits snugly into the coupler's rubber cups.

The earpiece of the handset rests on top of the coupler's microphone, so that incoming signals can be magnified, filtered, and recorded. For transmission purposes, the coupler's loudspeaker sits just beneath the handset's microphone (that is, its mouthpiece). That allows it literally to sing its modulated (that is, analog) version of the binary message it receives in serial form from your computer directly onto the public telephone line.

Although common and relatively inexpensive, this is not a particularly high-speed data communications arrangement, and speeds of 300 to 450 bits per second (bps) are typical. So is 1200 bps. Attaining faster transmission rates is possible, but the modems become significantly more expensive. How do these higher-priced units achieve higher transmission rates? Everything depends on the way in which the modem modulates the data prior to sending them over the phone line. We've been discussing frequency-shift keying (FSK), which is the most popular form of frequency modulation (that is, FM, as in AM/FM radio) for data communications. However, faster techniques involve the signal's phase instead of frequency. The process is called phase modulation (PM) or phase-shift keying (PSK). Finally, there is amplitude modulation (AM, the other half of AM/FM in car radios). Specifically, there is a four-level technique called quadrature-amplitude modulation (QAM) that readily permits speeds of 1800 to 9600 bps. Don't let any of these technical terms or their abbreviations throw you; we've mentioned them mainly so that the next time you encounter their names they'll seem a little more familiar. What is important to remember is that modems in this range are generally considered high-speed and tend to be considerably more expensive.

Well-behaved Computers

When most people think of data communication, they think of signal transmission; an acoustical or electrical message is sent from one point to another. However, even if two individuals speak the same language, say, English, there has to be some understanding between them as to when it is all right to speak and when it is appropriate to remain silent. Otherwise, conflict is nearly inevitable. Presented with this situation, civilized people usually say that politeness can be counted on to rescue the situation. Where computer networks are concerned, the comparable term is *protocol.*

There are famous etiquette books that describe in great detail how tricky personal situations involving weddings, death, divorce, and dignitaries are to be handled. But for the most part, people with a basic knowledge of the rules tend to trust their own intuition as to when and how to apply them. That isn't done in computer networks, where rigid adherence to a fixed set of guidelines is essential if reliable communication is to take place at all.

Before we look at the subject of data network protocol, let's note a few of the problems these rules of order are intended to solve. Some of the problems that are important in data communications networks we've met before; others, we haven't. For instance, it is obviously possible for one computer to send a message too quickly for the computer on the receiving end to capture accurately all the incoming information. How to handle this very common problem? A frequent solution is to use buffering, just as a microprocessor does with its peripherals (see Chapter 6). That way, incoming or outgoing messages, if they're short, can be stored temporarily until the receiving unit is ready to handle them.

Also, one computer may have to communicate with a variety of others, depending on the time of day, say, or the kind of information it is seeking. How can it tell one machine from the next? We encountered the problem before when we were discussing sheriffs and prisoners—or more accurately, microprocessors and memory cells. The solution was to use addressing. A similar technique is used in data communications networks, where the address of each machine distinguishes it from the rest.

Nevertheless, there are other problems that are quite different from those we've previously encountered. For example, when a microprocessor wants to communicate with one of its main memory cells as part of a WRITE operation, it puts the address of the cell on the address bus, puts the appropriate data on the data bus, and sends a WRITE signal on the control bus. That is, buses provide a physical connection between microprocessor and main memory, one that is used for communications purposes. The same goes for a typical conversation on the telephone, where copper wires (or more recently, optical fiber and microwave) that are overhead or underground carry the message. However, an increasing quantity of communication among computers makes use of orbiting satellites. In this case, there is a conspicuous delay in getting the message from one location to another, usually on the order of 700 milliseconds—that is, nearly three-quarters of a second. That may not seem long in terms of everyday events, but to computers, where nanoseconds (billionths of a second) are a common measure, it is an eternity, since three fourths of a second is 750 million of them.

The real question, though, is whether the message got there at all. Did noise disrupt it? Will sending it again mean that the machine on the receiving end gets the data once, or accidentally duplicates it? Sending a query and waiting for a response is time-consuming, but time-saving tricks have been found and satellite communications systems have been plummeting in cost, just as the cost of raw computing power (microprocessors) and internal (semiconductor) and external (tape and disk) memory have been. Also, and this is what's important, a modern space satellite allows at least 24 independent channels, each one more than 34 million hertz wide, in its 2 billion-hertz bandwidth. The equivalent of more than 100,000 voice-grade circuits can be carved out of this raw material. Similarly, the earth stations needed to communicate by satellite used to cost tens of millions of dollars, which strictly limited their customer base, but now individuals buy 5- or 10-meter dishes for personal purposes for less than $10,000.

Given the vast increase in the number and types of data communications networks, it is hardly surprising that there has been growing pressure on all parties involved—users, programmers, and manufacturers—to standardize the guidelines to be employed. That is where protocols come in. Notice that the word is plural: There are a variety of layers in a data communications network. It is important to see what they are, why they exist, and why a protocol is needed at *each* layer.

An analogy here is useful. If instead of merely sending a card, you decide to send yourself to a friend's wedding, events are set in motion on a number of different levels. For example, there is your RSVP—that is, the acknowledgment that you'll be there, so the host can anticipate your arrival. There is also the matter of getting to the proper location. This has nothing to do with weddings per se, since other people traveling on the same route that day might be heading in that direction for other purposes. Then, once there, there is the matter of expressing the appropriate sentiments. Finally, one must terminate the interchange and return home.

If we take a closer look at the entire episode from start to finish, we will see that it falls naturally into events that occur on a numbr of different levels, each of which supports—that is, services in some way—the levels above it. The service aspect is more important than the time sequence. In fact, the main reason people have difficulty grasping the basic principles of network architectures and their implementation is this: They insist on thinking about data communications in terms of what happens first, then what happens next, and so on, until the communication is complete. It is far more revealing to look at the event vertically—that is, each layer exists solely to provide services to the layers above it—as we'll see first in the wedding analogy and then in data communications networks in general.

The Layers Involved in Data Communication

The most basic layer is a physical one. If you own or rent a car that you alone will be using to take you to the party, this mechanical conveyance delivers one guest to the event. What does that correspond to in a data communications network? A bit. The *physical layer* of a network deals principally with mechanical and electrical issues, such as the right voltage needed to send a 1 and be certain that it is received as such. Modems, carrier waves and their modulation; parallel versus serial; full duplex versus half-duplex; and point-to-point versus multipoint (that is, the equivalent of a conference call) are all dealt with at this level.

What we've described thus far is the first layer of five:

TABLE 11-1

Session
Transport
Network
Data link
Physical

Don't let the stack of unfamiliar terms worry you; taking them one at a time—and always keeping mind that each exists merely to serve the purposes of the one above it—makes all of them easy to understand. Switching our focus to the top slot, the *session layer*, is helpful at this point. (It might be worthwhile to spend a few seconds memorizing the vertical order of the names of this five-layer cake. From the top down, the first letters are STNDP, and you add it to your mind, not your car's engine.)

The session layer is you at the wedding, making contact and having conversation with the friend who invited you. In a data communications network, the session layer is responsible for establishing, maintaining, and managing the interaction between the communicating parties (usually computers). It defines the rules that must be adhered to for effective communication by the session partners. By definition, a session is a connection between users, such as the one that might occur if you (actually, your computer) wanted to draw information from a remote data base in another state. The session layer is your interface into the network needed to obtain that information.

As Table 11-1 shows, the *transport layer* is directly beneath the session layer. What services does it provide its upstairs neighbor? The transport layer relieves the session layer of any concern about the *where*—the relative location—of the two parties who will be communicating. It permits them to behave as though they were face to face. In terms of the wedding analogy, the transport layer answers the question about where the event is to take place.

This is indeed a separate and distinct aspect of the situation, both in data communications networks and weddings. The wedding invitation may arrive in the mail with explicit directions included about how to get there, but whether it does or not, the specific route and vehicle you choose is ultimately up to you. Maybe you'll come on a bicycle, or if you are practicing for a marathon, you'll jog the 9 miles to the chapel. All that matters is that you be there.

In a data communications network it is particularly important that this layer be thought of as having a life of its own. Why? Because of the increasingly rapid changes in technology that are occurring in this area. Your friend can send you valid directions along with the invitation only because the roads that have been laid along the earth's surface are static, and the technology of the vehicles that use them (including your legs) changes relatively slowly. That is certainly not so where data communications equipment is concerned. If the road layout and vehicle technology were changing as fast as new equipment and techniques are being introduced in data networks, your friend's map would be obsolete by the time you got it in the mail. In short, the transport layer, by focusing on the question of where, isolates the session layer from the steady stream of innovations in communications hardware.

Perhaps it is clear now why there are two layers below the transport layer and above the physical layer. These in-between layers, the network and data link layers, answer, respectively, the routing questions (how to get there) and the question of how to take *each step* in the route—safely.

Framing the Data

These are two distinct sets of tasks, even though they may seem very much the same. Let's take the *data link layer* first. If the physical layer directly below it does its job well, 1s and 0s of good quality will be sent and received. But what do they mean? Something else has to be added to the bit stream if it is to become a meaningful message. The minimum we need to add is a sequence of bits that tells us when the transmission begins and another sequence of bits that tells us when it ends. That lengthens the transmission, of course, but so does saying "hello" and "goodbye" at the beginning and end of a phone conversation. The communication feels awkward and even confusing to us without it. If no goodbye is uttered, how do we know the conversation has been voluntarily terminated and not merely interrupted?

In data communications networks, it is common for the same byte-sized word, 0111 1110, to serve as both the hello and the goodbye. In either case, it is called a *flag*. After the hello, the next part of the message is the address, but in data communications networks it may well be the address of the sender instead of that of the receiver, in which case it is called the *broadcast address*. (You've probably heard radio and TV stations send exactly this information, typically at sign-on and sign-off, that is, when they are starting or concluding their broadcast day.)

After the address—or address field, as this portion of the transmission is technically named—comes the data. Before and after the data, though, are a sequence of bits dedicated to making certain that the data will be received as sent. If they haven't been, these bits tell the receiver to discard this particular data transmission. The two pieces of bread that sandwich the data are called, respectively, the *control field* (C) and the *frame check sequence* (FCS). The data link format we've been describing is known internationally as the *high-level data link control* (HDLC), and you'll be encountering the initials again if you're at all interested in the subject of data communications. Our framed chunk of data therefore looks like the one below (read it from left to right, since that is how it would be received):

Flag	Address field	Control field	Data	Frame check sequence	Flag

In short, the data link layer takes a raw stream of 0s and 1s provided it by the physical layer and, by adding some bits before and after the data, converts it into a data *frame*. Doing so not only makes the bit stream readable, it also goes far toward helping us recognize and eliminate transmission errors. In addition, it solves the problem we discussed earlier, connected with one computer transmitting information too quickly for another to capture it correctly.

The middle slot in our layer cake, the *network layer*, exists to relieve the transport layer above it of any concern about how to get the message from, say, point A to point B. Routing and relaying information, increasingly through intelligent terminals, is the function of the network layer.

The network layer is often called the *packet level*, and it is important for you to know why. What *is* a packet, and why is this concept of increasing significance in data communications networks?

Bits, Frames, and Packets

To gain some perspective on the matter, we should look briefly at what happens when you make an ordinary phone call. Computers at the phone company now do most of the work that telephone operators used to do manually, but it is worthwhile for us to go back to the earlier era, since it is easier to see what's going on in this setting. If you wanted to call a friend of yours on the other side of town, you gave the operator the number and she would perform a switching function for you—that is, she would select and then establish a physical connection between your phone and your friend's. Make no mistake about it, what you had at that moment was a dedicated pathway between the phones, one that depended on a continuous, copper-wire connection between the two residences. The pathway was yours and yours alone until you and your friend finished talking. This kind of switching is called *circuit switching*, and was designed with voice transmission in mind. Conversations were assumed to be continuous and extended.

Data communications networks, however, need a different kind of switching to work best. Since satellite and microwave are used increasingly in this area, no dedicated physical pathway is present between the two computers involved in the transmission, nor is any needed since the communication takes place at high speed and is generally brief. The key point here is this: To make certain that no dedicated pathway has to be put in place temporarily in order for data communication to occur, the data to be transmitted is broken up into smaller chunks, called packets. Each packet is numbered and then sent over *any* available route. Some of the packets may indeed end up traveling by a copper-wire pathway from source to destination, while others travel via satellite. It makes no difference—and that was the goal right from the start. The computer at the receiving end then proceeds to reassemble the message by arranging the packets in the proper order, regardless of the order in which they arrived. This type of transmission is called *packet switching*.

The wedding analogy affords us a good example of this technique in everyday life. If 48 people, all told, showed up for the ceremony and are now ready to be transported to the reception a mile away, it may be necessary to take them four at a time in the 12 cars that are available for the purpose. It really doesn't matter which car gets to the reception first, where we'll assume that everyone has been preassigned a seat. Nor does it matter which route the various cars choose to take, given the congestion on the roads. Once they've all arrived, the festivities can begin.

Many people encountering this material for the first time tend to be confused about the difference between a frame and a packet, particularly as regards their length. Keep in mind, then, that there is a maximum packet size for each network, and it is usually 1024 bits. Data transmissions that are of considerable length are divided up into the appropriate number of packets. Frame lengths are another matter entirely, and typically vary from 400 to 1200 bits, depending on the speed of the transmission. The higher the number of bits per second (bps) transmitted, the smaller the frame. For instance, at 9600 bps the frame length may be 1200 bits, whereas a satellite using 56,000 bps may utilize a frame length of 400 bits. It is also common for 127 frames to be sent as part of a single transmission. Then the computer on the receiving end issues a response—that is, it acknowledges the receipt of a transmission—and may add, "Where is frame 121?" Or, "Frame 86 arrived damaged, please transmit the message again."

Perhaps the best way to think about the difference is to recall that the bottom three layers of our data communications cake are, reading upwards, the physical layer, the data link layer, and the network layer. Frame is a data link layer concept (concerned with the imposition of meaning on a raw stream of bits), whereas packet is a network layer concept (concerned with making maximum use of a network as a shared resource). In fact, for shorthand purposes, layers 1, 2, and 3 may be thought of as concerned, respectively, with bits, frames, and packets.

Finding a Standard for Network Architectures

Let's spend a few minutes reviewing the most important points in the material we've been discussing, and add some needed historical details.

Computer manufacturers in the 1960s and 1970s were devoted to the strategy that customers should be captured. Any piece of equipment the customer bought should increase the chances that the next piece would be bought from the same manufacturer. What better way than to sell, as a first piece, a unit that won't work with equipment sold by anyone else? That was the dream. However, many of the companies that entered the business later, after the majors had become well established, deliberately made equipment that was compatible (industry jargon: "plug-compatible") with products already on the market. That way, hardware as well as software you'd already purchased could be used with new products—from a different manufacturer. Suffice it to say that in this intensely competitive field, cooperation and industry-wide standardization has been hard to come by.

However, in the early 1970s a powerful reason arose for *each* major manufacturer to make the machines comprising the company's entire line able to communicate with one another. Namely, some large firms had indeed been buying all their computers from just one manufacturer, say, IBM, and were now insisting that the machines be able to communicate readily with one another when necessary. Distributed computing—that is, different computers being dedicated to specific tasks, rather than each having to handle them all—and distributed data bases had by then become a widespread part of the data processing scene.

In 1974, IBM therefore introduced Systems Network Architecture (SNA), whch was to be used by IBM customers to construct their own *private* networks. SNA has been revised over the years, though, each time in the direction of making it more suitable to generalized communications networks. Digital Equipment, faced with similar demands from its customers, introduced DECNET, which is also frequently referred to as Digital Network Architecture (DNA), for its own customers' use in private networks. It has undergone revisions over time in the same direction as IBM's SNA. As you might have guessed, even today there are many differences between them; for instance, frames in DECNET must be multiples of 8, whereas SNA frames may be any length. Other companies moved quickly to enter the field by offering such proprietary products as Wangnet and Ethernet, which we'll take a closer look at later. There were government systems in operation by this time as well, with ARPANET from the Department of Defense being the first and best known (the initials stand for the Advanced Research Projects Agency; it's now called DARPA, the D standing for Defense).

Enter the ISO. The telecommunications field is rife with acronyms and abbreviations of all sorts, but these three letters stand for the International Standards Organization, a group whose members consist of standards organizations from around the world. If ever an area of technology needed some guidelines that firms and governments around the globe can follow and thus be better understood, the communications field is it. The result of ISO's extensive deliberations has been the creation of a seven-layer model for data communications networks (see Table 11-2).

TABLE 11-2

Applications	Layer 7
Presentation	
Session	.
Transport	.
Network	.
Data link	
Physical	Layer 1

We've already examined the first five layers (counting from the bottom, remember) of the proposed architecture in Table 11-2, and for most users, these are the important ones. The sixth, the presentation layer, is concerned with such things as text compression (abbreviations to make messages shorter). Think of this as a translation layer; you arrive at the wedding and find that the guests speak mainly Chinese. Layer 7, the applications layer, is concerned with such questions as how best to distribute data processing tasks so as to make optimum use of both the network and the computers attached to it, as well as any data bases they contain.

The two main reasons we've been discussing the ISO's model for computer network architectures are, first, that it has received global and growing acceptance. You'll undoubtedly be hearing more about it in the future. Second, and more important, this model not only encourages standardization in domestic and international data communications networks, it also gives people who understand it a framework that allows them to examine with real insight any existing or proposed network, whether it be public or private. (The annotated bibliography lists a number of readable and fascinating books that do just that.)

With this general picture in mind, we can far more readily understand the structure and operation of any given data communications network. That doesn't mean all networks will be the same in the near future. Neither the ISO nor any other international telecommunications agency would be presumptuous enough at this point to dictate how a proposed architecture should be *implemented*—that is, embodied in hardware and software—an impossibility anyway, given the rapid pace of advances in this area.

What is important to realize here, and in any additional reading you do in this field, is this:

1. Each layer of the network makes its contribution by adding something to the raw stream of bits in order to make the communication contained therein more meaningful. Where does it do the adding? Before and after the data; it appends a header and a trailer:

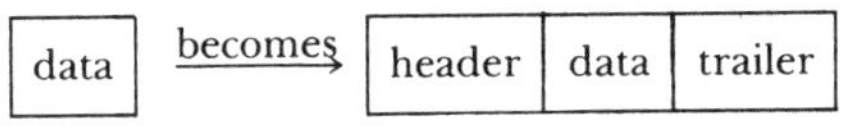

(Read from left to right, since that represents order of arrival.)

Sometimes it will first divide up the data (as in the case of level 3, the network layer, which you'll recall is also known as the packet level). Then it will add a header and trailer to each packet.

The computer on the receiving end, after making good use of all this appended information to interpret and correctly assemble the incoming transmission, discards the packaging and delivers the message to the recipient as if the added bits had never been there in the first place. This is the principle of *transparency* at work and is just what you'd expect from an effective modern network; the user doesn't really want to know about or be burdened in any way by all the intermediary handling required to get the data from point A to point B intact via a network that others also want to use.

2. Perhaps it is clear now why the word "protocol," when used with

respect to data communications networks, usually means protocol*s*. The plural is almost always more accurate because *each layer* has its own set of rules. If you are driving to the wedding, the maximum legal speed on the road may be 55 mph, and you have to drive on the right-hand side of any two-way streets. But that piece of highway protocol has nothing to do with expressing good wishes to the bride and groom once you arrive. And both of these separate sets of protocol are independent of the number of people you can put in an ordinary sedan, to take them from the chapel to the reception. If you try stuffing 15 people into this data communications equivalent of a packet ("A four-door packet? I thought they didn't make them any more."), someone is likely to be offended.

Local Area Networks (LANS) and Ethernet

Having discussed data communications networks in general, let's go back to the Office of the Future and look briefly at a popular local area network (LAN) that uses the Ethernet system. Since we're talking about *local* networks now, ones that are owned by a specific company or government agency, the distances over which data must travel are small (usually less than a mile) and the data transmission rates are high (typically 10 million bps). Needless to say, rates that high aren't available with the public telephone network, so instead of a copper cable that is already in place, we'll be looking at systems that use a high-bandwidth custom cable—coaxial or, increasingly, optical fiber—that has been installed expressly for the purpose of data communication.

Ethernet was developed at Xerox's Palo Alto Research Center in the early 1970s. In the late 1970s, an improved version was developed thanks to a joint venture by Xerox, Intel, and Digital Equipment. It makes fundamental use of a technique that can be described very simply, since we all use it when speaking. Namely, we can tell whether we're the only one giving voice to our thoughts at the moment by checking whether the words we hear belong to us and to us alone. That is, if we hear someone else's words *as well as* our own, we know that that person too is talking. Even if we were blind, and unable to see the other person's lips to double-check what our ears were telling us, we could still use the technique.

Constructing a device that listens to a cable isn't difficult. (Think of it as a mechanical replacement for Tonto having to put his ear to a railroad track to see if a train is coming.) The technical name for what the unit does is: *carrier sensing*. That is, it is sensing what, if anything, is on the carrier, the cable. Therefore a transmission unit (the mouth) that has a carrier-sensing mechanism attached to it (the ears) can avoid trying to send a message when another computer is already doing so. If the line is busy—that is, if there is currently a transmission on the line—all other transmitters know that they must wait.

Notice that no central device has to coordinate the transmitting activities of even a large number of transmitters attached to a network via this system. Why? Because each one has ears, and hence just like humans, can tell when it would cause a collision if it too began transmitting at that moment. Local area networks of this variety are called *contention*-type, since they are designed to prevent having two computers fight with one another for the transmission medium. When computers that want to send a message listen to what's on the cable before transmitting a message of their own, the network is referred to as a *carrier-sense network*. Since we're discussing telecommunications, we should mention at least one acronym that you're quite likely to encounter again if you do more reading in this area. There are many computers attached to the line, all of which may want access to it at one time or another. Ethernet may thus be thought of as a network that uses *carrier-sense multiple access with collision detection* (CSMA/CD).

Let's spend a moment seeing how this system fits into the ISO's seven-layer model. Ethernet has two layers in its architecture, the physical and the data link layers. (The other five are left up to the user to specify.) As you might expect, the physical layer is concerned primarily with transmitting and receiving high-quality bits, as well as sensing that messages are on the cable. The data link layer, on the other hand, is concerned with framing the message, addressing, and error detection, as well as avoiding collisions and handling any that do occur. It does so by backing off and retransmitting the message again later, as soon as the line is free.

Summing up, it should be clear now why local area networks are becoming of ever greater importance. Once a high-speed cable has been installed throughout an office, not only computers, but also telephones, printers, copiers, microprocessors, and peripherals of all sorts can be attached to it. Then, voice, text, images, and data can all be transmitted (in digital form) over the same facility—and can readily be plugged into international networks for worldwide transmission.

Funneling everything into one line might seem to be a recipe for disaster. When they first hear the idea, most people think the line would frequently be overcrowded and hence unusable, much like narrow tunnels and bridges into major cities are at rush hour. Fiber optics to the rescue. A coaxial cable, the first way in which Ethernet was implemented, has data tranmission speeds in the range of 5 to 100 million bps. But optical fibers are capable of transmission speeds of one to several hundred *billion* bps (gigabits per second), which will be used to minimize logjams. Also, if each transmitting computer has to send only one packet at a time, instead of just being able to commandeer the line and hold forth for as long as it wants with an unbroken stream of bits, there is usually room for other computers to get their messages sent too, a packet at a time.

The Hub of the Automated Office

The final topic we need to examine at least briefly is that of the private branch exchange (PBX). We've left it for last because, while it isn't difficult to understand, it is a concept and a product that is right at the heart of what automating the modern office is all about.

The best way to grasp what a PBX does is to think about the fact that most people who work in an office have a phone of their own. It allows them to contact other people in the building, as well as people in other cities or countries. To keep down the cost of connecting all those phones to one another, the telephone lines are first funneled into the modern equivalent of a switchboard. Remember, in olden days you'd have had to ask the switchboard operator to ring the bookkeeping department for you, to find out what happened to your paycheck. You couldn't do it yourself, since the phones were all linked to the switchboard, not directly to one another. This aspect of the firm's telephone switching operations was automated in recent decades, with AT&T's Centrex being a popular version that didn't require an operator as an intermediary. The only time you needed an operator was to find out general information or the extension of the particular party you wished to contact.

The cost savings under this arrangement of funneled phone lines, with or without an automated switchboard operator, are substantial. A simple statistic shows why. A company with 200 phones usually needs only 10 to 15 lines going from its switchboard to the local office of the telephone company in order to handle all of its incoming and outgoing calls, a nearly 95% decrease in the number of lines required.

If we switch our focus for a moment from phones to cars, we can gain an important insight into the role of PBXs. Suppose you are an extraterrestrial being making your first trip to Earth. Before you land on the planet, you survey the scene for a while from a few miles up. You can't see any people from that height, but you do notice something striking. Every morning between 7 and 9 a.m., cars drive into the city, and between 4 and 7 p.m., they leave. You therefore write in your notebook that the Earth is inhabited by shiny, mobile, multicolored boxes that spend their day clustered in cities and then disperse as the sun begins to set.

If we temporarily take the same people-missing-from-the-picture approach to telephones, we might think of each phone, on its own, as wanting to be in touch with all the others. Well then, why shouldn't computers feel the same way? After all, they're even more "human" than the phone, thanks to their CPUs and memories. Perhaps two computers want to get together and, just like people, exchange what's in their memories. If each phone can make contact with all the other phones in the world, computers should be able to do the same. The first question is whether a new set of cables is needed to link them all together. If so, does each firm with a lot of computers need a separate switchboard—a computer switchboard, as opposed to a telephone switchboard—so that they can contact one another, as well as computers located in other cities and countries?

Perhaps it's clear, then, why digital PBXs are rapidly becoming so popular. For they combine the abilities of both types of switchboard in *one* unit. They function as a communications controller, handling incoming and outgoing voice, data, and facsimile (for instance, blueprints) transmissions. Keep in mind that once a network is handling digital instead of analog signals, it becomes like a public highway on which any kind of vehicle can travel, here in binary form. Since PBXs are intelligent devices with CPUs of their own, they can be programmed to do a number of additional tasks that are very useful, such as finding the least expensive route for a long-distance call that one of the telephones *or* computers in the firm is making. (Since PBXs deal with phones and computers, not people, that is the reason we adopted the approach a few moments ago.)

By the way, the word "private" in the phrase "private branch exchange" means that the equipment belongs to the firm. The opposite of private in this case isn't public, it is "central office," and refers to equipment at the phone company, such as "central office digital switching equipment." Also, since computerized PBXs are thereby automated, the units are frequently referred to as "private automated branch exchanges" (PABX).

By now, you probably won't be surprised to hear that computer manufacturers and telecommunications companies have been anxious to pair up in recent years, so that neither misses out on the new developments in the important area where they overlap. IBM and Rolm, and Honeywell and L. M. Ericsson, one of Europe's leading PBX makers, are good examples. The two fields are drawing closer, stimulating one another in the process.

annotated bibliography

Since the primary purpose of this book is to give readers a running head-start that will allow them to comprehend better the large number of good technical works on the market, we mention a few here. In each category, the titles are listed in order of increasing difficulty.

Electronics

Computers are electronic machines, and a knowledge of the basics of electronics is therefore useful to understand not only the models now being sold, but also the new designs and equipment that will be coming off the drawing boards and out of the factories in years to come.

Tocci, Ronald J., *Fundamentals of Electronic Devices,* 3d ed. Charles E. Merrill Publishing Co., Columbus, Ohio, 1982.
The first 250 pages or so of this book provide a gentle introduction to the subject.

Tipler, Paul A., *Physics,* 2d ed. Worth Publishers, New York, 1982.
A good place to learn the rudiments of electricity and magnetism, and about elementary circuit theory.

Uffenbeck, John E., *Introduction to Electronics.* Prentice-Hall, Englewood Cliffs, N.J., 1982.
Written in a lively, readable style.

McGraw-Hill Encyclopedia of Electronics and Computers. McGraw-Hill Book Company, New York, 1984.
An excellent and well-illustrated place to learn about piezoelectricity and dozens of other subjects in the two fields.

Microprocessors and Microcomputers

Many books about microprocessors and their operations in computers assume little or no knowledge of electronics and instead discuss the workings of each device in terms of what it does at each step as part of the whole.

Khambata, Adi J., *Microprocessors/Microcomputers: Architecture, Software and Systems.* John Wiley & Sons, New York, 1982.
Keeps things simple enough so as not to overwhelm the reader, yet presents a good overview of the basics of the subject.

Mano, M. M., *Computer System Architecture,* 2d ed. Prentice-Hall, Englewood Cliffs, N.J., 1982.

Taub, Herbert, *Digital Circuits and Microprocessors.* McGraw-Hill Book Company, New York, 1982.
These two works are well written and will do much to deepen the reader's grasp of microprocessor operation.

Operating Systems

As you already know by now, a computer's operating system is as important as its hardware and applications programs. Keeping up with major developments in the field is worthwhile.

Davis, William S., *Operating Systems: A Systematic View,* 2d ed. Addison-Wesley Publishing Co., Reading, Mass., 1983.
Written in a relaxed, conversational style, the book discusses operating systems for large and small computers.

McGilton, H., and R. Morgan, *Introducing the UNIX System.* McGraw-Hill Book Company, New York, 1983.
Straightforward, easy to read, and quite useful.

Grant, C. W., and J. Butah, *Introduction to the UCSD p-system.* Sybex, Berkeley, Calif., 1982.
A practical and accessible discussion of a popular operating system that we didn't have a chance to cover, but one that is well worth knowing about.

Telecommunications

We've seen that office automation depends critically on telecommunications. So does the pleasure that many people get from using computers for personal, as opposed to business, purposes.

Glossbrenner, Alfred, *Complete Handbook of Personal Computer Communications.* St. Martin's Press, New York, 1983.
Short on technical details, long on fun. Provides the basic information needed to make contact with a variety of other computers and data bases.

Nichols, E. A., J. C. Nichols, and K. R. Musson, *Data Communications for Microcomputers.* McGraw-Hill Book Company, New York, 1982.
Conveys a reasonable amount of technical information about the subject in a readable manner. Includes useful hardware and software details.

Tanenbaum, Andrew S., *Computer Networks.* Prentice-Hall, Englewood Cliffs, N.J., 1981.
A serious overview of the subject that contains a substantial amount of information presented lucidly.

Data Structures

The subject of data structures has been mentioned only briefly in this book—for instance, graphs and trees, in connection with the UNIX operating system; stacks, in connection with handling interrupts; and pointers, in connection with stacks. However, the subject is both fascinating and important, one that provides great insight into everything from the structure of computer programs, on the one hand, to the relationship between software and hardware, on the other.

More specifically, the data you want to work with must find their way into the computer's memory in an orderly manner so that you can later retrieve and manipulate the data to obtain the answers you seek. A knowledge of data structures will allow you, among other things, to understand how memory space is best allocated to store the information.

It is worthwhile for you to become comfortable with a group of key technical terms, among them, arrays, queues, lists, and records, as well as trees, graphs, stacks, and pointers. Also, the concepts of dynamic storage allocation, recursion, searches, and sorts are important to know.

Augenstein, M., and A. Tenenbaum, *Data Structures Using Pascal,* Prentice-Hall, Englewood Cliffs, N.J., 1981.

Tremblay, J. P., and P. G. Sorenson, *An Introduction to Data Structures, with Applications,* 2d ed. McGraw-Hill Book Company, New York, 1984.

Beidler, John, *An Introduction to Data Structures,* Allyn and Bacon, Boston, 1982.

index

about the author

Srully Blotnick currently heads his own consulting firm, whose clients have included DuPont and IBM. Dr. Blotnick has received degrees from Rensselaer Polytechnic Institute and from Princeton, where he was a National Science Foundation Fellow. He has been a research statistician at Grumman Aircraft, and now writes a regular column for *Forbes* magazine.